A BOY from
CRACKERS NECK

A BOY from CRACKERS NECK

JOHN W. PEACE II

FOREWORD BY ADRIANA TRIGIANI

ISBN 979-8-8620-9072-7

Published by

TRIUMPH PRESS

www.TriumphPress.com

TESTIMONIALS

A Boy From Crackers Neck is full of wonderful reminiscences of a time and place very special in American history and culture. It reminds me of THE WALTONS, except set in the Appalachian Mountains of Southwestern Virginia. Peace captures the distinctive society and values of rural Virginia, from agriculture to coal mining; church, family, community, and traditional values. It is informative, moving, and humorous. The personal depictions of World War II are very illuminating and valuable. I highly recommend this book!

Garrett W. Sheldon
Professor Emeritus, University of Virginia College at Wise
Pastor, First Baptist Church, Big Stone Gap, Virginia

From a dairy farm in Big Stone Gap to B-17 missions over war-torn Europe, *A Boy From Crackers Neck* is filled with lessons from a true American hero whose story is riveting and important. Jimmie Galloway represents the courage, morals, and love of country that we should all emulate. It is because of men like Jimmie that we enjoy the freedoms and comforts we do today. His grandson, John Peace, has done an exceptional job weaving family history into the major events of the last century. John tells the story with so much detail, including the personalities and humor of the many characters in the life of his Papaw, Jimmie, that this book is hard to put down and you never want to end. It is among the best writing and storytelling of WWII-era history you will find anywhere.

Senator Tim Kaine (VA)
Armed Services Committee,
Foreign Relations Committee, and Former Governor of Virginia

The heart and soul of **A Boy From Crackers Neck** are the stages of overcoming life's frustrations and unfairness. The story describes simple, good, and humble people, born into poverty, who led astonishing lives, then become admired heroic figures. This is the American Dream that young, present-day Americans struggle to fully appreciate. Several figures in this story illustrate this point. For example, Jimmie Galloway, the B-17 bomber pilot on whom the book is based, comes from a family that all became legends in Crackers Neck and in the state. The cigar-smoking Staff Sargent, Slew Stallard, from back home that Jimmy ran into in Southampton became a well-known coach. Even the nice German engineer, a former 109 Messerschmidt pilot who adds a glimpse of the horrifying lives the German soldiers had to endure, became a true friend to an American bomber pilot.

This book has a warm and touching conclusion with a theme. The author, John Peace, is an unusually good storyteller with descriptions that are visual and thought-compelling. I love how John Peace begins with a picture on the cover of several young military trainees and ends with a description of the same picture. It is a human story of the troops in tragic situations and the "Lucky Bastards" who beat astounding odds. Both represent the greatest generation. Their stories are so uplifting, this book will deeply touch its readers and leave you so attached to the characters, you won't want it to end. That's the mark of a great book!

Kent O. Hansen MBA CLU CHfc
CEO and Founder of Generations
Financial Partners in Eugene Oregon

John Peace's biography of his grandpa in **A Boy from Crackers Neck** is an exhilarating and often tense adventure from beginning to end. The main character, among the many colorful people you meet, is United States Army Air Force Captain Jimmie Galloway whose life story is a rare first-hand collection of memories of pre, contemporaneous, and post WWII history. These stories were recited to John by his grandfather (whom he refers to as Papaw) much later in life. Readers will be motivated to keep reading until the book is suddenly finished in just one sitting. A Hollywood movie could never do true justice to this spectacular real-world ride.

Through **A Boy from Crackers Neck**, Peace has contributed to American history in a fashion few authors have achieved. It is a must-read, especially for younger generations who will benefit from an empathetic, compassionate, and heroic character from the past whose spirit and example are truly timeless.

The character of Jimmie "Papaw" Galloway was forged in rural Southwest Virginia where young men and women matured early of necessity. The responsibilities laid on Jimmie and his generation's shoulders are probably incomprehensible for younger readers today as they are unaccustomed to such periods of scarcity. It was a time when shirkers and hooligans were rare, as the U.S. lacked social safety nets. Families would simply go hungry if each able-bodied member did not work from dawn until dusk, all while looking after neighbors and their communities. The Depression Era forged exceptional American characters like Jimmie Galloway from the steel of a rural community that lacked any concepts of abundance or leisure. But the American spirit of these men, women, and their children never complained of the hardships and sacrifices defining them.

In his youth, Jimmie Galloway had already confronted the overwhelming tragedy of death as part of the coal mining industry. During WWII, it was exceeded by his experience as pilot in command of a B-17 executing near suicidal bombing missions over Europe, the scene of heretofore unimaginable industrial scale carnage. Captain Galloway and his duty-conscious crew faced those dangers day after day, voluntarily and without complaint, a level of disciplined patriotic commitment born of selfless service rarely found in our general population today. Jimmie Galloway is the epitome of America's greatest generation. The grit and idealistic positivism that these soldiers carried back with them is reflected in the spectacular society they built in the post-war peace.

Franz J. Gayl, USMC Ret.
Author of **Legacy of a Green Devil**

A Tribute to My Papaw, Captain Jimmie Galloway
"To him and those like him, God Bless!"
-John William Peace II

ACKNOWLEDGEMENTS

First and foremost, I owe a debt of gratitude to the remarkable individuals who played a pivotal role in bringing this book to life. At the forefront of this creative journey is my ever-inspiring muse, Cathy Swinney. She's not only my sounding board for ideas but also the wellspring of countless "mountain sayings" that paint the vivid tapestry of our region. I can't count the number of times I've surreptitiously reached for my smartphone notes app during our conversations, capturing the wisdom she imparts.

A heartfelt thank you to Mike Allen, whose candid remarks, spoken outside the hushed confines of a funeral home from our dear departed friend Ben Mullins, resonated deeply. His mention of the illustrious authors hailing from the Big Stone Gap area, those astute individuals who committed "our" stories to paper, sparked a revelation within me. While I may not possess the brilliance or eloquence of those esteemed writers, the notion took root – why not share the rich tapestry of stories from World War II veterans I've absorbed throughout my upbringing in this very community?

And then, there's my invaluable editor and publisher, Melanie Davis of Triumph Press. Melanie, you breathed life into this project and nurtured my aspirations. When I initially contemplated the idea of sharing these old Hillbilly tales, fear gripped me. I doubted whether these cherished narratives would resonate beyond my family and our close-knit community. I never set out to be a writer, but storytelling has forever coursed through my family. Melanie's expertise and unwavering support allowed these stories to venture beyond our hills and hollers, reaching the hearts of others. Her encouragement emboldened me to continue unearthing and recounting the myriad of mountain stories waiting to be told.

SPECIAL THANKS

I want to wholeheartedly thank my Cathy Regina for putting up with my typing in the evenings! She makes our home so beautiful, happy and filled with joy, which makes for such a great environment to write down stories. Special thanks to my mother, Brenda Peace, my Aunt Vicki Williams, and my Great-Aunt Virginia Lawson (who is 98 years young as of writing this) and to my brother, David Peace, for helping me gather stories and pictures. To my son, Trey Peace, and daughter, Shelby Peace, I hope I've done justice to your Great Grandfather's stories so you all can pass them on to your children and grandchildren.

CONTENTS

Foreword

Adriana Trigiani

———————～———————

John W. Peace II has written a glorious memoir about his grandfather, Jimmie Galloway, a decorated World War II bomber pilot and the family who shaped him. In true Appalachian tradition, John recounts the stories his grandfather shared with him, as he looked back on his experiences as one of *The Greatest Generation*. Stories of danger, daring and sometimes, even hilarity are described in detail. Wisdom comes from experience, and Jimmie Galloway had his share. Through John's recounting, we have a bird's eye view of the horrific conditions, acts of courage and moral tests that faced Jimmie on the battlefield and in life. Jimmie pushed through the worst and lived to tell the story. John's expert rendering of his grandfather's voice is a treasure.

Included in this memoir are heartwarming family stories, a pastoral portrait of life in Cracker's Neck Holler. The sumptuous farm table with fried chicken, okra, blueberry cobbler, mashed potatoes and skillet cornbread will take you home to the family table. You will recall the loyalty, love and support of neighbors and friends, the bonds that held together the community in Cracker's Neck holler. There is much warmth and affection on these pages, that the reader understood implicitly why Jimmie wanted to serve his country and return home to the place he loved. It's a hero's tale, in many ways. The boy from Cracker's Neck traveled the world but his heart was always home in the mountains of Virginia.

Jimmie's southwest Virginia "raising" was evident in his acts of caring and largesse to allies and enemies alike. When you're from southwest Virginia, you're an Appalachian, which can mean you are made of something. You possess an inner core of strength and purpose that shapes how you move through the world. Jimmie is the best example of an Appalachian, he is one with nature and his God, while his moral code was shaped by examples of faith in his own family.

There are colorful characters that leap off the page, from preachers to pilots to coal miners, enemies, allies, sinners and saints are described through the lens of Jimmie Galloway who loved people and wanted his grandson, the author John, to love them as much. At home, you will meet Brother Billy, Ma Galloway, Graham, John, Jenny, Grover Cleveland Galloway a/ka/ Uncle Bud and Brenda Helen. Jimmie's wife, Jean Compton, is the love of his life. Hardworking neighbors and farmers: Old Man Begley and Old Man Bloomer, add sass and color. There's a reverence for the land and the animals that provide sustenance. This book conjured so many images of life in a small town, by the end, you could fill a charm bracelet with reminders of the places you read about because they are dazzling and vivid.

There's a saying back home, "He never knew a stranger," and this is true of Jimmie. He leaned into his moral code when he went off to war and held on to those values tightly throughout some incomprehensible and frightening experiences. When Jimmie meets Tex Smith, William Masters, General Meade and Captain Fitzgerald, each affect his life in profound ways, and he has an impact on theirs.

Jimmie found his moral courage in the conviction of his beliefs, the bedrock of which are Appalachian. We have a long literary tradition in Appalachia, honest and truthful storytelling, in order to describe, celebrate and instruct. Appalachian authors also write to remember. Our stories are our treasures and should not be forgotten or lost in time. The life lessons taught to us by our elders are our treasures. John W. Peace II has written what he knows and has shared his grandfather Jimmie with the reader with authenticity and grace. This is a book I hope you will savor. It's a story that needs to be told, and as importantly, needs to be shared.

Adriana Trigiani

Beloved by millions of readers around the world for her "dazzling" novels, *(USA Today)* Adriana Trigiani is *The New York Times* bestselling author of twenty books in fiction and nonfiction. She has been published in 38 countries around the world. *The New York Times* calls her "a comedy writer with a heart of gold," She wrote the blockbuster *The Shoemaker's Wife*, the *Big Stone Gap* series, the *Valentine* trilogy and *Lucia, Lucia*. Trigiani's themes of love and work, with an emphasis upon craftsmanship and family life, have brought her legions of fans around the world. Their devotion has made Adriana one of "the reigning queens of women's fiction" *(USA Today)*. Visit her website at **www.adrianatrigiani.com**

PREFACE

The mourners filed out of their cars in the parking lot, their breaths visible in the unusually extreme freezing air. They paused to take in the sight of the Gilliam Funeral Home that used to be a Gold's Gym back in the 1980s. It was hard to believe that a building that had once been a hub of activity and fitness could now be a place of mourning and reflection. The Gilliam Funeral Home was now the centerpiece of the Gilliam family's small-town business empire and Carl Gilliam's presence at the funeral home brought a sense of reassurance and comfort to the mourners.

In the lobby, people continued to catch up with each other, sharing stories and memories of Jimmie Galloway. They spoke of his kindness, generosity, and unwavering love for his family and community. As they made their way out of the funeral home, the mourners passed by photos of Jim Galloway, showcasing his life, family, and many achievements.

Preacher Tony, who conducted the funeral, was a unique figure. Instead of the usual solemn expression associated with funerals, he wore a slight smile on his face, proud to be chosen to honor Jim Galloway. His warmth and charisma added to the celebratory atmosphere of the chapel which was filled with laughter, music, and memories. Preacher Tony spoke about Jim Galloway's life, sharing stories and reading his obituary. The mourners listened intently as he spoke of Jim's lifelong fascination with flying, and his many achievements in the military and life as a dairy farmer. They smiled as he recounted Jim's love for singing hymns and his penchant for sharing stories that kept people captive for hours.

As the service came to a close, the mourners left the chapel and gathered in the lobby once again. The sound of sniffles and quiet chatter filled the air as people comforted each other and shared more stories about Jim Galloway. The Gilliam family provided coffee and a variety of home-baked goods from town, a small gesture of appreciation for the community's support. The kindness of the community was not lost on the Galloway family who appreciated the outpouring of love and respect for their patriarch.

As the mourners made their way out of the funeral home, the bitter cold air hit them like a slap in the face. But the memories and stories of Jim Galloway warmed their hearts and they left with a sense of peace and closure. They knew that Jim had lived a long and fulfilling life and that his memory would continue in the hearts and minds of those who loved him.

For many of the mourners, the service was a reminder of the importance of community, connection, and history. In a time when it's easy to feel isolated and disconnected, events like Jim Galloway's funeral serve as a reminder of the importance of coming together to honor and support those we care about.

The following day, the Galloway family held a small burial service inside the mausoleum at Powell Valley Memorial Gardens. The ceremony was simple, yet poignant, with family members saying their final goodbyes to Jim as they laid him to rest. It was a solemn occasion, but also a celebration of Jim's life and the impact he had on those around him. As the months passed, the Galloway family found comfort in the memories of Jim and the support of their community.

The transformation of the Gold's Gym building into a funeral home reflected the ever-changing nature of life. It served as a poignant reminder that nothing stays the same forever and that we must embrace each new chapter with open arms. Jimmie Galloway's life had followed a similar pattern of transformation and growth, with different stages that brought new challenges and opportunities.

INTRODUCTION

I grew up on a dairy farm where I spent a lot of time with cows and my Papaw, Jimmie Galloway. I was perpetually at his side, helping to milk the Holsteins, riding on a tractor fender bouncing across the pastures and hearing his colorful stories of growing up during the Great Depression.

I had a speech impediment as a young boy that was a result of many, many terrible ear infections. With this disability, I was socially awkward, and going to school was not a pleasant experience. Lucky for me, between the ear infections and some plain old fashion "acting," I missed a lot of school. As a result, I had the best education money simply can't buy. Listening to Papaw Galloway, I learned far more than I could have ever discovered in the pages of a 1970s Rand McNally primary school textbook.

No matter how sick I was, or pretended to be, the sound of my Papaw's truck pulling up would heal my illness like an ol' time mountain preacher "laying hands on me." The healing power of hearing stories of the Greatest Generation was real and it is my hope that this book will pass along that healing to you. If not, well, at the very least, you'll have a bit of my priceless education as I share the people and places, I met through the stories of Captain Jimmie Galloway.

I can recall the exact moment Papaw opened up and shared the first of his WWII experiences. While he loved to tell stories and talk, he stayed quiet about his time in WWII until one fateful day; following the morning's milking of our dairy cows on the family farm, my Papaw and I relished a hearty breakfast and then caught a little satellite TV to keep up with the latest news before embarking on the rest of the day's work.

Seated in his Lazy-Boy recliner, Papaw entrusted me with the duties of being the TV remote, having me switch channels on the box sitting on top of the TV until he found something captivating to watch. Suddenly, he exclaimed, "Stop right there, let's watch this!"

I sidled over and settled down beside him wondering what had caught his attention. To my surprise, we were now witnessing some "Blue Blood" horse show at a London Country Club in England where riders decked out in fancy English attire with long coats, top hats, and such, gracefully maneuvered horses into a dressage (although at the time, I had no clue what that was).

After observing the horse show for a brief spell, I turned to Papaw and asked, "You want to watch *this*?" (I couldn't fathom why he would be interested in this display, given that we didn't possess any horses on the farm and I was highly allergic to the creatures, with no intention of owning one in the foreseeable future.)

He responded, "Hold on for a minute, Son. I recognize that place. I've been there. That was the Shell-Shock Hotel."

Now I was all confused, *Been there? Shell-Shock Hotel? What on earth are you talking about?*

Throughout my formative years, I had the privilege of standing right beside Papaw, hearing his tales of growing up in our community of Crackers Neck. I knew he had served as a B-17 Bomber Pilot during World War II, yet he possessed an uncanny knack for diverting the conversation if anyone attempted to prod him about his war exploits. He would politely address your query and then hastily change the topic, leaving no room for further discussion.

Over the years, many of his peers from the Greatest Generation would visit the farm to see him and I would often hear them recounting their own war stories, but Papaw had never revealed his experiences. But then, out of nowhere, he was seated in his recliner telling me about his participation in a tragic mission known as "Black Thursday" where none of his fellow squadron planes made it back. That fateful night on October 14, 1943, 291 B-17F Flying Fortress high-altitude heavy bombers, each carrying a crew of 10, attacked a ball-bearing plant near Schweinfurt, Bavaria. German antiaircraft artillery and 300 fighters shot down 60 of the aircraft. Six hundred crewmen were killed or taken prisoner and it is the largest Army Air Force loss of the war to date.

Papaw returned from that mission to sleep alone in the barracks. The following day, his commander granted him and his crew a pass to the Red Cross Center, which the men had nicknamed "Shell-Shock Hotel." It was surreal to see a horse show on TV that was taking place at the very location where my grandfather had once been in 1943.

At the time, I had no clue why he had kept his war stories under wraps, nor did I know that it had been nearly three decades since he had confided in anyone about his wartime experiences in such great detail, but once Papaw "unlocked that box," during the four years of my high school life I became the primary recipient of an outpouring of tales from his military service. Being the receptacle of such amazing and historical stories, I knew that one day I needed to write them down before they became lost.

I have titled this book **A Boy from Crackers Neck** as a way to introduce the small community my Papaw grew up in, located in Virginia where the coal industry was booming but everyday life was slow and impoverished. It is a story, not just about my Papaw, but of all those in his life… family, friends, and comrades… whose experiences capture the essence of existence from a time that it was so harsh, life seemed to have no value, yet these are the stories that make us who we are today!

I wrote this book from the stories I grew up with, stories I heard repeated many times over by these men of the Greatest Generation. Whenever they started telling a story, it never occurred to me to interrupt and say, "You've told me this before." I was always mesmerized, just like someone watching a favorite movie or listening to a favorite song many times over. Hearing these stories was comforting and I found myself transported to a different time and era. The men who shared these stories loved telling and hearing them as much as this current generation enjoys their social media on their phones.

I heard the stories I am sharing so many times, I wrote them in a way that takes you there as if you are witnessing the events in real-time. Although I had to use some imagination to describe them as if I was there, these stories were told so vividly, and so often, I assure you, everything you are reading is true to what I was told!

In this book, you will meet many colorful and fascinating people including Papaw Jimmie's parents, brothers, schoolmates, neighbors, and fellow veterans. Throughout many of the chapters, I will provide additional details and information in grey-shaded boxes that expand the story into the present. Come with me, and let's meet the boy from Crackers Neck!

ONE

Galloway Farm

———～———

The Galloway family was truly blessed. Brother Billy, the patriarch of the family and father to Papaw Jimmie, not only had a good cash-paying job at Stonega Coke & Coal, but he also managed to save enough money to buy a bottomland farm in Crackers Neck. The farm, called the "Rock Farm" by Billy's oldest son, Graham, was run by Billy's wife, Julie. She was a savvy businesswoman who always sought new ways to bring in income for the family. Despite her small stature, Julie commanded a presence on the farm. Even though she was barely five feet tall, she was known as the one who truly ran the operation. The farm was located on East Stone Gap Road and was surrounded by lush green fields and pastures with a small creek running through. It was dotted with cattle and chickens with a few hogs in the pen. The Rock Farm was a peaceful and idyllic place, a true reflection of the hard work and determination of the Galloway family.

In the early 1900s, four kids were hardly enough to make a decent-sized family, let alone a crowd. In those days, it wasn't uncommon for families to have ten or more children running around underfoot. But as much as these parents may have enjoyed a full house, they were all too familiar with the risks. Disease, accidents, and the hazards of daily living all took their toll and many of these kids didn't make it to see adulthood.

Paw was always fascinated by Old Man Begley's large brood of 12 kids from up in the Neck. "How do you manage to feed all of them in the house?" he asked in amazement one day after church.

Old Man Begley just chuckled and replied, "It's simple, really. We have a big, long picnic table in the kitchen. Whenever we have a new addition to the family, we just make the other kids slide down the bench to make room at the table. And if you fall off the end of the bench, well then, it's time to get a job!"

The Galloway clan was small compared to others in the Neck. It was comprised of Graham, the eldest son, Jimmie, who was three years his junior, and John, born just 11 months after Jimmie. And then there was Virginia, or Jenny for short. She was the only daughter in the family, born a couple of years after John. It seemed that Jenny was always in the kitchen with Ma or doing household chores with her.

Julie (hereafter referred to as Ma), was always looking for new ways to support the family and was famous for her bartering prowess. One year, she heard about the large number of workers from Poland and Czechoslovakia hired by the Stonega Coal Company and saw an opportunity to provide these workers with the geese they preferred for the holidays. After overhearing their complaints about only being able to find turkeys in the local stores, Ma ordered a delivery of baby geese from Sears and Roebuck and soon the local grocery stores in Big Stone Gap and Appalachia were offering dressed geese alongside their traditional turkeys. To reach a wider customer base, Ma even had Billy (hereafter referred to as Paw) deliver some of the dressed geese to the coal camps on his Harley Davidson motorcycle, despite his complaints about the smell in his saddlebags. However, the extra income made it all worth it. Along with selling the farm's tobacco crop, it helped make Christmas and winter more pleasant for the Galloway family. Ma's entrepreneurial spirit and business savvy were a testament to her determination to provide for her family.

With Ma's farm "hustle" money, all of the Galloway boys were kept in good church and school clothes. One thing Ma was known for was her love of brand-name clothes and grocery products. The boys always wore Pointer Brand overalls and Buster Brown church shoes. This love for quality brands sometimes caused people in the community to question her spending habits.

A fellow church lady once asked her, "Why do you spend so much money on your name brands, Julie? Have you outgrown your upbringing?"

Ma had a quick response, "You get what you pay for, and you're lucky to get that!"

Her husband, Brother Billy, also had a similar view on life and politics. He believed in getting the best quality for his money and his politics went by the motto, "You get what you VOTE for, and you're lucky to get that!" This meant that he took care in his personal life to make informed decisions and vote wisely, just as he did with his spending.

Brother Billy's own Grandfather had immigrated to America from Wales and Billy was fond of quoting an old Welch saying, "Manners Maketh' the Man!" He would explain to his family, churchgoers, or anyone else that would listen that the meaning of this saying is the best way to quickly judge a man's character. It is by observing a person's manners… words are only words, but *manners maketh' the man!*

Ma and Paw were never ignorant of the struggles of those around them. They made sure to give back to their community, often opening their doors to provide meals and a warm place to stay for travelers and members of the church who had fallen on hard times. They also made sure to give a portion of their earnings to the local church and to organizations helping families in need. Despite their own financial security, Ma and Paw always remained humble, never flaunting their meager wealth or status. They understood the importance of giving back and made it a priority in their lives. They were respected and loved by the people in their community, who admired their strong work ethic and charitable nature. The Galloway family was truly blessed and they made sure to spread that blessing to those around them.

The horse barn on the Galloway farm was also a source of pride for the family, known for its well-kept stalls and comfortable living quarters for the horses. In addition to the horses of the Galloway family, the barn served as a boarding facility for local horse owners, with the first border being Dr. Sutherland and his magnificent black Tennessee Walker horse named Colonel.

Uncle Bud (Grover Cleveland Galloway), Paw's older brother, lived in a small room attached to the back of the farmhouse and kept his trusty work mules in the rear stalls of the horse barn. Unlike his brother and many other farmers in Crackers Neck who had transitioned around this time to using tractors for field work, Uncle Bud was the exact opposite of his brother when it came to adapting to technology. Bud was proud to stick to the traditional methods and continued to use his two trusted mules, Doc and Buster, for all the heavy lifting on the farm. Bud had come to the mountain wilderness of Wise Co, VA long before King Coal.

Bud had been struggling to make ends meet and exhausted all other options, so he came to this wilderness country in the late 1800s with the first industrial wave of harvesting virgin timber. The small timber camps were dotted throughout the mountains, offering work to those who were willing to live in harsh conditions.

Life in the camps was far from luxurious. The cramped, unsanitary shacks housed multiple men with little privacy or comfort. The smell of sewage and waste was overwhelming and the constant threat of disease was ever-present.

For example, one evening, Uncle Bud approached the cook who was stirring up a batch of cornbread with his hands. Uncle Bud asked the cook where the wash pan was so that he could wash his hands before dinner.

The cook replied, "I don't know. I haven't been able to find that for three days."

Despite these severe conditions, back in those days Bud and fellow loggers were grateful just to have some paying work and a roof over their heads.

The days were long and arduous with Bud and the other men rising before dawn to begin work. The small railroad lines were developed to haul the huge timber out and, in the winter, Bud would use mules that were fitted with spiked horseshoes to drag logs down the frozen Clinch River to the train yards in Gate City. From there, the lumber companies would ship the timber all up and down the East Coast.

Bud had come to live with his brother's family after a terrible accident that left him with a bad limp. Paw had sent word to Bud that he didn't want him dead and buried without a tombstone or proper burial at some timber camp and offered him paid work and a place to lay his head if he would come home to the farm.

In addition to being a mentor and beloved family member, Uncle Bud also turned out to be a skilled farmer who knew the ins and outs of the trade. He passed down his knowledge to his brother's sons, Graham, Jimmie, and John, teaching them about the different seasons for planting and harvest, how to properly care for the mules and horses, and the best techniques for cultivating the fields. Uncle Bud was known for his green thumb and the family's vegetable garden flourished under his care. Every summer, the Galloway's had an abundance of fresh produce, from sweet corn to tomatoes to cucumbers, and Uncle Bud would often share some of this surplus with other families in the community. Beyond his practical skills and knowledge, Uncle Bud was a true surrogate father figure of the family, always there with a warm smile and a supportive word no matter what was happening in the world around them.

Life on the Galloway farm in the bottom land of Crackers Neck was filled with love, hard work, and a sense of community that was unbreakable.

As is usually the case, there are many stories behind the name of a town. One of the explanations for the unusual name of Crackers Neck comes from the fact it is a neck in the valley which was a rather "cracker jack" place in its beginning. The story goes that at a gathering of early settlers in the area (Henry Wells, Tom Johnson, Lee, and Andrew Galloway) they all became drunk in the home of "Old John Wells." He ordered them off his property, telling them that if they did not leave, he would crack their necks with a club.

There is more than one version of the name as well. In this book, it is called Crackers Neck, because that is how my family refers to it. It is also officially listed as Cracker Neck, without the plural, and Cracker's Neck, with a possessive apostrophe. Which name is the correct one might depend on the story being told about its origin as well as the version used by the original inhabitants.

Left: Galloway House. Right: Crackers Neck Airfield

Left: Galloway House Right: Galloway Horse Barn

TWO

Two Bushel Baby

The Galloway family was known for their keen skill in the art of bartering and made the most of the limited resources they had. Ma would trade eggs, chickens, and other produce from her farm with the local storekeepers in exchange for household items and groceries. Besides being a very good farmer, Uncle Bud was a skilled blacksmith and carpenter and he would trade his services with his neighbors for goods and services the family needed.

The bartering system was a way of life in the coalfields, a testament to the tight-knit farm community that existed in the region. Neighbors would come together and help each other out during tough times, relying on the skills and resources they had. Ma, Paw, and Uncle Bud were known for their generosity and fair dealings.

Even in times of scarcity and layoffs in the mines, the bartering system kept the community afloat and allowed people to survive. The Galloway family's bartering skills helped them to get by during the Great Depression and their reputation for fair dealings helped to establish them as respected members of the community. The bartering system was a symbol of the resilience and ingenuity of the mountain people of the coalfields and it served as a reminder of the importance of community and self-sufficiency during difficult times.

Jimmie's older brother, Graham, had a habit of calling him the nickname "Two Bushel" from time to time. It was a reference to the bartering system that was in place for doctor's visits, especially for delivering babies. For years, the common barter payment for a doctor to deliver a baby was one bushel of corn. However, by the time Jimmie was born three years after Graham, the price had gone up to two bushels. His brother Graham would jokingly say that Jimmie was worth twice as much as he was because he was a "Two Bushel Baby."

Even though John was the baby boy, he never acquired the nickname due to a little vanity on Ma's part. Jimmie and little brother John were born only eleven months apart. Ma had such a difficult delivery with Jimmie because of his large size and her small stature and body frame that she swore to the doctor that she would have no more children.

The doctor laughed and said, "Why, I'll be back in eleven months," followed by a large grin!

Ma replied, "You'll not see me in any eleven months!" So, when Ma became pregnant with John, she was too embarrassed to go to the doctor or even call the doctor when John was born at the house eleven months later. Thank goodness, for John's sake that Aunt Lytle turned out to be a good midwife in a pinch.

Down in the mountains, there's a saying, "Pistol Packing Momma!" and boy, let me tell you, that saying couldn't be more fitting for Ma. Her pistol packing skills may have saved her life once and even made the headlines of the local newspaper.

Paw, bless his soul, had gifted Ma a 22LR caliber revolver pistol for Christmas shortly after their wedding day. It was meant for her to use around the farm for safety and to shoot varmints when needed.

One fine evening, she heard a commotion that raised the hairs on the back of her neck. It was coming from her beloved chicken coop. Without hesitation, she sprinted down to the coop to investigate, finding a mountain lion rummaging through her flock of cherished chickens.

Most folks would have run for help, but not Ma. She fearlessly whipped out her pistol and put that lion down, defending her precious chickens with every bullet of her pistol. Ma's picture was in the local newspaper with her standing in front of her chicken coup holding her pistol with the dead predator at her feet.

She reached 98 years old and lived alone as a widow for the last 30, but no one ever feared for her safety due to her always packing "heat."

Ma may have stood at less than five feet, but she commanded respect like nobody's business. Her words were always honest, always in the right place, and you always knew where you stood with her. The woman was one of the most dedicated Christians to ever grace the earth, always making time each day for prayer and studying the scriptures in her well-worn King James Bible.

But let me tell you, there was one thing that could set the "wildcat" loose in her - the mere mention of the "Good Ole Days." One Christmas in the early 1990s, Little Granny's granddaughter, Vicki, had gifted her a fancy case of Mason jar mugs with handles. On Christmas Eve, when the Galloway family opened their presents, Ma, who was "Little Granny" to me and everyone else in those days, opened the box of glassware, took one of the mugs out, gave it a once-over, placed it back in the box, and returned the present to Vicki.

"That's a thoughtful gift, Sweetie, but I remember the days we had to drink from Mason jars, and I'm not going back!"

"But I thought it would remind you of the Good Ole Days!" Vicki expressed.

"The only good thing about the 'Good Ole Days' is that they're gone and over with," Little Granny replied. "My life goes all the way back to 1897 and there were never any Good Ole Days. Only the old folks with a BAD, bad memory would call them that. *Today*, we're living in the Good Days!"

Setting folks straight about the Good Ole Days wasn't just limited to family. Sometime in the 1980s, years after Brother Billy (Paw) had passed, Little

Granny was attending church to listen to a new preacher's sermon. That particular Sunday, the man spoke about "Getting back to basics in the Bible, going back to the Good Ole Days when life was cheaper, simpler, and more innocent."

As the congregation filed out, the new preacher made a mistake and asked Little Granny what she thought of his sermon, thinking the Good Ole Days talk would please her.

Little Granny had her words locked and loaded, "I know you meant well, Preacher, but you didn't know what you were talking about. Good Ole Days? When things were cheaper and more innocent? My memory is good. When were these days, Preacher?"

The man fumbled his words, "Well, I mean back when we had preachers in schools and things were cheaper. Maybe the 50s or 60s, back when The Andy Griffith Show took place?"

Little Granny stood up straight, using every inch of her five feet. "Let me start with the time when things were cheaper. I've lived to see bread in stores selling for five cents a loaf until now, when it's a dollar fifty. I prefer it at a dollar fifty; you know why? Because today with Paw's UMWA retirement, I lay down my dollar fifty and take my bread home. Back when it was five cents, we had NO money to buy bread and had to walk by it on the shelves at the store. What's good about cheap prices when nobody had money to buy anything?"

Little Granny took a deep breath. "Now, let's talk about the days when we had preachers giving sermons every week in schools. I raised three teenage boys with love and did my best to instill Christian values. But teenage boys have the attention span of a rooster and think of the same things as a rooster - about hens and fighting. What we need in schools is discipline and a few paddles, not preachers."

"In case you're yearning for the 'Good Ole Days,' let me assure you, they weren't all they're cracked up to be. Take the 1950s, for instance. Sure, Elvis was shaking his hips, but poor kids were getting drafted for the Korean War. And don't even get me started on women's rights. Back then, a woman couldn't even open a bank account without her husband's signature. And that's just for the white ladies. Think about the way minorities were treated under segregation laws. And let's not forget about the 60s and 70s. The Vietnam War was a nightmare and the country was rife with race riots and assassinations. The National Guard even opened fire on peaceful student protesters. So, if you're tempted to wax nostalgic about the 'Good Ole Days,' just remember they were full of strife and suffering."

"That Andy Griffith TV show, it's a great show, but it's all make-believe! Heck, did you not realize WHY all the characters on that show are happy all the time? None of them were married! The only one that was married was Ottis, the town drunk! Mayberry was just a pleasant dream of how we wish things were, not HOW they were."

Little Granny ended the conversation with, "God Bless you, young man, and I thank you for your efforts."

The result… no more sermons about the "Good Ole Days."

As mentioned, Ma was a master of the bartering system. She could turn all kinds of farm products into new clothes and other necessities for her children come school time. She only bought brands that she trusted and was known to walk away from deals that didn't meet her standards. Despite the poverty of the Great Depression, her children were well-fed and often brought delicious center-cut pork chops for lunch, much to Jimmie's chagrin during his high school years.

One day, Ma found out from one of the teachers that Jimmie had been trading her farm-grown pork chops for some canned SPAM at school. When confronted, Jimmie explained that he liked the store-bought meat and store-bought square bread because it was something that they couldn't afford at home. Although he still received a scolding, Jimmie continued to enjoy SPAM with his eggs for the rest of his life. It wasn't until Jimmie was a teenager that he finally had paper money of his own and would buy SPAM sandwiches down at Carmines in Big Stone Gap. The bartering system was a way of life for him and his family during the Great Depression, but he was grateful for the experiences and lessons it taught him about hard work and resourcefulness.

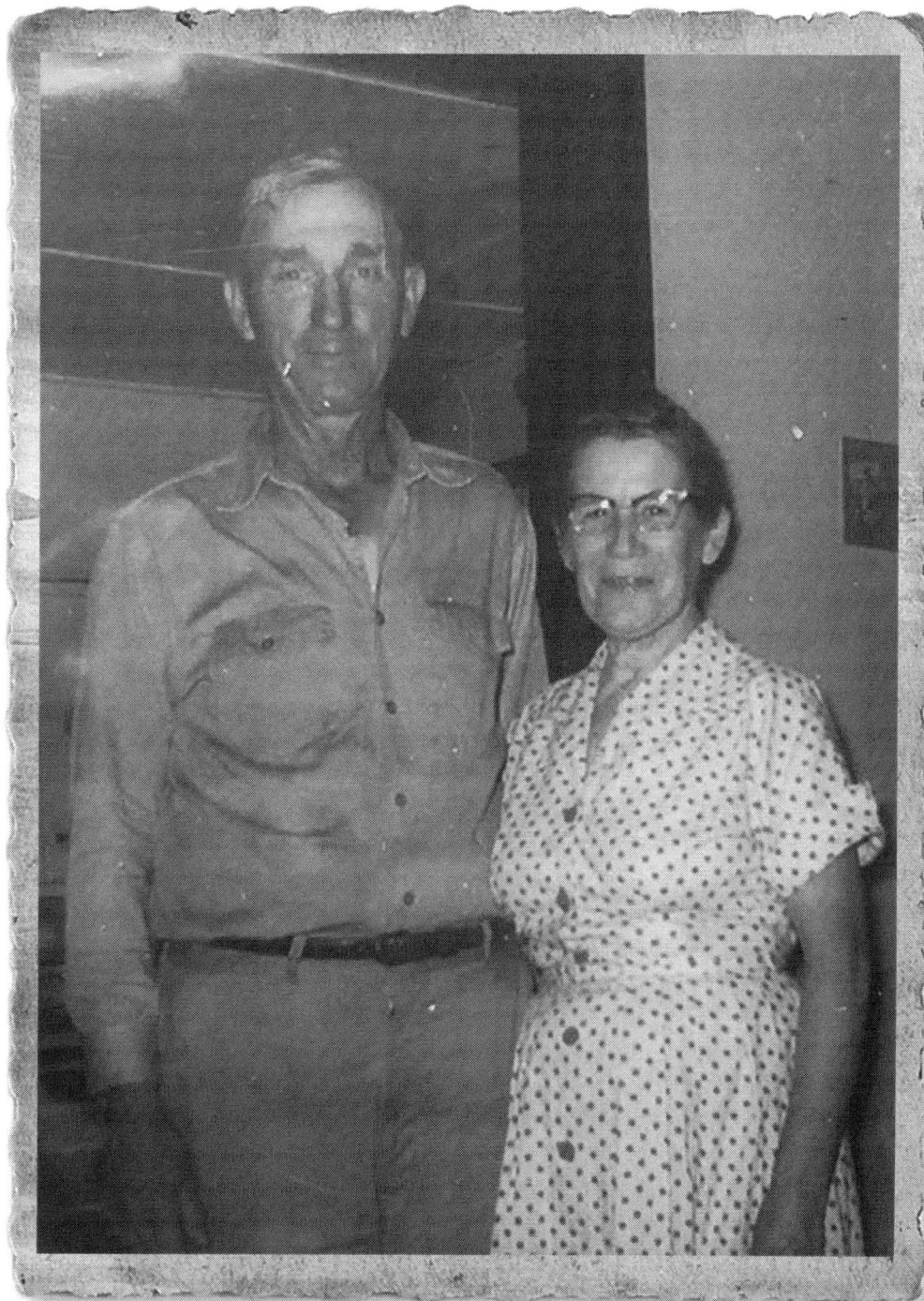

Left: Billy Galloway/Paw Right: Julie Galloway/Ma

50th Wedding Anniversary

THREE

Early Years on the Tobacco "Rock" Farm

———⌘———

"I damn hate this Rock Farm," barked Graham, tossing his hoe onto the ground.

"Yeah, me too," said six-year-old John as he pulled out a Camel cigarette and lit it up.

"Aw, come on, you two," interjected Jimmie, "We got work to do. Finish hoeing this tobacco row, and we'll catch them driving by in a minute. It'll make the effort worthwhile."

John took a long drag, exhaling smoke into the hot summer air, "I could use a break from this tobacco farming," he said.

Jimmie chuckled, "I hear you. I'm starting to feel like dirt's runnin' in my veins instead of blood."

As they wrapped up the last row, the trio ran up to the fence, propping their hoes against the gate. "Hey, remember when Ma caught you stealin' cigs from the coat closet at church last year?" Jimmie asked, trying to lighten the mood.

John took another drag and smiled, "Ah, those were the days. I can still see Ma's face when she caught me. But she started getting me my own Camels from her egg and goose money, so it all worked out."

"Yeah, did it really?" asked Graham, raising an eyebrow. "You been smokin' since you turned five years old, workin' farm chores for cigarettes and nothin' else."

John let out an "overly" raspy laugh. "Guess you're right. Should've listened to Ma and never started." Laughing while blowing smoke.

The tan Buick driven by the Fox sisters' chauffeur was a symbol of status and luxury in the eyes of the three boys. It was a sleek and shiny machine, with chrome accents that glinted in the sun; the sound of its engine was smooth and powerful. As it rolled by, the boys couldn't help but stare, marveling at the sight of the women who rode in such a fine automobile.

The Fox sisters were not just any well-to-do ladies, they were well-known in the area for their kinship to John Fox Jr., a local literary icon whose novels had put the region on the map.

John Fox Jr. was an American author, best known for his novel *The Trail of the Lonesome Pine*. Born in Kentucky in 1862, Fox grew up in the heart of the Appalachian Mountains, which would later become the setting for many of his stories.

The Trail of the Lonesome Pine tells the story of June Tolliver, a young woman living in the mountains of Virginia, and Jack Hale, an engineer who comes to the area to build a railroad. The two fall in love, but their relationship is threatened by the ongoing feud between the Tolliver and Falin families.

The novel was an instant success when it was first published in 1908 and became an instant bestseller, selling over a million copies in its first year alone. It remains one of Fox's most popular works. It was adapted for the stage and screen multiple times, including a 1936 film starring Henry Fonda.

This was the first movie on which Ma and Paw had ever splurged and took the boys to see. Graham thought it was boring but sure did think the lady actress playing June was pretty. Jimmie and John loved every minute of the movie.

In addition to *The Trail of the Lonesome Pine*, Fox wrote numerous other novels, short stories, and articles, many of which were set in the Appalachian Mountains. His writing focused on the people and culture of the region, often highlighting the poverty, isolation, and social injustices faced by its inhabitants. Fox died in 1919 at the age of 57, but his legacy as a writer and champion of Appalachian culture lives on.

The Trail of the Lonesome Pine remains a beloved classic, and is still taught in schools and universities today. The sister's association with him only added to their mystique and allure, and the boys felt a sense of reverence for the sisters and their family accomplishments.

The weekly drives that the Fox sisters took were a source of excitement for the boys who longed for adventure and a chance to explore the world beyond their small community. They imagined the thrill of cruising the countryside, feeling the wind in their hair and the sun on their faces. They also admired the sisters' simple pleasures, like stopping by Skeen's Store for RC Colas that were bottled over in Whitesburg KY and some local farm fresh pork skins, which seemed like a pleasurable luxury to the boys.

Jimmie looked at his brothers, "Heard Skeen's Store had barrels of fresh pork skins from the Dickensons'." They had just finished their yearly hog killing and had sold barrels of freshly cooked pork skins to local stores.

Jimmie really admired Terry and Stevie Dickenson's farming and timber operation from back in the day. Paw had allowed him to ride along while he showed a traveling chainsaw salesman their place in Maples Gap.

Terry and Stevie Dickenson were common-looking working men, but had by far the biggest and most profitable business operation in the area. They had bottomland in Crackers Neck where they farmed beef cattle, and up at Maples Gap, they had large tracts of timber that they cut and sold to local sawmills. From there, the timber would get sawed up and sold to the railroads for crossties and to local coal mines for mining timbers.

The Dickenson brothers weren't rich, but when they did buy something, it was quality and they were famous for taking care of equipment. Even up on the mountain timbering, the horse tack for pulling logs was cleaned every evening before being put up, horses brushed off and all saws given a wipe-down and sharpening at the end of the work day. Farm equipment was treated with the same upkeep.

The traveling salesman had stopped by the Galloway farm to talk to Paw about the latest technology of the 1930s, a Stilh motorized chainsaw. Now, these first chainsaws were not small. It took two stout men to operate the saw and, during the Great Depression years, they had a huge price tag of close to $50 or more!

"That sure is a great piece of modern technology there, young man, but we don't have any need or have the money to buy such a fine piece of equipment." Paw said, "but I do know who you might want to talk to, and if you end up selling them anything, you've earned your biscuits! Them boys know how to make money, and they know how to keep it more!" he said with a slight chuckle.

The salesman, not knowing the area well, offered Paw a dollar if he would lead him up the mountain and introduce him to Terry and Stevie. That's when Paw took Jimmie to see their operation up in the Gap. After the introductions and looking over the timber operation, Paw and Jimmie left the salesman and the Dickenson Boys to do their business.

Later that afternoon the salesman stopped by again grinning from ear to ear, "Thank you so much for taking me up to see Terry and Stevie!" the salesman said.

"I take it went well?" Paw replied.

"Well, they put me out of business!" the salesman chuckled

"Out of business?" Paw questioned.

"Yes, at first, I thought they were going to run me off the mountain when I told them price, but then we started my demonstration chainsaw up and I let them cut some trees and then size some logs! Lordy, not only did they order a new saw from me to be delivered, they wouldn't let me leave with my demonstration one. They bought it and every spare chain and part I had in the truck! I'm out of business until the company can ship me a new demonstration saw!" the salesman said, laughing with a grin.

In the eyes of the Galloway boys, the Fox sisters represented a world of possibilities and rich people's dreams, a world that was just beyond their reach. But even in their small and simple lives, they found joy and excitement in the sight of those who had a little more. It was a reminder that even in the midst of poverty and hardship of the Great Depression, there were small moments of beauty and wonder to be found in everyday life.

"Damn, when I get off this rock farm, I'm gonna make some money and buy me a car like that!" big brother Graham barked as the car drove away.

Jimmie had already lost interest in the car and was scanning the country airfield across the road on Skeen's farm, searching for any signs of activity. It was quiet, just cattle grazing on the country airstrip. Jimmie had been fascinated with planes since he was a young'un. Whenever a plane needed to land, the pilot would buzz the Galloway house across from the airfield and Jimmie and John would run the cows off the field through the gate to the next field. The pilot would circle until the field was clear and then come in for the landing. Jimmie would continue to lend his services at the airfield for years to come, eventually trading his cattle-herding work for flight training with some of the full-time pilots. He didn't know it then, but his pilot skills would shape the rest of his life. For now, he just knew he loved planes and would love flying them even more.

1920's Crackers Neck Airfield

FOUR

Skeen's Store

A few years later, when John was around 9 years old and Jimmie was 10, they walked up to Skeen's Store to spend their pennies on some chewing tobacco for Jimmie and cigarettes for John.

Skeen's Store was a small, rustic country shop located at the crossroads in Crackers Neck. Despite being in the midst of the Great Depression of the 1920s, the store remained open and bustling with activity as it was a popular destination for the surrounding rural community. Farmers and local residents would come to purchase essentials such as flour, sugar, and ammunition, as well as trade goods and gossip.

The building was made of rough-hewn, weathered sawmill boards and had a wooden porch that ran the length of it. The porch was a gathering place for people to socialize and catch up on the latest news. A hand-painted sign, barely legible, hung over the entrance, announcing the store's name in bold letters.

However, the Great Depression of the 1920s had indeed taken its toll on the store and its inventory was sparse. The shelves were lined with basic necessities such as flour, sugar, and beans, but there was very little in the way of luxury items. The shop was dimly lit with a single overhead light bulb casting a yellow glow over the counters and shelves. The wooden floorboards creaked underfoot and the air was heavy with the smell of sawdust and tobacco smoke. The store was run by a grizzled old man named Skeen who sat behind the counter on a wooden stool, always whittling away at a piece of wood, or so it seemed.

"I tell you what," said Jimmie, "if this politicking at Skeen's Store gets any more boring, I might just fall asleep right here on the counter."

John let out a loud cuss word, causing Jimmie to burst out laughing, "When did you learn to cuss like that?"

"Oh, you know, when Ma and Paw weren't around," said John with a mischievous grin. John being such a small kid, he had to compensate by being the loudest most foul-mouth young'un you ever heard. Only when Ma and Paw weren't around tho. The two of them continued their trip to Skeen's Store, joking and laughing all the way, despite the tough times on the Tobacco Rock Farm

As John and Jimmie approached the store, John took a drag from his Camel cigarette and turned to Jimmie. "Are you ready to find out what's going on in there?" he asked, his southern accent thicker than usual.

Jimmie nodded eagerly; his blue eyes wide with excitement. "I've never seen a Lincoln car before," he said, his voice filled with wonder as he looked at the big car parked in front of the store.

John chuckled and pushed open the door to Skeen's Store. The hum of excited voices filled the small space and the boys made their way through the crowd to the counter. They could see Mr. Skeen, the store owner, deep in conversation with a man in a suit surrounded by several other men in overalls.

John elbowed Jimmie and whispered, "Looks like we've stumbled upon the good stuff today, boy."

Jimmie stifled a giggle and leaned over to John. "Do you think they're talkin' about the election?"

John shrugged. "Could be anything. Maybe the bank's about to foreclose on some farm or somethin'. We'll never know if we don't go ask."

And with that, John stepped forward, his cigarette still dangling from his lips. "Excuse me, Mr. Skeen," he said, his voice surprisingly confident for an 8-year-old. "What's goin' on today?"

Mr. Skeen turned to him, a smile spreading across his face. "Well, if it isn't young John Galloway. And Jimmie too! What brings you boys to the store today?"

John shrugged nonchalantly. "Just needed some chew. And maybe a little gossip."

Mr. Skeen chuckled. "Well, I'll tell you what. These gentlemen here are from the Democratic Party, and they're lookin' for volunteers to help with the campaign."

John's eyes lit up with excitement and he turned to Jimmie, "We could help! We could be campaign volunteers!"

Jimmie nodded and the two boys eagerly joined the group, excited to be a part of the intrigue of the political world far from their Tobacco "Rock Farm."

The brothers, Jimmie and John Galloway, made their way through the crowded room of men and slid around to the back counter. Jimmie held up a penny, catching the attention of "Old Man" Skeen who was manning the counter. Skeen acknowledged the penny and put it in the pay jar on top of the counter. Jimmie then grabbed a drink and some Cracker Jacks for himself and John to share.

As they sat and snacked, they listened to the grumblings of the older men around them who were complaining about the lack of good-paying jobs and the possibility of another war in Europe. The WWI veterans in the group expressed their concerns about their sons and grandsons being sent to fight in a foreign war, just as they had.

In the center of the room, the Galloway brothers noticed a man who was unlike anyone they had ever seen before. Jimmie pointed at the man's shiny patent leather shoes, commenting that he must be rich. The boys sat near the egg bin and began to listen in on the grown-up conversation.

The well-dressed man was there to secure the miners' votes for the upcoming presidential election. He spoke in elaborate language, but the men around him seemed to be pleased with what they were hearing. Cheers erupted from the group when the man promised to support their right to unionize and to force the coal companies to pay higher wages. He empathized with the struggles the country was facing during the Great Depression.

Finally, the man promised the miners that if elected, he would do all he could to keep America out of any more wars in Europe. This promise, however, didn't seem to hold the attention of John who, by this point, was getting antsy. The sugar from his soda was kicking in and he lit a cigarette, stood up on a milk crate, and proclaimed, "I tell you what, we need to go to war on all this DAMN poverty around here! I'm tired of this shit! Can't afford to buy a damn thing because of all this poverty!"

All the men in the store turned their attention to John, momentarily caught off guard by the little boy's bold statement. But as he hung there with a cigarette dangling from his lip, the men started laughing. Jimmie held his breath, not sure if the man with the fancy shoes would be angry with John's outburst. But, when he saw the man staring at John with a straight face, he quickly grabbed John by the straps of his overalls and led him out of the store. Once the screen door slammed shut, both brothers started running home

The commercial for FDR continued to play over the radio and Paw listened intently, nodding his head in agreement with the candidate's promise to end the Great Depression. The Galloway family was doing ok, but knew so many families that were struggling to make ends meet, just like many families across the country. The Great Depression had hit them hard and they were eager for any solution to their financial struggles.

As the commercial ended and the Grand Ole Opry resumed, Ma sat back in her rocking chair and said, "It's about time someone stood up for the little folks. Maybe this Roosevelt fella will be the one to make a difference."

Jimmie and John couldn't help but feel a sense of pride as they thought about the man in the fancy shoes who had listened to John's outburst at the general store. The fact that a presidential candidate was now using similar language made them feel like their voice was being heard and that change was possible.

From that day on, the Galloway family followed FDR's campaign closely, hoping and praying that he would indeed deliver on his promise of a "Fair Deal" and bring an end to the hardships they faced. They knew that this election had the potential to change their lives and the lives of countless others in their community.

Ma had a tough upbringing as one of 13 siblings who were all orphans at a very early age. At the young age of 14, she married William "Billy" Galloway and became the matriarch of their family. Although small in stature, she was a force to be reckoned with and ran the household with an iron fist while her husband had the final say in all family matters. He worked as a foreman at the Stonega Coal Company during the week and was a self-educated preacher at Big Springs Church on the weekends, known to the community as "Brother Billy." Despite the onset of the Great Depression in the late 1920s, Paw earned enough money from his job to pay the bills while Ma supplemented their income with her farm enterprises.

FIVE

Brother Billy

———~———

Brother Billy Galloway, or Paw as his family called him, was a unique individual in the small community of Crackers Neck. He was not only a devout Free Will Baptist preacher but also an avid reader, educator, and early adopter of technology. Despite never having the chance to attend a traditional seminary school, he was highly knowledgeable and well-read, having educated himself through mail-order correspondence courses. His study room was a testament to his dedication and hard work, with shelves filled with books and stacks of meticulously prepared sermons, typed up on his trusty Victor typewriter. When he received a new study chapter from the correspondence course, he would spend hours researching the answers. If he received a graded paper back with a mistake, he would study the issue to make sure he never made the same mistake again.

Brother Billy's progressive ideas and beliefs were both revered and controversial within his congregation. His love for technology and incorporating it into his life and the church caused two significant scandals within the community. Some members felt that his embrace of modernity went against the teachings of the Baptist faith, while others saw him as a trailblazer and visionary, bringing the gospel into the modern age. Despite the controversy, Brother Billy remained steadfast in his beliefs and continued to preach with passion and conviction. He had a magnetic personality and was well-loved by many in the community who saw him as a charismatic leader who truly cared about their well-being.

The first big scandal at Big Spring Church was when Brother Billy became one of the first residents of Crackers Neck to install a telephone in his home. At the time, many Southern Baptist preachers in the area were against the new technology, preaching that the telephone was a tool of the devil that would only spread lies, gossip, and neglect of household duties by wives. Despite the opposition, Brother Billy saw the potential benefits of the telephone and embraced it wholeheartedly.

Decades later, when the internet became widespread, Jimmie remembered the controversy surrounding the telephone and chuckled at a similar sermon he heard at Oak Grove Baptist Church. That future preacher was warning about the dangers of the internet and how it was spreading sin. Jimmie realized that the controversy his Paw was part of in his youth was repeating itself and reflected on the power of technology and how it can shape and be shaped by society's beliefs and values.

The second technology-related scandal involving Brother Billy was when he became one of the first residents of Crackers Neck to own a television set. Again, this caused a huge stir among the Southern Baptist preachers in the area who believed that the television was a tool of the devil and was spreading sin into our God-Fearing homes. They argued that TV shows, which they perceived as being full of lust, greed, and deviant behavior, were corrupting children and housewives. One preacher even proclaimed that you could see the "Marks of the Devil" - TV antennas - sticking up from homes in Big Stone Gap that had supposedly lost their way with the Lord.

Despite the criticism and opposition, he faced, Brother Billy remained steadfast in his belief that technology was a powerful tool that could be used for good. He was a visionary, always seeking out new ways to connect with others and share his message of faith. His unwavering spirit and passion for spreading the gospel touched the lives of countless people and inspired them to embrace new technologies and use them to spread positivity and hope.

Furthest Right: Brother Billy Galloway

SIX

Not One but Two
Murders at Church

In the rural mountain areas of those days, church attendance was considered mandatory and those who didn't attend were often looked down upon as heathens or drunkards. The church was the central pillar of the community and people would gather there not just for religious services but also for social events like potlucks, fairs, and charity drives.

On some pretty days, the Big Springs Church would be so full that all the windows would be raised and seats unfolded outside so the overflow crowd could hear Brother Billy preach. The sound of his booming voice would echo across the fields and reverberate through the trees. It was a spectacle to behold, with people of all ages sitting under the sun, taking in the gospel, and socializing with their friends and family. It was not just a religious duty, but a social event that brought the community together.

The young men and women would also use the church as a place to court each other. The boys would sit on one side of the church and the girls on the other, sneaking glances at each other and exchanging shy smiles. After the service, they would linger outside, chatting and laughing, taking walks together, and maybe even sharing a sweet kiss. Church was not only a place to worship, but also a place to find love and companionship.

Even the non-churchgoers were lured by the allure of community and the grandeur of the event and would show up on such special occasions. It was an opportunity to catch up with the neighbors, hear the latest gossip, and indulge in the simple pleasures of life. For most folks, the sound of Brother Billy's sermons brought comfort and served as a source of motivation, reinforcing their faith and their position in the world. However, the church was not immune to the world of sin.

During the 1930s, the population of Wise County, VA swelled to over 40,000, enticed by the logging and mining jobs. Just imagine such a massive population and only one police chief, a daytime deputy, and a nighttime deputy in the town of Big Stone Gap, VA. East Stone Gap wasn't even a proper town, and hence there was no police department. During those years, the elected county sheriff's office wasn't much better, with just a sheriff and six full-time deputies to serve the whole county day and night. Moreover, a considerable expanse of the county had no telephone facilities to even call law enforcement. In other words, the only law someone had was the knife or pistol they carried.

Combine these two scenarios of extensive social gatherings in church and meager law enforcement and you get a recipe for man's law to sometimes override divine law. It was during Brother Billy's reign as preacher at Big Springs Church when these two worlds collided, with disastrous consequences.

The scene at Big Springs Church was always a sight to behold on Sundays with folks from all walks of life coming together for prayer, worship, and fellowship. But on that fateful Sunday, the peaceful atmosphere was shattered by the sound of a razor slicing through flesh.

Albert Spears, a rugged man with a fiery temper, had been simmering with rage for weeks over rumors of his wife's affair with Deputy Sheriff Sam Dixon. He couldn't stand the thought of the man who had betrayed him walking around free and happy in his community while he suffered in silence. So, he made the decision to take matters into his own hands.

As the congregation began to sing their first hymn, Albert slipped into the back pew and sat directly behind Sam. The piano player started the tempo and the voices of the choir rose in song, but the notes were soon drowned out by the sickening sound of metal slicing through flesh.

Sam Dixon's throat was cut from ear to ear, blood gushing out of the wound and staining the Sunday clothes of those nearby. The shocked congregation screamed and scattered, some running for the doors and others cowering in fear.

Albert sat calmly in his seat, still holding the razor in his hand as the other churchgoers watched in horror. It was a scene that would be etched into their memories forever.

A few years passed since the tragic event of Albert Spears and his straight razor, yet the memory of it lingered in the minds of those who witnessed it. Once again, Big Springs Church was the scene of another church goer violent streak, as another murder occurred on its steps.

This time it was over money, a common vice that had a way of turning peaceful neighbors into bitter enemies. George Chandler and James Adams had been disputing over property lines and James had hired the Dickenson Brothers to cut down trees that he claimed belonged to him. But George disagreed, and tensions between the two escalated until they culminated on the front stoop of the church.

People had come to church that day seeking solace and spiritual guidance, but what they got instead was a scene out of the wild west. The two men began yelling at each other and it quickly became clear that this was no ordinary argument. In a flash, George pulled out a pistol and shot James point blank.

The sound of the gunshot echoed through the church sending everyone into a panic. People were screaming and running for cover, while others tried to tend to James' lifeless body. The Dickenson Brothers, who had been hired to cut down the disputed trees, stood frozen in shock, unsure of what to do next. The authorities were called, but as with the previous murder, justice was swift and brutal. George was arrested and thrown into the Wise County Jail, later sentenced to a light 15 years in prison due to the circumstances of the ongoing feud between neighbors.

Big Springs Church / Crackers Neck

SEVEN
The Explosion

———————～————————

The story of the Stonega Coke and Coal Company began in the early 20th century in Southwest Virginia, a land full of mountains and coal mines. The company was formed in 1902 by a group of Yankee businessmen from Philadelphia, who saw the rich coal seams in the area and the potential for profits to be extracted from the mountains.

The company built a massive complex of mines, coke ovens, and coal processing plants in the heart of the mountains and soon became one of the largest coal producers in the region. The workers, mostly immigrants from all over the East Coast and Europe, labored in the mines and at the coke ovens, enduring long hours and dangerous conditions. The company town of Stonega grew up around the mines, a collection of company-owned houses, stores, and churches.

The coal camps had everything the workers needed, from a hospital to a post office to a movie theater. But it was a company town, and the workers had little say in their daily lives due to company police. Even the church preachers were hired by the company and answered to their calling.

The mining operations of the Stonega Coke and Coal Company were a marvel of engineering and technology for production, but not necessarily for miner safety. The mines were dug deep into the earth with miles of tunnels and rail lines crisscrossing the underground network. The coke ovens used a complex system of heating and cooling to turn the coal into coke, a vital ingredient in the steel-making process.

Despite the impressive technology and the profits flowing to the company owners, life for the workers in Stonega was hard and dirty. The twelve-hour work shifts, six days a week, was standard. That plus extremely dangerous working conditions took a toll on the miners and their families. There were accidents and injuries, and catching the black lung disease was a constant threat.

The Stonega coal loading tipple where Brother Billy worked was just as rough and dirty a place. The coal dust and grime covered every surface, from the walls and floor to the machinery and the workers themselves. The sound of coal being shoveled, weighed, and loaded onto rail cars echoed throughout the tipple. The air was thick with the scent of coal dust, oil, and sweat from the hard-working laborers. The machines, though necessary for the work, were loud and dangerous, and the workers were constantly on guard to avoid injury.

Despite the harsh conditions of the coal-loading tipple, Brother Billy had a small clean office located at the far end of the tipple. It was a cramped space, filled with papers and ledgers, but it was his refuge from the chaos and noise of the loading area. The walls were covered with railroad maps, mining charts, and schedules, and the desk was cluttered with inkwells, quills, and stacks of invoices.

Brother Billy was in charge of keeping the records of the coal production and shipments and he took his job seriously. He was meticulous in his record-keeping, making sure that every detail was logged accurately and in a timely manner. The coal tipple always looked a mess, but to Brother Billy, it was a sign of the hard work he put in every day to keep the tipple running smoothly. Despite the dirty and rough exterior of the coal-loading tipple, Brother Billy's office was a well-organized haven that reflected dedication to his work and commitment to doing his job correctly.

It was a typical day at the Stonega Coke & Coal's tipple up at the Bullitt Mine operation. Brother Billy Galloway was going about his usual routine of ensuring the orderly work and efficiency of the coal shipments and movement of equipment, when, suddenly, disaster struck. The tranquil repetitive hum of the mine machinery was shattered by a loud and powerful explosion that originated from Bullitt Mine portal.

The sound of the mine explosion was deafening. It was unlike anything Brother Billy had ever heard before, a mix of a thunderclap and a high-pitched scream. He could feel the vibrations in his chest as if a giant hand was squeezing his heart. He immediately jumped up from his desk and ran to the window. He could see a thick cloud of black smoke rising from the mine entrance.

Men were running in all directions, their screams adding to the cacophony of noise. Brother Billy felt helpless, watching the chaos unfold from his safe office. He knew that this was no ordinary accident; something terrible had happened down in the mines.

Billy's heart was pounding as he approached the mine entrance and scene of the explosion. The area was in chaos, with miners running and shouting, trying to escape the dangerous gasses that were seeping out of the mine. Billy was not afraid, however. He had seen similar disasters like this before and knew what had to be done.

He assessed the situation quickly, taking in the extent of the damage and the position of the trapped miners. He could see that the explosion had caused a cave-in, burying several of the coal miners beneath the rubble. With no time to waste, he began issuing orders to the rescue workers, directing them to the areas where the trapped miners were most likely to be found.

Billy worked tirelessly, his adrenaline kicking in as he led the rescue efforts. He was the voice of calm and reason in the midst of the chaos, making sure that his workers were safe and that the rescue operation was proceeding smoothly. Despite the dangerous conditions, he never lost his cool and was able to make quick, effective decisions that ultimately helped to save lives.

After about two hours of intense rescue efforts, the bodies of sixteen miners and four ponies were brought out of the mine shaft by the rescue team. Billy was devastated by the loss of life and the tragedy that had occurred. He knew the risks that the miners took every day, but he still couldn't shake off the feeling of guilt and responsibility. He was well respected by his peers and the miners for his compassion and leadership and the loss of life under his supervision weighed heavily on him.

Just as the events of the tragedy had started to settle down, a fancy Cadillac Model 61 car pulled up. The Model 61 was a luxury car of the 1930s and this one was no exception. The sleek black paint was polished to a high shine, reflecting the surrounding trees and sky. The enclosed cab provided a comfortable interior with plush seats and large glass windows offering a clear view of the countryside. The hood was adorned with a shining chrome radiator indicator and the wheels were fitted with whitewall tires that added to the car's overall appearance.

As Mr. Kelley stepped out of the automobile, the door creaked softly on its hinges, adding a touch of sophistication to the car's design. Onlookers couldn't help but be impressed by the car's beauty and elegance, a symbol of Mr. Kelley's wealth and status with the coal company.

Mr. Kelley stood and looked around with an air of confidence and power. He was dressed in a finely tailored three-piece suit, the material a deep shade of navy blue that matched his polished shoes. A crisp white shirt, complete with a starched collar, was topped off with a silver tie pin and a red silk handkerchief peeking out of his breast pocket. A matching fedora hat sat on top of his well-groomed head, casting a shadow over his dark and piercing eyes

He had received a wire about the explosion at the miner's office in Big Stone Gap and had decided to come and assess the situation for himself. Billy approached Mr. Kelley, ready to face the consequences of what had happened and to do whatever was necessary to prevent a similar tragedy from happening again. This accident was going to cost the company money and coal production due to the deaths of so many experienced miners.

Superintendent Kelley caught Billy's attention and motioned him into the coal tipple's office.

"What in the devil happened to those DAMN ponies?" Kelley barked. "They're going to cost the company three dollars apiece to replace!"

Billy was outraged by the Superintendent's callousness towards the human lives lost in the explosion. He had worked in the mines for years and had seen the dangerous conditions that the miners faced daily. He had lost friends and coworkers before, but this tragedy hit close to home and the Superintendent's attitude was insulting.

"Ponies?! Sixteen men died here today! How can you be so heartless?" Billy exclaimed, his voice rising with anger. "These were fathers, husbands, and sons. They had families who depended on them, and now they are gone."

The Superintendent scowled at Billy's outburst, "Listen here, Galloway. I'm the Company Superintendent and I'm here to get answers. It doesn't cost the company a damn penny to replace men. Hell, there's already a line of unemployed men up at the Miner Building in Big Stone looking to take their places. So, unless you want to join them in being unemployed, you'd better start talking."

Billy took a deep breath and tried to calm himself because as much as Mr. Kelley's words were callous and cold-hearted, he knew they were truthful. Men would be lined up to apply for the same jobs that had killed the men before them. He also knew that speaking out against the company could lead to his immediate dismissal, but he couldn't remain silent in the face of such injustice. He decided to take a stand and speak his mind. "You know what happened, Superintendent. The conditions in the mines are unacceptable. The ventilation is poor and the ponies are overworked. Another tragedy like this is inevitable unless something changes," Billy said, his voice firm and resolute.

The Superintendent rolled his eyes, "Save your excuses for someone who cares, Galloway. The company is spending a lot of money to modernize the mines and the ponies are essential to the operation. We can't afford to lose any more of them."

"I'm not making excuses, Superintendent. I'm speaking the truth. The miners deserve better working conditions, and the ponies deserve to be treated with dignity and respect. It's time for the company to take responsibility for the well-being of its workers and even the animals," Billy said, his eyes blazing with determination.

The Superintendent looked at Billy with disdain and then turned to leave. "I expect a better attitude when we meet again, Galloway," he warned as he stepped out of the office.

As the tensions subsided, Company Police arrived on the scene to maintain order and dispose of the bodies. Each deceased miner was identified and wrapped in large burlap tobacco bundling sheets, then loaded onto a Dodge flatbed truck that one of the policemen had brought up with them.

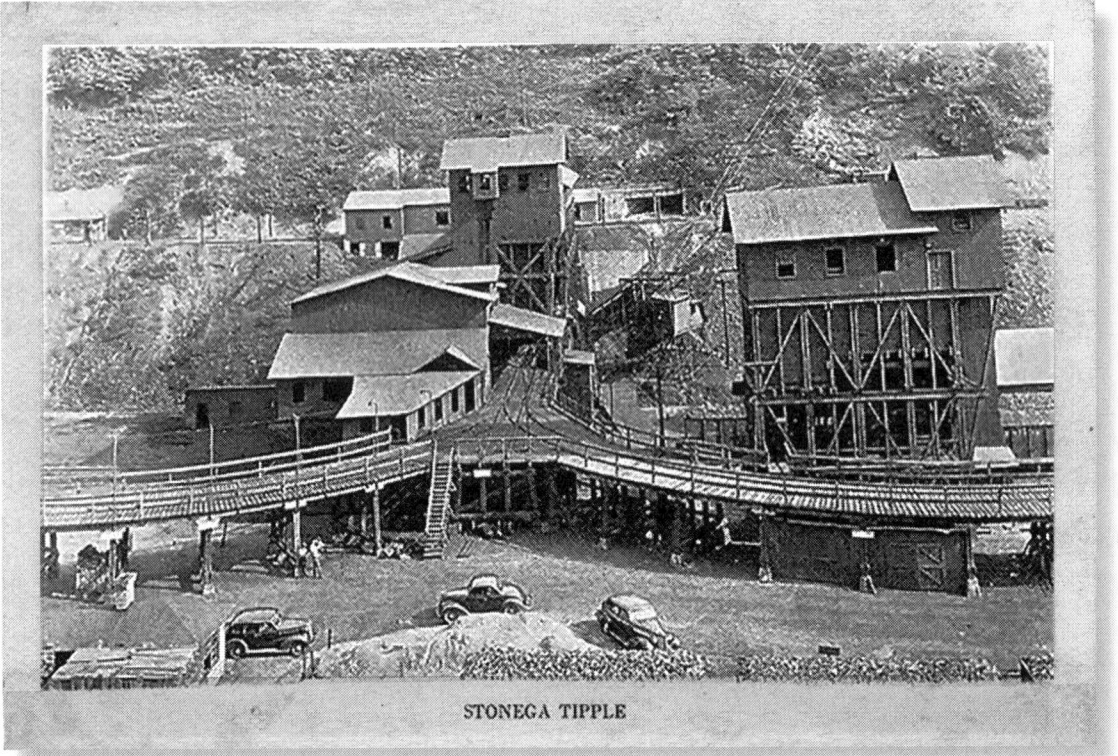

STONEGA TIPPLE

Open flame lamps on their helmet !

EIGHT
The Aftermath

———~———

Life was tough for the families who lived in the coal camps that dotted the Appalachian Mountains around the coal mines. These remote, isolated communities were built to house the workers who toiled in the mines deep underground, extracting the coal that powered the country's factories and trains.

The coal camp houses were simple, wooden structures that were cramped and often crowded but did have some modern utilities of electricity and running water. Most of the houses were only one or two bedrooms with a kitchen and a combined living/dining area. There was little room for a lot of furniture and families often had to make do with just a few pieces of furniture and a small amount of personal possessions.

Despite the cramped quarters, the coal camp houses were a symbol of hope and opportunity for the families who lived in them. For many of these families, the coal camps represented a chance to escape poverty and make a better life for themselves. They came from all over the country, from cities and across Europe and local farms alike, in search of work and a better future.

The streets of the coal camps were often unpaved and littered with coal dust, but the houses were surrounded by small gardens and fruit trees. The gardens were a source of pride for the families and a way to grow fresh produce and brighten up the otherwise drab surroundings.

In the aftermath of the explosion, the nearby coal camps of Stonega and Pardee were in a state of mourning and suffering. The company showed little compassion for the families of the fallen miners, leaving the responsibility of burying their loved ones to them. The bodies of the miners were transported to their families' company homes, accompanied by a cruel note left by the Company Police that informed them of the company's demand for them to vacate their homes within three days. The families were given no time to grieve or properly bury their loved ones and instead were left to struggle with the added burden of losing their homes along with their livelihoods.

The company's only "concession" was to offer the deceased miner's job to one of his sons, if he was old enough to work. However, this offer was conditional and came with strings attached. Before any employment could commence, the Company Police would come to collect any debts owed to the Company Store.

The coal companies paid their workers in script money during those years, meaning that they were dependent on the Company Store for all of their basic necessities. The workers were forced to purchase from the store at exorbitant prices and often found themselves in debt to the company. Exchanging the script for currency would result in a loss of value, leaving the workers at the mercy of the company, which demanded their "loyalty" in exchange for their survival.

Billy was deeply affected by the treatment of the workers and the injustice inflicted upon them. Despite the obstacles, Billy remained determined to fight for the rights of the workers and bring an end to the injustices inflicted upon them. Later that month, he and several of the other coal miners from the Stonega mines attended their first United Mine Workers of America recruiting meeting at one of the Baptist churches in Appalachia.

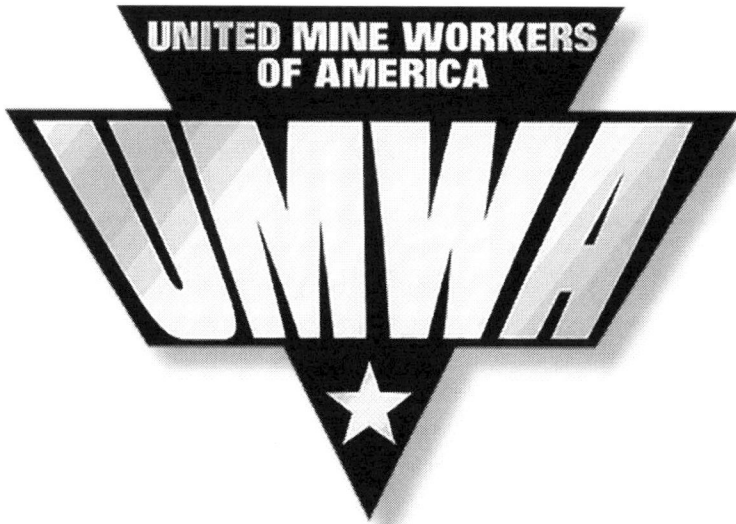

Actual script money from Stonega Coke & Coal Co.

NINE

The Cost of Coal

—————— ◠◡ ——————

Billy's passion for establishing a local chapter of the United Mine Workers of America (UMWA) was fueled by the Portal 1 Mine explosion, which claimed the lives of many miners and left their families devastated. He saw first-hand the human toll of the coal industry and was determined to do something about it. He used his sermons as a platform to raise awareness about the plight of miners and their families, who were largely immigrants from Europe and faced discrimination and exploitation from the coal companies that controlled their lives.

Billy threw himself into promoting the UMWA, preaching and unionizing with an unwavering spirit. He wanted to provide his fellow workers with better wages, shorter hours, and safer working conditions. He knew that the union was their only hope of achieving this and that they had to stand together in the face of opposition.

The UMWA was formed in the early 1900s and by the 1920s, it had gained real momentum in the coalfields of Southwest Virginia and Eastern Kentucky. The miners organized strikes, protests, and other forms of activism to fight against the coal companies. They faced opposition from the coal companies and the government, who used their power and influence to try and break the union.

One of the most famous incidents in the early days of the UMWA was the Matewan Massacre in 1920. The miners in Matewan, West Virginia, were on strike when the coal company hired a group of armed men to break it up. The miners, led by Sheriff Sid Hatfield, fought back resulting in a gun battle in the streets and the deaths of seven men, including Sheriff Hatfield. The incident became a rallying point for miners across the country and helped to galvanize support for the UMWA.

Despite the challenges, Billy remained undeterred. He knew that the cost of coal was far higher than any company could ever calculate and he was determined to fight for the rights of miners. As he stood before his congregation, he felt a sense of purpose he had never experienced before. He was determined to bring change to the coal camps of Appalachia and to provide opportunities for his boys so they would never have to work down in the coal mines. By the end of the 1920s, the UMWA had tens of thousands of members and the miners had made great strides in their fight for better working conditions. However, the fight was far from over and the UMWA continues to fight for the rights of miners to this day.

Brother Billy made the statement at the first union meeting at the local 118, "My boys nor your family's lives will ever be seen as worth less than some work ponies!"

Coal camps/houses were duplexes with two families per housing unit

TEN

Going to See a Cob-Roller

The boys eagerly jumped into the bed of Paw's Ford Model T pickup truck after leaving church on a beautiful Sunday morning. The ride was bumpy and dusty, but they didn't care. They were thrilled just to be with their beloved father who drove them back home to the family farm. Once they arrived, Paw instructed the boys to quickly change out of their Sunday best clothes and meet him on the front porch.

When they were all ready, they set out on a walk down Egan Rd with Paw leading the way. The boys were filled with excitement and curiosity, eager to find out what adventure their father had in store for them.

"Where we headed to, Paw?" asked John, his voice laced with excitement.

"We're off to see the biggest cob-roller hog you ever did see," Paw replied, his eyes twinkling with amusement.

"Cob-roller?" John queried; his curiosity piqued.

"That's right, Son. This hog is so big, its belly touches the ground and could roll a cob of corn in front of it," Paw explained.

As they walked up the winding valley road towards the Bloomer farm, the boys could feel their anticipation rising. The warm sun beat down on their faces and the sound of their boots crunching on gravel filled the air.

As they approached the farm, Old Man Bloomer spotted them from a quarter mile away and was ready to greet them with a friendly "Howdy" as they entered the garden gate. Bloomer asked if they were there to see the "cob-roller," and Paw replied, "Reckon we are."

Bloomer explained that since word got out about the hog, he had received many visitors eager to catch a glimpse of the largest hog ever seen in these parts.

"Come on over to the pen, and I'll show him to you," Bloomer said, leading the way.

The boys (Jimmie, John, and Graham) eagerly approached the hog pen with Jimmie leading the way and Graham being a bit less interested. Despite this, Graham had heard that Old Man Bloomer had a good-looking daughter who attended school up the mountain at Norton High School.

As they gazed into the hog pen, the boys' eyes widened in amazement at the sight of the massive hog. The beast lay sprawled out in the sun, snorting contentedly as the boys leaned over the fence to get a better look.

Paw grinned at the boys' excitement, happy to have given them a little pleasure on this lazy Sunday afternoon.

He was pleased to have shared this little adventure with his boys, but he knew that there were more dangerous adventures ahead of them in life. As they stood there, he said a silent prayer for their safety and well-being, knowing that the world would bring many dangers and disappointments to their doorsteps. But for now, he was content to enjoy the simple pleasures of life with his boys, watching them grow and learn about the world around them. And in that moment, nothing else mattered.

After admiring the "cob-roller" hog and exchanging polite conversation with Old Man Bloomer, Paw, Jimmie, John, and Graham set out on their walk back home to Crackers Neck. The warm afternoon sun beat down on the boys, but the sight of the rolling hills in Powell Valley and the greenery was a welcome distraction. They took their time walking back, stopping to admire wildflowers and search for crawdads in the nearby creek.

As they walked, Jimmie and John chattered excitedly about the hog and how big he was. Graham was quiet, lost in thought about the good-looking daughter of Old Man Bloomer as he had gotten to say a few pleasantries to her. The thought of meeting a girl from Norton High School had made quite an impression on him and made the long walk much shorter.

Paw walked ahead of the boys, a gentle smile on his lips. He was happy to have had this chance to spend time with his sons, even though his job at the coal mines and his responsibilities as a preacher kept him busy. On weekends, he performed many weddings, leaving little time for family one on one time.

As they approached the gravel road that led up to Crackers Neck, Paw picked up the pace. The boys had to jog to keep up with him. He was eager to get back home and rest his weary feet, but he knew that his boys would never forget this special day they had together.

When they finally arrived back at their house, the boys hugged Paw, thanking him for the adventure. They knew that time spent with him was precious and that memories like these would last a lifetime. They said goodbye, ran inside, and settled down for a good night's sleep, ready for school in the morning.

1930s Powells Valley

ELEVEN
Technology Comes to the Farm

―――――――――― ～ ――――――――――

Jimmie and Paw were on their way to a Virginia Tech Extension meeting in Pennington Gap to learn about a new product called "Hybrid Seed Corn." As they drove down the road in their old Ford Model T truck, Jimmie expressed his concern about getting another flat tire. Paw replied that he hoped they wouldn't, as he was running low on patches.

Back in those days, flat tires and breakdowns were a common occurrence and Jimmie couldn't recall a time when they drove, or anyone else drove anywhere, without encountering these problems. Despite what people may say about things being made better in the past, modern-day vehicles and equipment are of much higher quality than those in the "Good Old Days."

After fixing the flat tire, Jimmie and Paw drove through Dryden and headed towards Pennington Gap High School where the Virginia Extension meeting was being held. They were eager to learn about this new product that could potentially revolutionize the way they farmed.

Jimmie turned to Paw, his eyes full of curiosity, "What exactly is an Extension Agent?"

Paw took a moment to collect his thoughts. "Well, Son, the Virginia Extension Service, also known as the Cooperative Extension Service, has been around since the early 1900s, twenty years or so before you were born. They're a group of highly trained college-educated individuals that work for Virginia Polytechnic

Institute (VPI) who come out to rural communities to help farmers and families improve their way of life."

He continued, "In the days past, farmers were isolated and had limited access to the latest farming techniques and scientific research. The Extension Service changed all that by sending agents out to offer advice on everything from pest control to soil management. They even provided training in home economics, nutrition, and other skills to improve the quality of life for rural families."

Paw went on to explain how the Extension Service had expanded to offer services to a wider range of people, including urban communities and 4-H youth programs in the public schools.

"The Extension Service is a true testament to the power of knowledge and education," Paw concluded. "It's helped current generations of farmers and families to improve their lives and build stronger, better communities."

The Virginia Extension Service had done it again, bringing the latest innovations in farming to rural communities. Agent Fowler and Agent Cawood had set up shop in the high school auditorium, filling tables with literature on hybrid seed corn.

As the presentation began, the agents displayed charts and diagrams showing how the new hybrid corn outperformed the old open-pollinated varieties. They spoke of the increased revenue and the improved efficiency of livestock digestion. But when Agent Cawood asked if there were any questions, the room fell silent.

Agent Cawood began to pace, searching for something to spark interest. Then, he spoke of something he had heard from other farmers, but didn't have any scientific research on. Hybrid seed corn could produce a little more corn whisky per bushel than the old open-pollinated varieties.

Preacher Culbertson, sitting in the front row, confirmed the statement by standing up and facing the crowd. "Folks these fine young men are telling the Gospel truth, you'll get a couple more quarts per mash run every time!"

Suddenly, the audience of farmers came to life with hands in the air and clipboards passed around to sign up for more information. Agent Fowler and Cawood found out that in the mountains of Southwest Virginia, more corn was sold by the quart than by the bushel.

Jimmie learned an important lesson that day. He saw the power of knowing your customer and speaking their language.

The creation of America's Land Grant Colleges, as mandated by the Morrill Act of 1862, revolutionized higher education not only in the United States but also around the world. Prior to the Morrill Act, higher education in the United States and around the world was mainly reserved for the elite, with private institutions catering to the wealthy and religious groups. The Land Grant Colleges were established with the goal of making higher education more accessible to the general population and promoting practical, hands-on education in agriculture, engineering, and other fields.

The Land Grant Colleges were unique in several ways. First, they were publicly funded institutions which meant that they were more affordable and accessible to a wider range of students. Second, they were designed to provide practical, vocational education that was relevant to the needs of the country and its economy. Finally, they were mandated to engage in research that would benefit their local communities and the nation as a whole.

The impact of the Land Grant Colleges was profound. By making higher education more accessible and relevant, they helped transform the United States into an industrial and agricultural powerhouse. Their emphasis on research also helped to spur innovation and technological advancements, which had ripple effects throughout the economy and society.

The Land Grant model was so successful that it was adopted by other countries around the world, including Canada, Australia, and India. Today, there are more than 1,000 Land Grant Colleges and Universities around the world, and they continue to play a vital role in promoting education, research, and economic development.

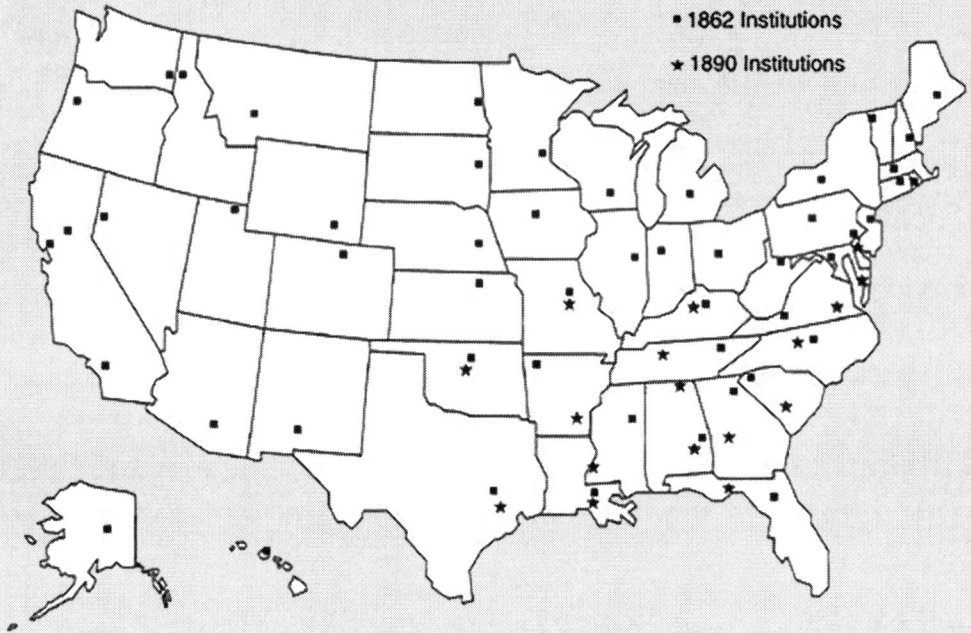

NIFA LAND-GRANT COLLEGES AND UNIVERSITIES

■ 1862 Institutions
★ 1890 Institutions

TWELVE

The High School Years:
Late 1930s

———————

In the hollers and foothills surrounding East Stone Gap High School, children from Crackers Neck, Maples Gap, and Powell Valley would make the daily trek on foot. The walk to school was a time for exploration and discovery with students traversing winding dirt roads and babbling creeks. They would often walk in groups, chattering and laughing along the way, discussing their hopes and dreams for the future. Sometimes they would find themselves walking alongside wildlife, with deer, rabbits, and squirrels darting across their paths.

During the winter months, when the snow would blanket the ground and the icy wind would chill their bones, the students would don thick coats, hats, and gloves. They would trudge through the snow, their boots sinking deep into the drifts. Despite the harsh conditions, they never missed a day of school, determined to get the education they knew was their ticket to a better life.

In the spring, the students would marvel at the blooming wildflowers and the leaves budding on the trees signifying the end of winter and the start of a new season. The girls would sometimes gather the flowers and weave them into crowns and necklaces, giggling and smiling at their creations.

In the fall, they would witness the leaves changing colors, red, yellow, and orange. They would kick up the fallen leaves and breathe in the crisp air. The fall was also a time of harvest and they would often stop along the way to pick apples or help gather the crops from the local farms.

The walk to school was a time for friendship with students from different backgrounds and neighborhoods coming together to learn and grow up together. The students shared a bond, formed by their shared experiences, hardships, and small triumphs. They knew that the schooling they received at East Stone Gap High School could pave the way for a brighter future and they were willing to walk miles every day to make that dream a reality. Or, in Graham's case, Paw made sure he walked to school each day, often calling the school from his office at the coal tipple to make sure he did.

The years spent at East Stone Gap High School were filled with moments that left an indelible mark on the Galloway boys and fellow students. Despite the hardship and scarcity that many of them faced at home, the students at East Stone Gap never felt they were missing out on anything.

The teachers were strict but fair and their teachings inspired the students to work hard and learn. Every day, the students would gather in the schoolyard, surrounded by tall oak trees that provided relief from the heat of the day. Their laughter echoed through the halls along with the sound of games like tag and marbles.

The schoolyard was a picturesque sight with its freshly painted white fence, soft green grass, and wildflowers blooming along the fence line. The school building was a grand stone and brick structure with large windows that flooded the classrooms with natural light. The halls were lined with wooden lockers and the classrooms were filled with rows of wooden desks and chairs. The blackboards were always immaculate and the walls adorned with posters and maps helped students learn about geography and history. The building had a distinct aroma, a mix of chalk dust, old wood, and musty books from the library. The library was a sanctuary for quiet study, filled with rows of books and plush armchairs. It was a place where students could retreat from the clamor of the schoolyard and delve into the world of books and learning.

Jimmie's time in school was noteworthy, with his lunchtime shenanigans earning him a reputation among his peers. His mother's home-cooked meals were always a hit, but Jimmie craved something more exciting. The SPAM lunch meat, with its square slices of bread, was a delicacy to him. Growing up on the family farm, Ma never bought meat or store-bought "square" bread! Jimmie never imagined that his simple act of lunch trading would lead to such a severe punishment from his mother.

As the years went by, Jimmie realized that the lessons he learned in and outside of the classroom would guide him well in life. The importance of honesty, hard work, and perseverance were lessons that he carried with him throughout his life. He also never forgot the taste of that Spam lunch meat and the exciting experiences that it brought him.

As the late 1930s bled into the 1940s, the world was changing fast. The Great Depression was ending, and unknown at the time was that World War II was about to begin. The students of East Stone Gap School would soon face trials they had never fathomed.

East Stone Gap High School

THIRTEEN

A Football Hero for the East Stone Gap Tigers

The nurse raised an eyebrow as Jimmie proudly recounted his youthful high school football days of 60 years ago to her.

"And how did you hurt your knee that you now need a knee replacement for?" she asked, her voice laced with a heavy dose of skepticism.

Jimmie sat up a little straighter, a grin spreading across his face as he prepared to regale her with tales of the East Stone Gap Tigers. "I was playing football for the Tigers, of course," he said, his voice tinged with nostalgia. "We were up against our biggest rivals, the Big Stone Gap Buccaneers. Coach Smith called for a toss sweep, and I was playing running back. As I caught the ball from the quarterback and ran towards the sidelines, I planted my left foot to cut back right. At that moment, I felt a burning sensation in my knee."

The nurse shook her head and sighed. "I guess it wasn't worth it, was it?"

Jimmie's smile didn't falter. "Listen here, Sweetie," he said while eyeballing the nurse. "Back in my day, if you didn't play football, you couldn't carry the girls' books home from school! What's a knee replacement or two!"

Football was more than just a game in the coalfields, it was a way of life. And for Jimmie and his teammates, being a football hero for the East Stone Gap Tigers was a point of pride they carried with them throughout their lives.

Led by Coach Al Smith, a former WWI sergeant who believed in tough love, the Tigers were a force to be reckoned with on the gridiron during the 1930s. As a World War I veteran, Coach Smith had seen some of the most brutal and intense battles in Europe. He was a proud American soldier veteran who joined the Army right after the United States declared war on Germany in 1917.

Coach had always been a fierce competitor and a man of great discipline and these qualities served him well in the brutal trench warfare he experienced on the Western Front. Coach was initially assigned to the 77th Division which was made up of, as he would say, "Damn Yankee" soldiers from New York City.

He quickly rose through the ranks due to his courage, leadership, and strategic thinking. In the late summer of 1918, the 77th Division was sent to the front lines to participate in the Battle of the Somme.

Coach and his fellow soldiers endured unimaginable horrors during the battle. They were forced to fight in cramped, muddy trenches that were infested with rats and other vermin. They were constantly under attack from enemy soldiers, artillery, and gas attacks. Coach saw many of his comrades fall to the ground, never to rise again. Despite the constant danger and treacherous conditions, Coach remained steadfast and determined. He led his men with courage and resolve, often exposing himself to enemy fire to inspire his troops. He was wounded several times during the battle, but he refused to leave the front lines until he was ordered to do so by his superiors.

When the Battle of the Somme ended in November 1918, Coach was hailed as a hero by his fellow soldiers. He had earned numerous medals for his bravery, including the Distinguished Service Cross and the Purple Heart. Coach would always carry the memories of the battle with him, but he was proud to have served his country and to have fought alongside his fellow Americans.

His experiences on the battlefield had hardened him greatly, but they had also taught him valuable lessons about discipline, perseverance, and leadership. He brought these lessons with him when he returned home to East Stone Gap and took up coaching football.

But Coach Smith's dedication to his country and his team went deeper than just his own personal experiences. His grandfather had fought for the Union during the Civil War and had instilled in him a sense of duty and honor that stayed with him throughout his life.

In the hills and coalfields of Southwest Virginia, the Civil War brought about a fierce division among the people of the hill country. The mountains were filled with pockets of people loyal to the North or the South, with few willing to cross the lines.

But there was one man, Coach Smith's grandfather, who didn't shy away from fighting for what he believed in, even if it meant taking up arms against his neighbors. Born and raised near the town of Jonesville, Virginia, the young man grew up with a fierce sense of justice and a desire to see the Union succeed. He had heard stories of the evils of slavery and was convinced that the North was fighting for a just cause and not for these rich plantation folks with slaves.

Despite the dangers and the opposition of many around him, he made the decision to join the Union Army. It was a decision that would change his life and his family's lives forever.

As he marched with the Union soldiers, he faced many challenges. He was met with hostility and anger from many in his community. He was even accused of being a traitor by some of his own family members. But he pressed on, fighting alongside his fellow soldiers, and proving his loyalty to the cause.

He had fought in some of the bloodiest battles of the war, including the Battle of Gettysburg, where he was wounded in battle. Despite the pain, he continued to fight with determination and courage, earning a reputation as one of the toughest soldiers in his regiment.

His bravery and tenacity earned him a battlefield promotion to Sergeant and he was later awarded many Medals of Honor for his actions on the battlefield.

After the war, he returned to his hometown, where he was met with a mix of disdain and respect. Some still saw him as a traitor, while others recognized his bravery and the sacrifices he had made.

But regardless of how he was perceived, he was proud of the decisions he had made and the role he played in fighting for what he believed in. His legacy lived on through the generations of his family, including his grandson, Coach Al Smith of East Stone Gap.

As a coach, he used these family and life experiences as teaching lessons to inspire his players and build a sense of camaraderie and respect among them. He believed in tough love, pushing his football players to their limits and beyond, but always with the goal of building their character and strength. He knew that the lessons they learned on the field would stay with them for the rest of their lives, just as the lessons he had learned on the battlefield had stayed with him.

And so, every day, Coach Smith would stand on the practice field, shouting out commands and pushing his boys to give their all. He would crack the old horse and buggy whip on their rear ends when they needed a little extra motivation, but he would also be there to lend a hand when they stumbled or fell. He was tough, but he was fair, and his players knew that he would always have their backs.

In the end, Coach Smith's dedication and hard work paid off. The East Stone Gap Tigers became one of the most respected football teams in the coalfields, feared by their opponents for their "toughness" and respected by their fans. One of Coach's most cherished newspaper clippings was of the rival team's coach calling his "boys" a bunch of "Brutal Thugs and their fans aren't much better!" in the newspaper. And while many of his players went on to lead successful lives in many different fields, they always remembered the lessons they had learned under the watchful eye of Coach Al Smith, the World War I sergeant who had become a legendary football coach.

Coach Smith was also a resourceful man, making sure his teams had everything they needed to be successful, including a 4-man blocking sled made of old sawmill lumber and shoulder padding made from old feed sacks. He would stand above his boys on a perch as they fired out and drove the sled up and down the practice field.

But Coach Smith's methods weren't all fun and games. If he didn't think one of his boys was pulling their weight, he had that old horse and buggy whip that he would crack on the boy's rear end to motivate and toughen them up at the same time. Despite the tough methods, Coach Smith was well-loved by his players, including Jimmie, who knew it was all for their own good.

During Jimmie's junior year, he was determined to lead the Tigers to the district championship. Their biggest obstacle was the gritty Bulldogs of Appalachia. In a defining moment of his high school career, Jimmie put on an electrifying performance against the Bulldogs, but the game remained close and time was running out.

That's when Coach Smith hatched a cunning plan using Jimmie as a decoy and calling plays that would bamboozle the Bulldogs' defense while the other halfback, A.K. Fraley, carried the ball. A.K. had been tearing up the field, but on the fifth play of the drive, he slammed into a Bulldogs player and collapsed in agony, clutching his arm.

Jimmie, the team captain, immediately called a timeout.

Coach Smith stomped out onto the field; his face twisted in anger. "What the hell is going on, Jimmie?" he barked.

"A.K.'s hurt real bad, Coach," Jimmie replied. "His arm looks as crooked as a politician's word."

Coach Smith glared at A.K., his eyes full of contempt, "Are you turning yellow on me, A.K.?" he snarled, before storming back to the sidelines.

Despite the excruciating pain, A.K. refused to leave the game, tying some old bandanas that Dr. Ford gave him tightly around his arm and gritting his teeth. It was a moment that epitomized the gritty, never-say-die spirit of football in the coalfields where players were expected to embody that same toughness both on and off the field.

In the end, the East Stone Gap Tigers emerged victorious, lifting A.K. up on their shoulders and carrying him off the field as the hero of the game.

For Jimmie and his teammates, football was more than just a sport, it was a symbol of toughness and resilience that they carried with them throughout their lives. And little did they know at the time, but their toughness and resilience would be needed to save the world from tyranny in just a few short years.

After the game, Dr. Ford took A.K. for an X-ray of his arm. Diagnosis: broken arm. Football in the coalfields is a tough business!

It was the early 1970s and Jimmie was going over the day's milk deliveries at Clinch Haven Farms which he had just purchased from Mr. Terpstra. As he was reviewing the reports, his old football halfback teammate, A.K. Fraley, stuck his head in the door and motioned Jimmie over.

Jimmie greeted him warmly, "Great to see you, A.K. What's going on?"

A.K. responded, "I came by to see if I could borrow a Ford alternator to put on my coal truck and get it back up and running. Wade down in the mechanics shed said you all had an extra one."

Jimmie, looking confused, asked, "Of course, you can borrow one, A.K., but are they out of them down at the parts store? They usually keep a bunch of them."

A.K. looked around and closed the door. "Well, Jim, don't tell anyone, but I'm broke right now and I've used up all my credit at the parts store. Everything will be all right if I can get my coal truck going and sell some coal this week. I'll pay you back next week right after I make my payroll!"

And pay him back he did. A.K. Fraley and his family sold a lot of coal over the years and turned Fraley Coal Company into a very successful business, employing many good people from East Stone Gap, Crackers Neck, and the surrounding communities. It was yet another example of the fearlessness and grit of the Greatest Generation.

1930s East Stone Gap Football Game

FOURTEEN

The First Night-time Football Game in Wise County

~

As the week leading up to the game against the Coeburn Blue Knights approached, the halls of East Stone Gap High School were filled with excitement and anticipation. Everyone was talking about the upcoming game, which was set to be a historic event. It wasn't just any regular game – it was going to be the first night game ever played in Southwest Virginia.

The local coal mine owner at Paramont Coal Mines had spared no expense, installing lights up on Skull Hill at the football stadium during the summer. The Coeburn Blue Knights playing the visiting East Stone Gap Tigers were going to be the first game to christen the lights on this Friday night.

It was a moment that would go down in history and everyone in the town and the surrounding towns were talking about it. Until then, football games in Southwest Virginia were played right after school as soon as the visiting team could arrive. But this game was different. This game was special. The entire community was coming together to witness this historic modern event and the excitement was contagious. Everyone knew that this was a moment they would never forget.

Jimmie and the rest of the team arrived up on Skull Hill around 6 pm to begin warm-ups before the game that would start at 7 pm. It was already getting dark and the lights had been on for some time, but there was a huge problem! The coaches and all the referees were meeting at the 50-yard line to discuss it. The problem was, even though the lights were on, it was still so dark you couldn't even see the football if you were more than a few feet away.

Coach Smith said, "Boys, we have a big problem here. Even though the lights are on, it's still too damn dark to see the ball."

"Yes, I agree. We need to find a solution quickly, the game starts in an hour," the referee added.

Jimmie suggested, "What if we paint the ball white? It'll be easier to see in the dark."

Coach Smith, "That's a great idea, Jimmie. But where are we going to find paint this close to game time?"

"I can go get some paint from the hardware store. It's just a few minutes away," offered Dr. Ford.

Coach Smith agreed, "Okay, let's do it. We need to find two dollars for the paint though." Then Coach Smith took out two dollars from the gas money toolbox and gave it to Dr. Ford.

The whole stadium was a buzz as to what was going on. About 30 minutes later, Dr. Ford was back with a pint of white house paint from the Coeburn hardware store. All the game footballs were gathered up and the painting commenced. The dark brown footballs were as white as the enamel countertops down at Bessie's dinner in Appalachia. To dry the football faster, Harold Lester had volunteered to start up his Dodge truck and let the hot exhaust from the engine dry the paint on the footballs in a few minutes.

The Tigers had a good game but lost the game 14-7. As Jimmie left the field after the game, you couldn't even read the number 8 on his game jersey from all the white paint that had rubbed off the footballs from carrying the "Rock." Jimmie exclaimed, "Even though we lost, this was an amazing experience. The first night-game in SWVA and the white-painted footballs added to the memory!"

FIFTEEN

A Pistol Across the Gym Floor

—————～—————

Basketball wasn't Jimmie's favorite sport, but he was glad it was an option during the freezing winter months. He would much rather be in a warm gym practicing basketball than outside in the cold doing farm work. Besides, he couldn't deny that the cheerleaders at the games were a lot more attractive than Uncle Bud's old work mules, Doc and Buster, down on the farm. Growing up, Jimmie enjoyed watching the cheerleaders perform their routines during the games and he couldn't help but feel a bit envious of the basketball players who got to spend so much time with them. He didn't have much interest in playing basketball himself, but he was a pretty good athlete and became one of the better players on the team.

The East Stone Gap High School gymnasium, built in the early 1930s during the start of the Great Depression, was a shining example of the community's commitment to education and athletics. The two-story brick building stood tall and proud on the edge of town, its clean lines and symmetrical architecture a testament to the skill and craftsmanship of the local builders. The gymnasium's exterior was adorned with a large stone archway that led to double doors made of solid oak.

Inside, the gymnasium was spacious and well-lit with large windows that let in a lot of outside light during the day. The basketball court, the focal point of the space, was shiny and new, its polished hardwood floors gleaming under the bright lights for the day. The bleachers, which went all the way down to the playing floor, were made of sturdy wood and provided ample seating for the spectators.

The air in the gymnasium was thick with the smell of chewing tobacco and cigarettes which were still acceptable in public places in those days. But despite this, the building was well-maintained with freshly painted walls and clean floors. The sound of bouncing basketballs echoed off the walls, punctuated by the occasional whistle or shout from the coach.

Overall, the East Stone Gap High School gymnasium was a source of pride for the community. In a time of economic hardship, the building was a symbol of hope and progress, a tangible representation of the community's commitment to its young people and their future even as many students went home to poverty.

The basketball stadium at East Stone Gap High School this Saturday night was a sea of excitement as the rival team, the Norton Raiders, arrived for the game. The fans were already in full voice, shouting insults and jeers at the opposing team as they made their way onto the court. The players were rough and aggressive, throwing themselves into each other as they went for the ball. The referees were letting a lot go, allowing the players to play with a level of physicality that would have normally resulted in fouls.

In one particularly rough play, Jimmie was elbowed in the eye under the basket, causing it to bleed profusely like a stuck pig. The players around him started throwing punches and the benches soon emptied as the fight spilled onto the court. East Stone's Coach Fleenor, a towering figure at 6 foot 2 inches, tried to break up the altercation but as he stood up, his foot caught the edge of the scorer's table and he stumbled, falling to the hardwood floor.

As he hit the floor, his trusty .38 Smith & Wesson revolver pistol fell out of his pocket and slid all the way across the hardwood court. The unique and bold sound of the pistol hitting the floor echoed while sliding across the basketball court. The crowd immediately hushed as a church service during silent prayer, all eyes fixed on the gun.

As Coach Fleenor calmly walked across the court to retrieve the pistol, Jimmie found humor in the situation and leaned over to his teammates. He whispered, "That's how you shut up a rowdy crowd, boys. Forget throwing elbows or talking smack, just bring a gun!"

His teammates chuckled nervously, but then one of them quipped back, "I don't know if I want to mess with Coach Fleenor now. He's got a gun and he knows how to use it!"

Jimmie replied, "Yeah, we better watch ourselves or we might end up with some extra ventilation holes!" The teammates laughed again as the tension in the gym had definitely dissipated. Coach Fleenor had certainly, although unintentionally, made his point: *no-nonsense and NO fighting on his basketball court.*

The referees eventually blew their whistles, signaling for the players to return to their benches. The game resumed, but now with a much more gentlemanly spirit as the players were cautious not to provoke any further conflict. As the game progressed, the fans grew more and more riled up, shouting encouragement to their team and jeering the opposition. Despite the rough start, the basketball game was intense and thrilling, with both teams determined to come out on top.

In the end, the East Stone Gap team emerged victorious, winning by a narrow margin. The fans erupted into cheers, congratulating the players as they left the court. It had been a wild and unforgettable night, one that would be talked about for years to come, a testament to the fierce competitiveness and passionate fans of East Stone Gap Tigers.

East Stone Gap High School

SIXTEEN
Gone with the Wind:
Senior Year 1940

The students of East Stone Gap High School were buzzing with excitement as they were given a surprise day off from school to go see the premier of *Gone with the Wind* down in Big Stone Gap. *Gone with the Wind* was a massive movie during Jimmie's senior year. Released in 1939, the film was a huge critical and commercial success and during the early spring of 1940, it finally made it to the coalfields of Southwest Virginia. It was directed by Victor Fleming and starred Vivien Leigh and Clark Gable, both of whom became legends in their own right due to the film's impact. All the students were buzzing with anticipation, all except two students.

Despite the cold, crisp March air, the students and teachers made the journey on foot to Big Stone Gap where the movie was being shown at the local cinema. The walk was over three miles, but the students were in high spirits and didn't mind the journey.

On the downtown Main Street of Big Stone Gap, there was a quaint movie theater known as The Earle. Despite its small size, The Earle was the hub of entertainment for the area and the source of many fond memories for the town's residents.

The exterior of the theater was a modest brick building with a large, illuminated sign above the entrance that read "The Earle Theatre." The entrance was grand, with a red carpet leading up to the ticket booth and the sound of the ticket dispenser ringing echoed through the street. Stepping inside, patrons were greeted by a small, cramped lobby with posters of the latest films adorning the walls. The air was thick with the smell of fresh popcorn which was popped on-site and sold for just a nickel a bag. The theater itself was a simple room with a small stage at the front, a large screen, and rows of wooden seats that creaked when sat on. The seats were padded and upholstered in red velvet and the walls were adorned with gold-leaf accents and elegant sconces that provided dim, romantic lighting. The Earle Theater only had one screen, so there was only one showing at a time. But for the people of Big Stone Gap, it was more than enough… normally. They would gather with their friends and neighbors, sit back and enjoy the magic of the movies. Despite its small size and limited resources, The Earle was a cherished landmark in the town and its memories would be cherished by the residents of Big Stone Gap for generations to come.

When the faculty and students arrived in downtown Big Stone Gap, they were greeted with the sight of a long line stretching down the street and around the corner from The Earle Theater. The small movie theater was not equipped to handle the large number of students, so they had to break them into smaller groups and watch the movie in three shifts throughout the day. For many of the students, this was their first-ever trip to a movie theater and even more were seeing a movie for the first time. Being from a poor area, many of the students had never been exposed to the luxury of cinema and were overjoyed at the opportunity.

Jimmie and Woodrow had always been the best of friends, growing up in the same rough neighborhood in East Stone Gap. They often found themselves in trouble, always seeking adventure and a good time. As they walked towards Big Stone Gap with the rest of their classmates and teachers, they made a plan to sneak away and make the most of the day.

"Hey Woodrow, you know what would be a good idea?" Jimmie whispered.

"What?" Woodrow replied.

"Instead of going to see that Civil War movie, let's sneak away and go down to Daughtery's Store in Big Stone Gap. I heard they got a bottle of wine I can buy for us."

Woodrow's eyes lit up with excitement. "Hell yeah, let's do it."

Woodrow grew up really hard in a large family with 12 siblings up the mountain in the small area of Chandler Mountain. His father worked as a logger, but he was also an alcoholic and often struggled to provide for the family even when work was good.

Despite the difficult circumstances, Woodrow was determined to make a better life for himself. Growing up, Woodrow's home was a hostile environment. His father's alcoholism made him volatile and there was never enough food to go around. Despite this, Woodrow never let his circumstances hold him back. He was a hard worker, always doing odd jobs around the community to help provide for his family.

Education was never a priority for Woodrow. He didn't care about getting good grades and the idea of college wasn't an option for a poor teenager like him. The primary reason Woodrow went to school was that most days it was the only source of food he had. Jimmie's Ma would pack what looked to be a grocery sack for him to take to school for lunch. Back in the 30s, there were no public-school lunches, so the only food school kids had was what they brought with them.

Ma packed so much food for Jimmie because she knew she was packing for Woodrow too. Ma would pray for Woodrow thinking about how that poor young man would go from Friday's school lunch all the way to lunch on Mondays with very little or nothing to eat.

All Woodrow wanted was a life where he didn't have to worry about going hungry or living in fear of getting beat up. He dreamed of having a job that would provide him with enough money to take care of himself and his family. Despite the challenges he faced, Woodrow never lost hope. He saw Jimmie, his best friend, as a symbol of what he could achieve. Jimmie was smart and always had big plans for the future. He encouraged Woodrow to believe that he too could have a better life.

Woodrow, in fact, ended up having a much better life. Eventually, he would marry a young lady from down in Lee County whose father was the sheriff. Back in those days, the sheriff "ran" the county, so when his daughter married Woodrow, he bought them a nice farm to live on. From there Woodrow discovered he was quite good at cattle trading and became famous in the region for his ability to just look at cattle and figure their weight right in the field. That skill allowed him to make a fine life for his family and food was never a worry again!

As the two boys managed to slip away unnoticed and made their way to Abbie's, a small store that sold everything from candy to alcohol. Jimmie had a little pocket money from helping at the airport and bought a bottle of wine. Then they made their way down to the river where they spent the day skipping rocks, walking around town, and enjoying each other's company. As they sat on the banks of the river, sipping their wine, Jimmie and Woodrow talked about everything under the sun.

"Hey Jimmie, do you ever think about leaving East Stone Gap and these mountains?" Woodrow asked.

"Yeah, all the time," Jimmie replied. "I want to fly planes and see the world, you know? There's got to be more to life than this."

"I feel you, man," Woodrow said. "I don't want to spend my whole life working in the coal mines or logging like my dad. I want to do something big, something better."

"Me too, Woodrow. We can do anything we set our minds to," Jimmie said, his eyes shining with determination.

They talked about their dreams for hours, discussing different possibilities and planning their futures. As the sun began to set, they realized they had to get back to the movie theater to sneak in and watch the end of the last showing that day.

"Hey Woodrow, you know what? This has been the best day ever," Jimmie said with a grin.

"Yeah, I know," Woodrow replied, smiling widely. "We should do this more often." And so, the two boys spent the day in Big Stone Gap making memories that would last a lifetime. They were two best friends, enjoying their youth and each other's company, completely carefree and happy.

Little did the boys know how their lives were going to change and they would be doing something bigger and more important.

In the early '90s, we had just finished planting our main cornfield when Woodrow Franklin's late-model diesel Ford Lariat pickup appeared on the horizon. As he stepped out of the truck, Papaw greeted him with a familiar quip between the two, "Glad to see you have two shoes on your feet; you must be doing good Woodrow."

Woodrow laughed, "Life IS good!" Pulling out some Red Man chewing tobacco and offering some to us.

Curiosity piqued; I asked about the meaning behind the shoe joke. Woodrow explained that it was a nod to their shared past of poverty and struggle in the old days. He told the story of how he once walked into East Stone High School with just one shoe on and when the principal asked if he had lost one, Woodrow replied, "No Sir, I found one!"

Woodrow looked at me and said, "John William, if you got a pair of shoes on your feet and a belly full of food, today is the best day of your life!"

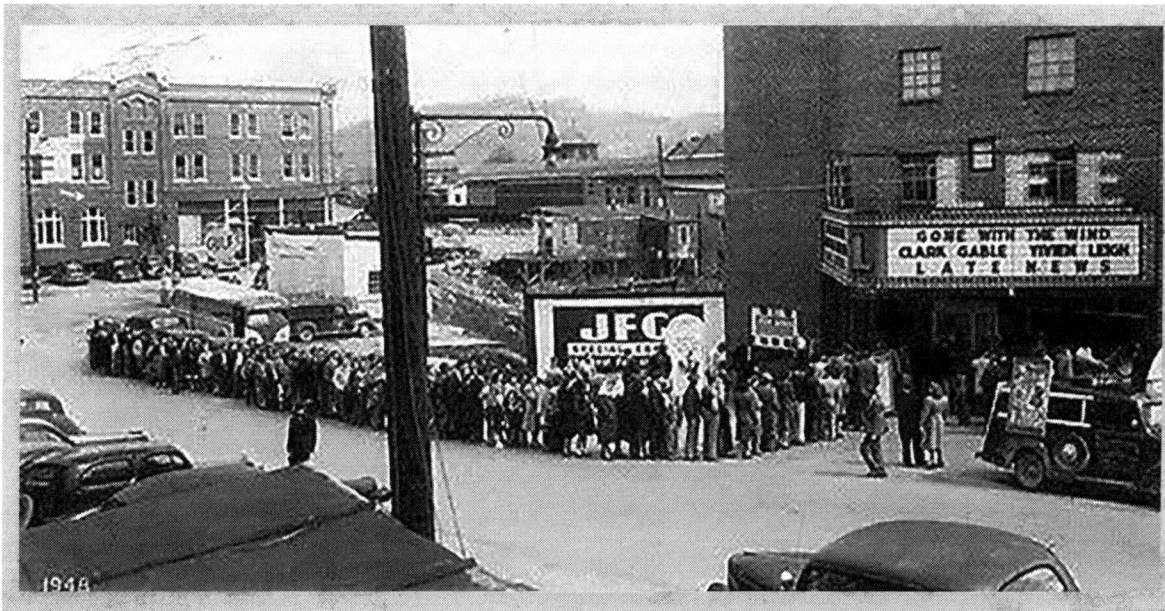

People lined up to see Gone with The Wind / Lee County VA

SEVENTEEN
Getting the News

———————~———————

Jimmie and his brothers were known around both towns for their wild and teenage carefree ways. They had a reputation for always finding the party and their pockets always seemed to have a little extra jingle in them at the end of the week. On the weekends when Ma and Paw were out of town officiating marriages in the area, the Galloway boys would hop on the coal trains passing through East Stone Gap and ride them down to Big Stone Gap or Appalachia, a town with a booming coal industry and a reputation for its bars and brothels.

Graham, being the oldest and boldest of the brothers, was the first to venture into the seedy nightlife of Appalachia. He would spend his nights hopping from bar to bar, soaking up the raucous atmosphere and the lively music pouring out of the jukeboxes. Before long, Jimmie and John were right there beside him, eager to experience all that Appalachia had to offer.

As Graham would say, you could hear the jukeboxes start playing as the train made its way toward Appalachia. The town seemed to have an energy all its own, fueled by the endless supply of coal and the men who worked the mines and the Galloway brothers were right in the thick of it, living life to the fullest.

When Graham graduated high school and joined the Navy in the spring of 1938, Jimmie and John took up the mantle of keeping the family tradition alive. They continued to ride the coal trains down to Appalachia, still searching for the next big party or wild adventure. The Galloway brothers may have been "loveable" troublemakers, but they knew how to have a good time.

Finding good times in the town of Appalachia or any of the local coal towns was an easy task to accomplish. To keep the coal mines running and coal miners happy, the local law enforcement was obliged by the Coal Companies to look the other way on the Federal Alcohol Prohibition laws and the local "Cat Houses" brothels.

You could venture over the mountain to Jenkins Kentucky to the Dew Drop Inn which had a huge sign that said "Drop into Dew Drop's for Whisky, Beer & Gin." The town of Pound, Virginia had the famous Red Onion Bar and Grill, while Norton had the Copper Kettle with live Bluegrass Mountain Music on the weekends. The county seat of Wise had the Esso Inn and the Beverly Hills Bar that was literally right across the street from the sheriff's office. Big Stone Gap and Appalachia had what was considered the wilder drinking and partying establishments. Down below Dip Crossing of the Wildcat Section of Big Stone, you had the Bloody Bucket bar that held boxing matches in the back lot for miners to wager on while drinking. Come on up the road on Route 23, you had the Rock House and the Sunset Inn and downtown Big Stone had the Pavilion and Liberty Cafe, both serving beer and some of the best Apple-Jack and Apple Brandy produced from up in Wise and the other apple orchards that found out selling apples in a mason jar was a lot more profitable than selling apples by the bushel.

The Galloway boys had a favorite spot to spend their weekends, and it was none other than downtown Appalachia. Main Street was divided by vice: on one side, you had the gambling and drinking bars and, across the street, the infamous "Cat Houses." Among the numerous drinking establishments, Jimmie favored Shelton Gilliam's place. The biggest of them all, it had a massive bar along the side wall across from the dance floor and a spacious back room full of pool and betting tables where miners could pull ball tickets (wagers) on local and national sporting events. The rooms of Gilliam's had a secret weapon: holes in the floor along the walls. These were used by drinkers to quickly dump their alcohol during occasional state police or "G-Men" raids. At one end of Main Street, you had the Coffee House and at the other end of the street, African American miners would frequent Sam's making it another popular spot for the Galloway boys to spend their weekends listening to Jazz and Blues Music of the day.

It was a bullet whizzing by his ear at Shelton Gilliam's that brought Jimmie and the Bronx-bred Jewish attorney, Mr. Gladstone, together. The shooting had taken place at Shelton Gilliam's place on a wild weekend and Attorney Gladstone had summoned Jimmie to give a statement of the event he had witnessed on behalf of his client.

Jimmie was intrigued by Mr. Gladstone who had an air of sophistication and spoke with a New York City accent. After giving his statement, Jimmie couldn't help but ask the attorney, "Mr. Gladstone, what in the world brought a Jewish lawyer from the Bronx to the coal town of Appalachia, Virginia?"

Mr. Gladstone had immediately grown to like young Jimmie and had purchased dressed geese from his Ma for years during the holidays. He smiled and began his personal story:

"Well, young man, I ask myself that same question sometimes. I was graduating from New York City Law School in the spring of 1930 during the Great Depression with a wife and two young daughters at home and no job prospects in sight. I asked my professor for advice on how to feed my family. He told me about a recent news article in the New York Times about a coal town in Southwest Virginia with the highest per capita murder rate in the whole country. I thought *that sounds like a place where I could make some money as a lawyer!*

The newly graduated attorney had pawned some inherited jewelry, booked a train to Bristol, Virginia, and taken a bus to Big Stone Gap. As he rode in a cab up to Appalachia, he braced himself for the worst. "I was really expecting to see dead bodies in the streets!" he chuckled. "But I didn't quite find that. Instead, I found plenty of defendants and customers in need of legal representation. The local bars, brothels, paychecks, and weekends can keep an attorney quite busy, let me tell you!" Now, almost a decade later, Attorney Gladstone could confidently say that the coal business had been good to his family.

Jimmie's days of bar-hopping and boozing came to a sudden halt with the arrival of an ice cream sandwich. It just so happened that Jean Compton, a senior at Big Stone High School and former Miss Big Stone Gap beauty pageant winner, had been hired part-time by Pet Dairy to make ice cream sandwiches alongside her best friend. These frozen treats were hand-crafted by cutting the vanilla ice cream into small rectangles and placing them between two thin cakes… all by hand. At the end of each workday, the company would allow any broken or damaged sandwiches to be given away to the workers at the processing plant.

Jimmie quickly caught Jean's eye and before long, the largest broken sandwich of the day was saved for him. After hanging up his work jacket, Jean would beckon Jimmie over, reach into the cooler and produce the prized frozen delicacy. Their playful courtship continued for a few weeks until Jean's mother, known as Momma Compton, disapproved of their relationship. She warned her daughter with a stern voice, "All you'll get from that wild flyboy, Jimmie Galloway, is a reputation."

Jimmie was the star football player at East Stone Gap and Jean's mother wasn't too pleased with her daughter going out with the "wild high school football star." She had heard of some of Jimmie's escapades of hopping trains and riding down to Appalachia to frequent its plentiful bars. But Jean couldn't resist Jimmie's charm and good looks and the two quickly fell in love.

Despite different high schools and backgrounds, Jimmie and Jean's love was strong and they were determined to make their relationship work. After graduating from East Stone Gap High School in the spring of 1941, Jimmie married who he thought was the prettiest girl in town. After their wedding, they moved into a small house on Jimmie's family farm and started their life together as newlyweds.

Jimmie had gotten his pilot's license during the spring but pilot's jobs were few and far between during these hard times. So, he felt lucky to have landed a job downtown Big Stone Gap at the Pet Dairy milk processing plant. He had graduated from high school just a few months ago and had already started a family with Jean. It wasn't easy to find work during the summer of 1941, but Jimmie's determination paid off. He was grateful for the steady work and the benefits that came with it.

The job at the dairy plant was hard work, but it was a job that provided for his growing family. The plant processed milk from local farmers and distributed it to the surrounding communities. Jimmie worked long hours, often coming home late at night covered in milk and sweat. But he knew that his hard work was helping to provide for his wife and upcoming baby.

As Jimmie arrived at the Pet Dairy plant each day, he was greeted by the sweet smell of milk and the loud clanging of machinery. The plant was a hive of activity, with workers moving back and forth, pushing carts, and hauling milk jugs. The work was hard, and the hours were long, but Jimmie was grateful to be employed.

Pet Dairy was one of the largest milk processing plants in the region, serving the surrounding coal camps and communities all across Southwest Virginia. The milk was brought in fresh each day from local farms from Powell Valley, down through Scott and Lee County, all the way down to Rose Hill. The workers would pasteurize and bottle it, getting it ready for distribution. Jimmie's job was to operate the bottling machine, making sure the milk was filled to the correct level and that the bottles were capped and labeled correctly.

The work was repetitive, but it required precision and focus. Jimmie would spend hours each day tending to the machines, making sure that everything was running smoothly. He took pride in his work, knowing that the milk he was bottling would be consumed by families across the region, providing some reassuring job security.

At the end of a long day, Jimmie would trudge out of the Pet Dairy processing plant, his body aching, and his mind weary. But the sight of his Paw's familiar Harley Davidson motorcycle would always bring a smile to his face. If he was lucky enough to get off work early, he could catch a ride home with Paw as he made his way back from his job up in Stonega.

The two men would often swap stories and jokes as they rode through the winding mountain roads with the sound of the motorcycle's engine providing a steady hum beneath their conversation. Jimmie always felt a sense of pride riding on the back of Paw's bike, holding on tight as they zoomed down the road. As they approached their home in the heart of Crackers Neck, the men would share a final laugh, reminiscing about their day and the struggles and triumphs they had experienced.

Sundays were the only days off back then. It was a given that families would wake up early, take care of the household and farm chores, and get ready for church. This December morning was unusually warm and Jimmie asked his pregnant wife, Jean, "Do you feel like walking to church this morning or do you want to take the Ford?"

Jean responded, "I think the short walk will do my aching back some good."

His Paw (Brother Billy) had just wrapped up an especially moving sermon about "Looking inward at your own sins instead of your neighbors' sin."

There was the usual full church house of members that day and afterward, Brother Billy asked the Elders of the church to stay after service to look over the new upcoming church budget for the next year.

Brother Billy said, "I promise not to keep you so long as to let your dinners get cold!" with a slight chuckle.

The elders of the church gathered in the small meeting room behind the altar to discuss the church budget for the upcoming year. They pored over the numbers, discussing how best to allocate funds for various programs and projects. The discussion was cordial with each elder sharing their opinion and offering suggestions for how to make the most of the church's limited resources.

At one point, they even took a break to enjoy some of Sister Betty's homemade cookies and coffee which she had prepared for the occasion. It was a good meeting, and by the end, they had a solid plan for how to move forward with the budget.

Brother Billy looked down at his watch, showing the time as 12:50 p.m., and said, "Told you gentlemen that I would get you out of here before your dinners got cold."

Jimmie and his wife were sitting on a church pew waiting for Paw to finish the meeting when, suddenly, they saw Rob Davis hurrying towards them with an unusually quick pace, carrying under his arm what looked to be a radio of some kind.

As Rob Davis approached them, Jimmie could see the urgency on his face. He wondered what could be so important for Rob to be in such a hurry.

As he got closer, Rob handed Jimmie the old Philco radio and said, "Turn it to the WLSD station, quick!"

Jimmie quickly took the radio to the back office where the Elders were meeting and turned the radio on. The voice of a news announcer filled the church room.

The announcer sounded frantic as he shouted, "We interrupt this program for a special news bulletin. The Japanese have just attacked Pearl Harbor. I repeat, the Japanese have attacked Pearl Harbor Naval Base! The attack came just before 8:00 a.m. Hawaiian time," the announcer said. "It was a coordinated assault by the Japanese military on the American Pacific Fleet stationed at Pearl Harbor. The damage is extensive and the loss of life is still being calculated. The President of the United States has called for a state of war with Japan."

The news hit Jimmie like a sack of taters. He had heard of the tensions between the United States and Japan, but he never expected an attack on American soil.

Everything changed at that moment and Jimmie knew his life and the lives of those around him would never be the same.

Paw looked up from the radio he was eyeing and asked Jimmie and Jean, "Where's your Ma?"

Jimmie replied, "She already walked home to finish making dinner."

Paw said, "Let's go. We need to find out about your brother Graham."

"Go find out where John is and tell him to come home to be with his Ma! Tell him no cussing and just do as I ask, PLEASE!" Paw said urgently as he headed towards the door. Jimmie quickly nodded and ran out to find John. He knew that his brother, Graham, had joined the Navy a couple of years ago and was stationed on the West Coast, but he didn't quite know why he was so worried.

As he made his way through Crackers Neck, he couldn't help but feel a sense of unease. Finally, he spotted John chatting with some friends outside the Skeens General Store.

"John, you need to come home to Ma's right away. Something has happened in Hawaii and we don't know about Graham," Jimmie said, his voice trembling with fear.

John's expression turned serious as he realized the gravity of the situation. "What happened? Is he okay?"

"I don't know, Paw just said to come home and be with Ma. He needs you to come back without any fuss," Jimmie replied.

John put his cigarette out, nodded in understanding and quickly followed Jimmie back to their home. As they approached, they saw the worry etched on their mother's face and Jimmie knew in that exact moment their lives would never be the same.

As the radio crackled in the background, the Galloway men gathered around the kitchen table, their faces etched with concern and worry. The smell of fresh coffee wafted through the air mixing with the scent of fresh biscuits baking in the oven. The kitchen was small and cozy with mismatched chairs gathered around the wooden table. The linoleum floors were worn and scuffed, evidence of years of use.

Sister Jenny sat in the corner, hands clasped tightly in her lap, and her eyes red-rimmed from tears. Ma sat at the head of the table, a look of disbelief on her face as she tried to process the news. The radio announcer's voice was a constant hum in the background, a reminder that the world outside was a lot smaller and even more dangerous.

Paw, a rugged man with calloused hands and a weathered face, sat at the foot of the table, his eyes fixed on the radio. He spoke in a low voice, his words measured and deliberate, as he explained the details of the last letter they had received from Graham. The room was heavy with an oppressive weight of fear and the tension was so strong you could bend a horseshoe in half. The men sat in stoic silence, each one grappling with the same internal demons of doubt and apprehension for the uncertain future ahead

Paw somberly informed the boys that the last letter they had received from Graham three weeks ago indicated that he had been promoted to Electrician's Mate Chief Petty Officer and was transferred from San Diego to be stationed at Pearl Harbor, aboard the USS West Virginia. The news hit the family hard and the gravity of the situation settled in with Jimmie and John as they began to grasp the enormity of what had happened.

Ma finally stood up with a serious, but calm look and said, "Our family's saving grace is that we all know your brother Graham well. The radio announcer said the attack on Pearl Harbor happened early this Sunday morning there. Knowing my son, Graham, he was probably still at a bar or in the brig. It might be the only time I hope and pray Graham was out drinking and bar hopping, chasing women! But let's not jump to conclusions. We must stay hopeful and wait for any news about Graham."

After a week of unrest and unpleasant waiting, a telegram from the United States Navy was delivered to the Galloway home. As the whole family gathered, Ma opened and read the news, she smiled and said, "He's alive!"

John, the youngest brother, was a senior at East Stone High School at the time, and Jimmie had a baby due in the spring. Paw knew that his sons' first impulse was to join their brother Graham in the war effort. With a stern expression, he addressed the boys, "I know both of you want to serve in the military, just like your brother. I won't stop you, but I ask that you wait until summer. John, you need to finish high school. Jimmie, you have a baby on the way and need to be here for Jean and spend some time with your new child before you ship out. If this war is as bad as we think, waiting a little longer won't hurt."

It was a crisp morning of December 8th, 1941 when Jimmie walked through the front doors of the Pet Dairy milk processing plant. He had graduated from East Stone Gap High School just six months prior and was excited to start his first job in the real world after working the summer at the downtown bus station. But the bombing of Pearl Harbor and the start of World War II changed all his plans for himself and his family.

The plant was bustling with activity as workers in white coats and hairnets moved quickly from one machine to the next, checking gauges and filling orders. Jimmie was assigned to the pasteurization department where he would be responsible for ensuring that the milk was heated to the proper temperature to kill any harmful bacteria.

He donned his white coat and hairnet and joined the team at his assigned station. His co-workers were a mix of experienced dairy workers and recent high school graduates like himself, all working together to keep the plant running smoothly. The plant was a large, cavernous building with concrete floors and metal rafters supporting the roof. The noise of the machines was almost deafening as they whirred and hummed, the sound of the bottling line particularly loud as it churned out bottles at a dizzying pace.

The first step in the pasteurization process was to transfer the raw milk into large tanks where it would be heated to a specific temperature for a set amount of time. Jimmie carefully monitored the temperature gauges, making small adjustments as needed to keep the milk at the correct temperature.

As the milk passed through the pasteurization process, Jimmie and his team kept a watchful eye on every step. They had to ensure that the milk was safe and healthy for human consumption and any misstep in the process could be costly.

Once the milk had been pasteurized, it was transferred to the bottling line where it would be filled into glass bottles and capped with foil. The machines on the bottling line were large and complex with dozens of moving parts that had to work together in perfect harmony.

Jimmie's job was to make sure that everything was running smoothly and to quickly troubleshoot any issues that arose. Jimmie's job wasn't just about monitoring the machines, though. He was also responsible for keeping the work area clean and ensuring that all the equipment was sanitized between batches. This was a critical part of the process as any contamination could spoil the milk and render it unusable.

Despite the long hours and the challenging work, Jimmie enjoyed his job at the processing plant. He was proud to be doing his part to help feed the country and he felt like he was part of something bigger than himself. But he couldn't help but think about his brother Graham serving in the Navy in the Pacific. It was a hard and difficult decision, but he knew he would be joining the military this summer. He couldn't have two brothers serving without him, no matter how mad it made his wife Jean.

Jimmie working his first job out of high school at the Pet Dairy

Pet Dairy with employees and delivery trucks lined up

EIGHTEEN
Off to Army Flight School

The three of them slept together in the front bedroom off from the living room that night with their infant daughter, Brenda Helen. Jean sobbed most of the night with Jimmie holding her tight and asking her not to cry because he had to go. He promised to keep in contact writing letters and to do his utmost to return to Jean and his baby daughter.

The next morning, Jean and Jimmie walked to the bus station together for what might be their final goodbye. Dad's younger brother, John, was already there. Jimmie and his brother were going to join the newly formed Army Air Corps together. The Greyhound bus pulled into the station and Jean and Jimmie embraced and kissed as all couples do before deployment.

Going to Knoxville by bus was a long and tiresome trip. The bus stopped for anyone standing beside the road that flagged them down. There were people of all ages, from children to the elderly if you had payment for fare. There were six young men about John's age, fresh from high school or younger. They were going to join the war effort also. Mountain men folk had a long history of serving their country.

As the bus rattled down the bumpy road, Jimmie couldn't help but feel a little nervous as John was brimming with enthusiasm, "I want to fly the fighter planes; I want to see some action!"

Jimmie replied with a wry smile, "You can have the glory, John. I've got a wife and baby to think about. I'm applying for bomber training since it pays extra and has a bigger G.I. insurance payout just in case, I don't make it back."

John looked at his brother, "You always were the practical one, Jimmie."

Jimmie grinned, "You mean I'm the one with a brain. You know, I heard that being a bomber pilot is pretty cushy. You get to sit in a big comfy chair and push buttons all day while your crew does all the work."

John raised an eyebrow and replied, "Cushy, huh? I don't know about that. I heard bomber pilots have to fly for hours on end, dodging enemy fire, and hoping they don't get shot down. Sounds pretty nerve-wracking to me."

Jimmie chuckled, "Well, at least they have a good view up there. The fighter jocks are stuck in a tiny cockpit all day with no legroom. How are you going to handle that, Johnny boy?"

John leaned back in his seat, grinning. "Hey, I'm a natural-born pilot. I could fly a kite if I had to. Plus, I heard that fighter pilots are the real heroes of the war and get ALL the good-looking girls. Plus, you get to take the enemy head-on, guns blazing."

Jimmie shook his head, "Well, good luck with that. I'd rather stay up high and avoid all that danger."

John laughed. "Yeah, you always were a bit of a scaredy-cat. But don't worry, I'll protect you."

He turned to John and said, "What if I crash one of those bombers? My wife and baby are depending on me to make it home."

John, always the joker, took a draw of his cigarette and replied, "Well, Jimbo, if you do crash, just make sure you land on a soft target. Like a pillow factory or a marshmallow farm."

Jimmie couldn't help but laugh at John's absurd suggestion, "I'll keep that in mind," he said with a grin.

As the bus made its way through the rolling hills of Tennessee, the brothers looked out the window at the passing scenery.

"You know," John said, "I always thought we'd be farmers, coal miners, or preachers like Paw."

Jimmie nodded in agreement. "Yeah, but we were meant for something bigger than this. We were born to fly."

John chuckled. "Or crash, depending on how good you are." They both laughed at that, enjoying the light-hearted banter that eased their nerves about the journey ahead.

When they arrived in Knoxville, the eight young men asked for directions to the recruiting office. It was only a block away. They walked in and went to different recruiter's desks. Jimmie and John went to the Army Air Corps recruiter and signed the necessary forms. That was all that there was to it. The recruiter escorted them to the train station, bought them tickets to Richmond, Virginia for their physicals, wished them the best of luck, and thanked them for their service to their country. Jimmie and John had literally left home with nothing but the clothes on their backs.

The trip from Knoxville, TN to Richmond, VA seemed like such a huge adventure for the boys. They slept in the train seats, talked to the other new recruits, smoked, and ate in the diner car. The food was delicious and was served by African-American waiters. The food was served in China bowls and silver platters. The coffee was served in silver serving pots. They ate on China plates that were trimmed in gold. Jimmie and John had never seen anything like it. The price of their tickets included meals for the eighteen-hour trip.

Once they got near Richmond, they started seeing the city skyline and skyscraper buildings. The buildings looked white and perfectly spaced. Everything was so clean. The train pulled into the magnificent railroad station.

"Wonder where we'll go?" asked John.

"I don't know, but I'm sure that someone will be here for us," answered Jimmie.

Sure enough, a recruiter held up a sign with Army Air Corps written on it. Jimmie and John were the only two to go with this recruiter. The other young men went with Army and Marine recruiters.

The recruiter said, "Welcome. I am Sergeant Wade and I'll take you to the armory where you will receive your physicals."

They jumped into an Army Jeep and Sergeant Wade drove them through the city traffic with the greatest of ease, whipping in and out of the lanes of traffic. Soon, they reached their destination and lined up for their physicals.

From years of slaving on that damn "Rock Farm" and working in the processing plant, the brothers were in excellent physical shape and had no medical problems. They passed their physicals with ease, then signed more papers and were sworn in.

Still wearing their clothes from home, they boarded the train back to Nashville, TN. This was an extra-long trip because the train was first routed through Atlanta and then north to Nashville.

Jimmie and John received more testing. These tests were psychological in nature, but the brothers had no idea at the time. The psychologist tested their aptitude, academic skills, and emotional well-being. Having scored above average in all areas, they were accepted and reported to Berry Field where they received their military uniforms.

John remarked, "Wish the girls back home could see me in my uniform!" as he gazed in the bathroom mirror.

With their new enlistment, the brothers had beds in the barracks and nicely pressed uniforms to wear. The shower was the most impressive thing of all, just having hot water on tap. That was *"Rich Folk stuff!"*

Next, they got their military buzz haircuts and supper in the mess hall served on metal shingles. Exhausted, they immediately went to bed and didn't awaken until revelry at 6:00 a.m. Coursework for the military began on the very first day of the Army Air Corps.

During World War II, the United States Army Air Corp established several airfields in Arkansas for advanced training of military pilots. One such airfield was the Camden Army Air Field, located approximately five miles southwest of Camden, Arkansas. The airfield was used for bomber crew training and was in operation from 1942 to 1945. It was home to the 456th Bombardment Group, which trained with B-24 Liberator bombers and the B-17 Flying Fortresses.

At its peak, the airfield had over 4,000 personnel, including 500 officers and 3,500 enlisted men. The 456th Bomb Group was a highly decorated unit, earning several Distinguished Unit Citations for their efforts in combat. The group flew missions in the European Theater of Operations, including attacks on German oil refineries and strategic targets in France

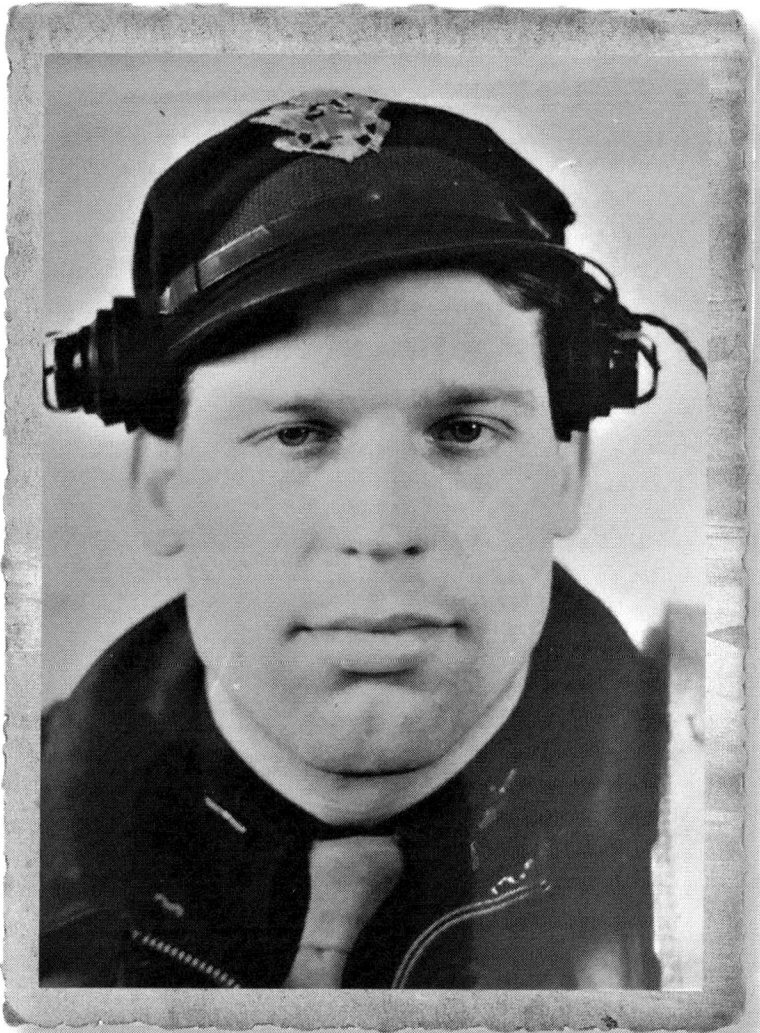

Jimmie right out of flight school after getting his wings

NINETEEN
Drafting The Crew

Jimmie couldn't help but feel a guilty pleasure every day he spent in the military. While he missed his wife and baby girl back in Crackers Neck terribly, he couldn't deny that he loved military life.

Back home on the farm, everything ran on a schedule - planting tobacco at a certain time of year, harvesting it at a certain time, and selling the crop at a certain time. Daily activities were done at the same time every day, like feeding the animals and gathering the eggs. Even his job at Pet Dairy had a set routine for every activity.

The military was no different. Physical fitness activities started at 0500 hours, breakfast was served at 0650 hours, and schooling followed. Everything was done according to a schedule and Jimmie found comfort in the routine. It gave him a sense of order and purpose in a world that felt otherwise chaotic with a war going on.

Jimmie had never gone to bed with an empty stomach, nor had his siblings. But he knew that he was surrounded by hunger during the Great Depression. Friends, family, neighbors - nearly everyone he met had experienced some level of hunger. Ma and Paw were fortunate enough to have a farm and always did their best to feed as many people as they could.

In the military, however, everyone had plenty of food. The mess hall was a sight to behold for Jimmie and every other new recruit. The quality of the food may not have been as good as Ma's cooking, but there was one thing all military mess halls had that she didn't: quantity. There was food everywhere! While the main course of meat might sometimes run low, the sides were endless.

Jimmie noticed that the men who had grown up hungry the worst were the ones who loaded up their trays and ate every bite without complaint. And they always made sure to fill their pockets and take some food back to the barracks as if the mess hall might disappear overnight. That fear of hunger never left them, even in the midst of plenty.

The greenbacks that Second Lieutenant Jimmie Galloway was making were no small beans. At $161 per month, he was making more money than he had ever made in his life, not to mention the additional $20 per month for hazard bomber crew pay. No one in training with him had ever made that kind of dough and they were all walking around with a bit more swagger in their step because of it.

Jimmie decided to keep the $20 hazard bomber crew pay for himself as a little extra spending cash, but the rest of his earnings were headed straight back to his wife and their daughter, Brenda Helen Galloway. Jean had written to him about their new savings account at the Big Stone Gap Bank & Trust. It was a proud moment for them both, but when Jean opened the account, the bank manager couldn't help but joke, "Who did Jimmie kill to get so much money?" He laughed, but Jean knew the answer. Her husband was putting his life on the line every day, and he was earning every penny

Jimmie was on top of the world, having just graduated with his Air Corps Wings from basic flight training and advanced Twin Engine training in Columbus, Mississippi. The sense of accomplishment was overwhelming and he couldn't wait to take the next step in his journey as a pilot.

As he boarded the train to Chanute, Illinois, for B-17 training, Jimmie couldn't help but feel a sense of nervousness. The Flying Fortress was a massive plane compared to anything he had flown before, and he knew it would take a lot of skill and determination to master it. Arriving at Chanute Air Force Base, the airfield was a hub of activity with planes taking off and landing every few minutes. He knew this was the big leagues now, and he was ready to step up to the challenge.

Over the next few weeks, Jimmie immersed himself in the world of the B-17. He learned every inch of the massive plane, from the cockpit to the tail gunner's turret. He studied the mechanics of the engines and the intricate systems that kept the plane in the air. And, of course, he practiced his flying skills, taking the B-17 up into the skies time and time again.

It wasn't easy, but Jimmie was determined. He pushed himself harder than he ever had before and, slowly but surely, he began to master the Flying Fortress. He even began to enjoy the feeling of being in control of such a massive machine.

As the end of his training approached, Jimmie was confident in his skills. He had proven himself to be a capable pilot, ready to take on the challenges of flying in combat, and he knew that no matter what lay ahead, he was ready for it. Or at least he felt that way.

Jimmie arrived at MacDill Field in Tampa Bay, Florida with a sense of anticipation and a touch of apprehension. He had already completed his basic flight training, and advanced twin-engine training, but he knew that B-17 crew training would be a whole new level of intensity. The idea of being responsible for the lives of nine other men was daunting, to say the least.

As he stepped off the transport plane, the humid Florida air hit him like a wall. He wiped the sweat from his brow and made his way to the barracks to settle in. The next morning, he was supposed to meet Major Graham with the other pilots so they could pick their crews, much like a draft day of a sports franchise. The pilots would have personnel records of gunners, navigators, bombardiers, radio operators, and the like. Pilots would choose the men they felt most comfortable with and such.

Jimmie hadn't taken two steps out of the barracks this important morning when a corporal handed him a message to immediately report to the medical building. Somehow during transferring his medical records, they had lost his T.B. screening and he needed to come by first before heading over to his pilot's meeting. Jimmie looked at his watch, knowing this was probably going to make him run late.

Running him late, it did. As Jimmie reached the pilot's meeting room, Major Graham had Jimmie explain his tardiness.

Major Graham barked, "Damn doctors, they should have let you come pick your crew first and then done their fucking tests. Anyway, you're here now, but I don't recommend what crew officers we have left! All the other pilots have picked their crews."

Jimmie replied, "Sir, why do you say that? What's wrong with them?"

Major Graham handed Jimmie their personnel files and Jimmie started to scan through them. "Sir, hell, all but two of these men are college graduates from top-notch colleges that I even recognize. Why didn't the other pilots want them as their crew?"

Major Graham, "Damn, Son, where are you from? Stupid hillbilly; you don't recognize the names or see their religious affiliation? The college boys are God Damn JEWS and that one there named Smitty is almost a midget in size and that tall one has NO schooling at all and is a troublemaker from Texas, I can tell! You don't want this crew son. I'll have a new batch of crews to pick from coming in next week. You can wait until then."

Jimmie was still scanning over the personnel files, his copilot, Bob Burkenfield, was even the quarterback of the Boston University football team. As he was thinking to himself how the only two Jews he had ever met back home were Attorney Gladstone and Old Man Cohens, who owned a department store in Norton, they sure did seem like fine fellows to him! Paw had always told him that if you ever got the choice of who you worked with, choose fellow workers who were smart. Dumbasses and fools would get you killed in the mines quicker than anything.

Jimmie asked the Major if he could have a few minutes to talk to some of the men before he made his decision.

Major Couch replied, "Take a few minutes and let me know. I'll be over at my office."

Jimmie was going to bite the bullet and wanted to find out how the two non-Jewish airmen felt about working with the other Jews. Jimmie motioned for Tex and Smitty to come out while the other airmen stayed in the meeting room.

Jimmie said, "Tex Smith from Texarkana, Texas, is that your real name?"

Tex replied, "Yes Sir, believe it or not, Tex Smith is my official name. Is it my God-given name? I have no idea. I was an orphan from birth, Sir."

Jimmie straightened his back, "I got one simple question for both of you. The rest of the crew in there are Jewish; do either one of you have a problem flying with them and living with them?"

Tex grinned from ear to ear, "Sir, I don't have any damn religion and from what I'm hearing about the war and the slaughterhouse meat grinder we're heading into, we better partner up with some buddies that have some damn religion. I hear that Jews have all kinds of religion, maybe some will rub off on us!"

Smitty responded, "I agree with Tex! I hear the chances of us living through our tour are pretty damn thin, Sir! Some religion sounds ok with me!"

So, the crew of Little Helen was born.

Jimmie always said, "I didn't pick my Jewish bomber crew because I was a just and moral person, the fact is, I WAS an uninformed hillbilly that didn't know I was supposed to hate Jews! I really didn't know any, so I didn't know any better, but to like the Jews and the Catholics. I didn't know any Catholics either."

This was a time when the world was changing and not always for the better. Eugenics was becoming a popular topic and some of the most influential people in the country were embracing it with open arms.

The American Nazi party was spreading like wildfire and the message of hate, bigotry, and anti-Semitics… blaming Jews for the Great Depression… was spreading. It was the 1920s and 1930s; America had just gotten out of the Great War (WWI) and was on the brink of another war. Eugenics was the pseudoscience that argued for the sterilization of those deemed "unfit" for society. People with disabilities, immigrants, and persons of color were often targeted for sterilization under the guise of improving society.

Famous people such as Alexander Graham Bell, President Woodrow Wilson, Winston Churchill, John D. Rockefeller, and H.G. Wells were embracing this ideology. Leaders of the movement like Charles Davenport and Harry Laughlin had prominent positions in the scientific community. Even President Theodore Roosevelt was a vocal supporter of eugenics and, for about 30 years, from the early 1900s until the 1930s, America had an active and popular eugenics movement.

But it wasn't just the elite who were spreading these ideas. The American Nazi party, under the leadership of George Lincoln Rockwell, was gaining traction in the United States. Rockwell's message of white supremacy and eugenics resonated with many, poor and rich alike, including some prominent celebrities like Henry Ford and Charles Lindbergh who were known anti-Semites and supporters of eugenics. It was a dark time in American history and the echoes of that time can still be felt today. The lessons of the past should never be forgotten; we must always be vigilant against hate and bigotry in all its forms.

Little Helen Flight Crew
(Bottom Row L to R: Kimmel, Cline, Smitty, Isaac, Stapp
Top Row: L to R: Tex Smith, Bob Burkenfield, Jimmie Galloway,
Marty Livengood)

Little Helen officers in front of barracks at Tampa Bay
Below: *Back side of the picture*

TWENTY

7 Ft Tall with a Cigarette

Jimmie and John had been thick as thieves since childhood, so when it came time for John to ship off to Luke Field in Arizona for fighter pilot training, Jimmie felt the emptiness inside. Jimmie himself was headed to Fort Campbell in Arkansas for twin-engine airplane training with plans to graduate with his wings in Columbus, Mississippi. After that, B-17 training in Chanute, IL, and eventually the assembly of his bomber crew in Tampa Bay, Florida, before shipping off to war.

As John was about to board his transport plane to Arizona, Jimmie tried to hide his emotions as he shook his brother's hand, but couldn't help leaning in for a slight hug. "Don't do anything stupid and get yourself killed, John Boy!" Jimmie said, his voice slightly cracking.

John, taking a drag of his Camel cigarette, gave a small smirk before responding, "You too, big brother. You too." And with that, he boarded the plane, leaving both brothers to face their own futures alone for the first time in their lives.

John found fighter school bookwork to be grueling, often wishing he had paid more attention in Mrs. Gembach's algebra class back in East Stone Gap High School. But he was a natural when it came to flying and it showed in his skills. Even flying bi-planes out of Crackers Neck Airfield, John always had the ability to make a plane run faster and longer than any other pilot could. Back in the days before computers and fuel injection engines, planes' fuel-air mixtures would be constantly adjusted by pilots as they flew. Even being able to read the clouds and weather and find those wonderful tailwinds to fly fast and save fuel, John could sniff them out like a night champion Walker dog coonhound.

John may not have been the most technically proficient dog-fighter pilot, but he could fly fast and far, and this caught the attention of a new military unit called the Office of Strategic Services (OSS).

The OSS was a top-secret agency formed during World War II to conduct espionage, gather intelligence, and perform covert operations. It was later reorganized and renamed the Central Intelligence Agency (CIA), but during the war, it was the OSS that recognized John's talents.

At first, John was hesitant to join the OSS, as he was loyal to his fighter squadron and wanted to stay with them and see active combat against the Nazis. But the OSS convinced him that he could still fly, just for a different cause. So, John agreed to join and soon he found himself in the thick of things, performing long-distance delivery runs of top-secret documents and valuable troop V-Mail from airfields around Washington D.C. and New York City to combat theaters of England, North Africa, and then Northern Italy, as the war progressed.

The O.S.S. had commissioned a fleet of brand-new P-51 Mustangs that had been fitted with extra fuel tanks and extra storage by omitting the customary six .50 caliber machine guns and ammo. The P-51 Mustang was a long-range, single-seat fighter and fighter-bomber used during World War II. It was designed in the United States in 1940 by North American Aviation and quickly became one of the most famous and effective aircraft of the war.

The Mustang was originally designed to be a high-altitude interceptor, but it was later adapted for ground attack and escort duties. It was powered by a Packard-built Rolls-Royce Merlin engine, which gave it a top speed of over 400 mph and a range of more than 1,000 miles.

The P-51 was armed with six .50 caliber machine guns and could carry up to 2,000 pounds of bombs or rockets. It was also equipped with advanced avionics including a radio compass and an autopilot which made it easier for pilots to fly long distances.

John had a natural talent for making a Mustang soar at top speed. The factory specs claimed the Mustang's top speed was 437 mph, even with their most skilled test pilots at the helm. But John had managed to clock his Mustang at an impressive 450 mph, all while casually puffing away on a Camel cigarette. It was no wonder that his skills at speed caught the attention of the Office of Strategic Services (OSS), which later became the Central Intelligence Agency.

After graduating from flight school, John was assigned his specially equipped O.S.S. Mustang and given orders to fly from Arizona to a secret airfield north of Washington D.C. to begin missions of flying top secret military documents to Europe. He was given three days to report, which gave John an idea for a quick stopover. His destination? Crackers Neck Airfield to see the folks.

The Mustang purred like a kitten as John cruised above the clouds, the sun beating down on his aviator sunglasses. He felt a sense of pride as he flew his beloved aircraft. After all, it was more than just a plane to him - it was an extension of himself.

As he made his descent to Crackers Neck Airfield, he couldn't help but feel a sense of nostalgia. This was where he learned to fly, where he first took to the skies and felt truly alive. He was looking forward to catching up with the old-timers and showing off his new bird. Man, how the girls were going to be impressed with his plane and fancy uniform of the U.S. Army Air Corps fighter pilot.

As he taxied his P-51 Mustang onto the grassy runway of Crackers Neck Airfield, a rush of excitement at the thought of seeing Ma and Uncle Bud rushed over him. John knew Paw would be up at the coal tipple on a Tuesday, but he didn't mind, he would see him tonight when he got home. Seeing Ma and Uncle Bud right away was enough to make the detour worthwhile and then head out to D.C. in the morning.

John shut off the engine and jumped out of the cockpit, stretching his legs and feeling the familiar crunch of grass sod under his boots. As he made his way towards the mechanics shed, that sense of nostalgia continued to wash over him. This airfield held so many memories for him.

When he finally reached the front porch of Ma's farmhouse, John could hear the sound of Uncle Bud's fiddle playing a lively tune inside. He pushed open the screen door and was greeted with the familiar sight of Ma cooking up a storm in the kitchen and Uncle Bud tapping his foot to the beat of his own music.

"Well, I'll be," Ma exclaimed, wiping her hands on her apron and giving John a big hug. "Look at you, all grown up and fancy in that uniform."

John smiled at the familiar warmth of Ma's embrace. "Good to see you too, Ma," he said, before turning to Uncle Bud. "Hey there, old man. Still making all the young ladies swoon with that fiddle of yours?"

Uncle Bud laughed and shook his head, "Nah, I'm afraid these old bones ain't what they used to be. But I still know how to make 'em tap their toes, you can bet on that."

For the next few hours, John sat around the kitchen table catching up with Ma and Uncle Bud over a hearty lunch of fried chicken and mashed potatoes.

Shortly after 2 p.m., Ma caught sight of a parade of cars and trucks heading towards their house, even the city bus had joined in.

"What on earth is all this coming our way?" Ma asked, peering out of the kitchen window.

At that moment, there was a knock on the front door, prompting John to get up from the kitchen table and answer it. Standing on the porch was Bill Hendricks, the editor of The Post newspaper.

"We received a report of a fancy Army airplane landing on the airfield and I'm here to find out about it. I take it I knocked on the right door!" Bill said.

John responded, "You sure did, but what's with all these other people?" as he pointed to the busload of students and sightseers making their way towards their house.

Bill exclaimed, "The principals at both East Stone Gap and Big Stone Gap High Schools heard about your fancy fighter plane being at Crackers Neck and they decided to let school out early so the students could come and see for themselves. You better get out here and meet your admirers!"

John wasted no time grabbing his pilot's cap, making a few minor adjustments to his uniform in front of the mirror, and straightening his tie. He was ready to meet his eager fans.

That following week, John was on the cover of The Post standing in front of his Mustang fighter plane looking seven feet tall and holding his Camel cigarette. That week in Crackers Neck and the surrounding communities, even Clark Gable wasn't as famous as John was, and that suited him quite well!

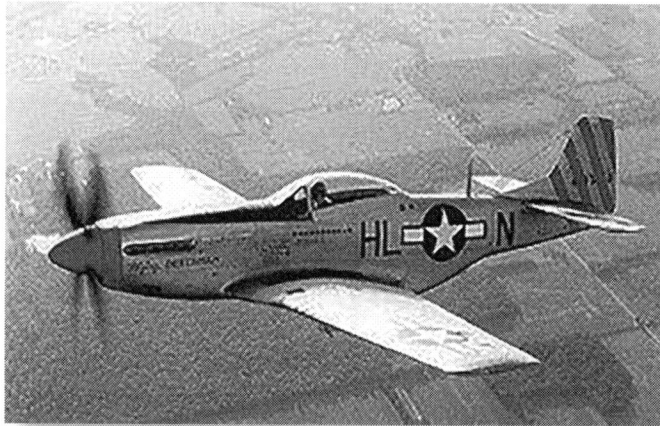

P51 Mustang

Captain John Galloway

GALLOWAY JOHN W
AO 817919

In the thick of the Battle of Waterloo, Napoleon Bonaparte, that little French General, spun out a phrase that's stuck around, "An army marches on its stomach." Not a truer message has been said about keeping a fighting force on its toes. But the grizzled warriors of the 20th Century, right through to the boys today, know there's more to it than that. What keeps a soldier's heart in the fight, what keeps him puttin' one boot in front of the other, is the love of what's waiting back home. And nothin' stokes that fire more than a piece of MAIL from the home front!

As G.K. Chesterton, that sharp-witted English bloke, once said, "The true soldier fights, not because he hates what is in front of him, but because he loves what is behind him."

At the height of World War II, Uncle Sam had over three million boys in uniform stompin' around the European theater alone. Now, you think about trying to deliver all that mail, all those "pieces of home," to every GI Joe and Jane with a rifle and a helmet, and you got yourself a problem the size of the Atlantic Ocean. The task of moving that much mail was no Sunday drive; it was a logistical nightmare that would make even the steeliest quartermaster break out in a cold sweat.

The 1942 Annual Report to the Postmaster General laid it out plain and simple: "At the Post Office, War, and Navy Departments, we know the score. We understand that a steady flow of words from moms, pals, and sweethearts back home, it's like fuel to a flame. It stiffens the spine, sparks the patriotic fire, eases the sting of loneliness, and lights a fire under the men and women out there in the thick of it, miles away from home and familiar faces."

The military mail system during the Big One, well, it was a sight to behold. Letters and packages were flying back and forth across oceans like never before. Army post offices, fleet post offices, U.S. post offices… they were all drowning in a sea of envelopes and parcels. Every year, the tide rose higher. By '45, the Army Postal Service was wrestling with *2.5 billion* pieces of mail, and Navy post offices had their hands full with *8 million* more. To keep the mail moving to every corner of the globe took a system as wide as the world itself, and a little bit of Yankee ingenuity. Enter V-mail, short for "Victory mail." Now, this was a smart play designed to shrink down the space needed for mail, freeing up room for bullets, beans, and bandages.

The V-mail system was only in play between June '42 and November '45, but in that time, over one billion items hitched a ride. The fancy name was the "Army Micro Photographic Mail Service," but all you really need to know is that it was a way to make a letter as small as a flea, then blow it back up again at its final destination. It was, as War Department Pamphlet No. 21-1 put it, "an expeditious mail program which provides for quick mail service to and from soldiers overseas. A special form is used which permits the letter to be photographed in microfilm. The small film is transported and then reproduced and delivered. Use of V-mail is urged because it greatly furthers the war effort by saving shipping and airplane space."

In the early days of May 1942, Uncle Sam shook hands with the camera whizzes over at Kodak, striking up a deal for that V-mail microfilming magic. Then, on June 12th, President Franklin D. Roosevelt got his hands on the first two V-mails. A few weeks later, on July 1st, the V-mail service kicked into high gear.

The key to the whole V-mail operation was the use of one-sheet-fits-all stationery. It was a letter and envelope all rolled into one, a smart little package even before you got to the microfilming part. This one-two punch of a form was cooked up by the brainiacs at the Government Printing Office and handed out free of charge at post offices, two sheets per GI Joe or Jane per day.

Smithsonian
National Postal Museum

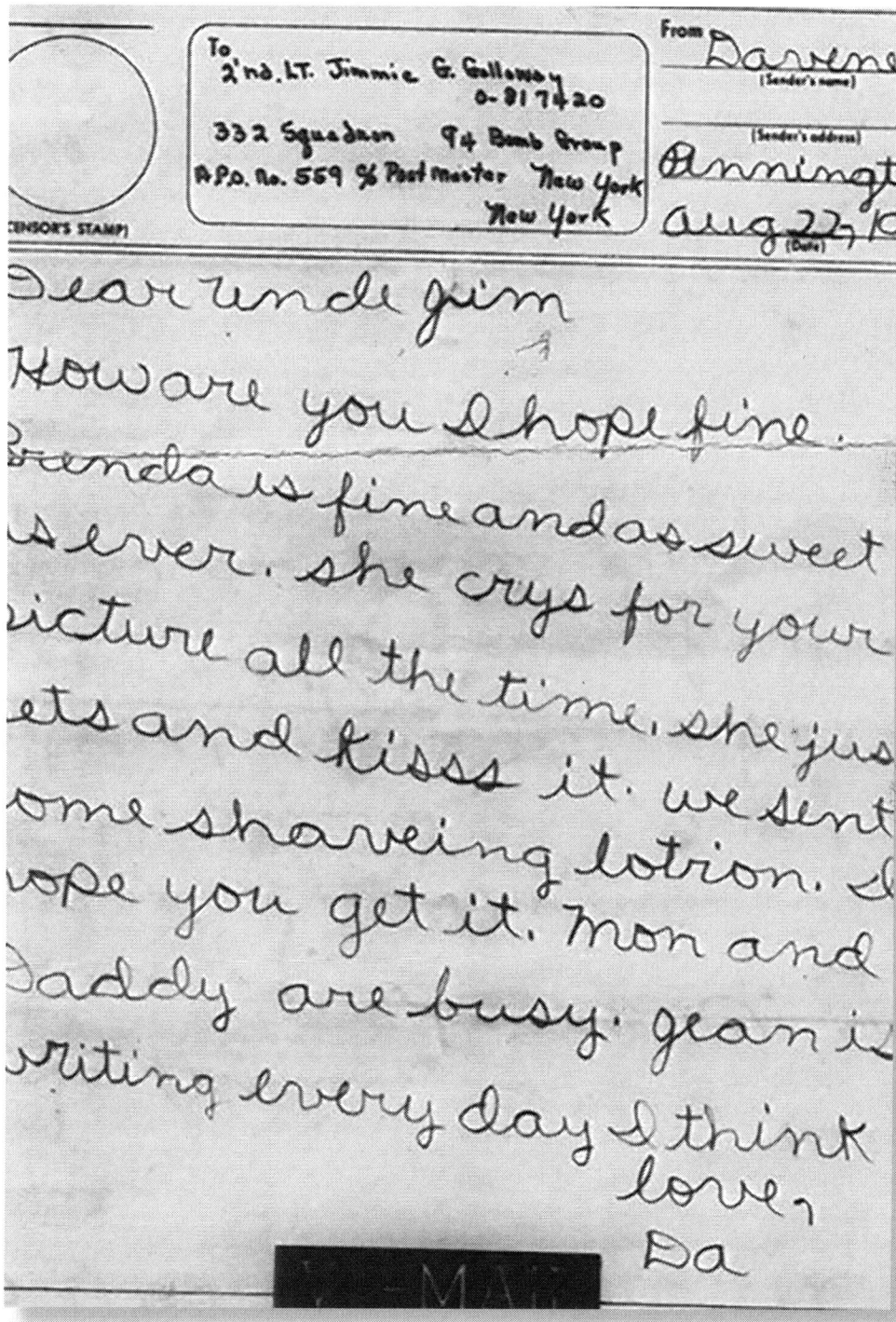

To
2'nd. LT. Jimmie G. Galloway
0-817420
332 Squadron 94 Bomb Group
A.P.O. No. 559 % Post master New York
New York

(CENSOR'S STAMP)

From Darlene
(Sender's name)

(Sender's address)
Anningt
aug 22, 10
(Date)

Dear Uncle Jim
How are you I hope fine.
Brenda is fine and as sweet
as ever. she crys for your
picture all the time. she jus
ets and kisss it. we sent
ome shaveing lotrion. I
ope you get it. mon and
Daddy are busy. gean is
riting every day I think
love,
Da

One of Jimmie's actual V-mail letters

123

TWENTY-ONE
Long Boat Ride to England

A s the day of their departure finally arrived, Jimmie and his crew boarded the ship laden with all their gear and equipment. The vessel was loaded to the brim with soldiers and airmen all heading towards various destinations across England. The faces of the men were filled with uneasy tension, as everyone knew that they were venturing into the very heart of the warzone.

> Throughout World War II, an estimated 1.5 million American GIs were shipped to England. They were a crucial part of the Allied Forces fighting against Nazi Germany and its Axis partners. From 1942 onwards, the GIs arrived in England with the majority of them coming as part of the work up to D-Day in 1944. They were then stationed at bases across the country.

Jimmie had never set foot on a boat before and the thought of seasickness was nagging at him. But as he laid eyes on their transport, the mighty R.M.S Tamaroa, all his worries vanished.

This British beauty was a beast, capable of carrying a staggering 1,700 passengers as well as mail and freight. A twin-screw steamship, weighing in at a whopping 12,375 tons, she was constructed in 1922 by the Belfast-based Harland

& Wolff for Thompson's Aberdeen Line and was originally named Sophocles. Her purpose was to support the Australian passenger service. In 1926, she was chartered by Shaw, Savill & Albion, and renamed Tamaroa. Six years later, in 1932, the company took full ownership of the ship. She was used to run between New Zealand and Great Britain before being repurposed as a troop ship during World War II.

R.M.S. Tamaroa / Troop Carrier

Up until this time, Jimmie felt that his life in the military was full of plenty: plenty of food, clothes, the best boots he had ever owned, health care, and excitement. Due to Old Coach Smith's toughness as a football coach, even the drill sergeants and physical training in basic training didn't seem too bad.

As the R.M.S. Tamaroa joined with the other ships of the armada heading to WWII, Jimmie and his crew stood on the top deck taking in the vast ocean view on the first evening. They observed the positioning of the Tamaroa and the other ships and Bob, the co-pilot, inquisitively asked one of the ship's crew about it.

The shipmate gave them a shocking response: all the troop-carrying ships were surrounding the cargo ships carrying fuel and war equipment for protection.

Tex, feeling a little angered by the situation, spoke up and asked, "Protect them from what?"

The shipmate responded with a solemn tone, "Nazi U-boat Wolfpack attacks."

Tex's anger turned into disbelief, "So, you mean to say that the Navy Brass would rather lose a ship carrying 1700 G.I.s in the cold North Atlantic than one of their precious fuel ships?!"

The shipmate replied, "That's the way they see it. It's harder to get more fuel than to get more G.I.s for the war effort."

Jimmie couldn't help but think of his Paw and how the coal miners were treated by the big coal companies back home. The men were viewed as cheap and disposable, worth less than the mules and ponies.

On the second day of sailing, it was a moonless night, the sea was rough, and the wind was howling as the transport ship slowly made its way through the North Atlantic. The ship was one of many in a convoy heading towards England with a stop in Belfast, Ireland to resupply the Allied war effort. The men aboard the ship were mostly young soldiers, sailors, and airmen, eager to make it to their destination, but also acutely aware of the danger that lurked beneath the waves. The German "Wolfpacks" were the stuff of nightmares and the men knew that they were always just one torpedo away from a watery grave. Every sailor aboard the ship was on high alert, their eyes scanning the dark, choppy waters for any sign of a periscope while the sound of the engines and the creaking of the ship filled the air.

One night, they received a warning that a German "Wolfpack" submarine was in the area, and the ship's captain ordered everyone to go below deck and stay there until further notice, announcing "NO smoking and NO lights!"

Jimmie's aircrew huddled together in the cramped quarters, their hearts pounding with fear. They could hear the distant rumble of explosions and the hiss of torpedoes in the water and they knew that the submarine was getting closer. Every moment felt like an eternity, and the fear was almost suffocating.

Miraculously, the ship managed to evade the U-boat and they continued their journey to Belfast, Northern Ireland. When they finally arrived, the crew felt a sense of relief that they had made it through the treacherous waters of the

Atlantic, but they knew that they were still facing great danger as they prepared to confront the enemy in the skies over Europe.

As Jimmie and his crew disembarked from their ship at the Belfast port, they were greeted by the sight of a fleet of waiting trucks that would transport them to the Belfast Air Base for the next leg of their journey.

Jimmie looked over to Bob, sweat starting to bead up on his forehead from the stuffy ride in the back of the truck, "Wish we had a few days to explore Belfast. This is the first foreign country I've ever been in and all I'm seeing of it is from the back of this truck," he said wistfully.

Bob nodded in agreement; his eyes fixed on the passing greenery of the Irish countryside, "Supposedly, my family's ancestors came through Ireland," he said. "It would have been nice to take a look around and see if I could find any traces of them."

Jimmie chuckled, "I know what you mean. I've heard stories about my granddaddy's granddaddy coming from these parts, but it all feels like a distant memory now."

As the truck rumbled on, they both fell into a comfortable silence, lost in their thoughts of what could have been. The lush fields and rolling hills of Ireland passed by them in a blur, a fleeting glimpse of a foreign land that they would never fully explore.

The trucks bounced and rumbled along the winding roads, the drivers skillfully maneuvering around sharp turns and dodging potholes along the way. As they reached the air base, they could see the waiting DC-3 transport plane on the tarmac, its propellers already churning and ready to take off.

The flight crew went through their final checks as the men settled into their seats, the roar of the engines filling their ears. As they took off and gained altitude, the crew couldn't help but feel a sense of unease. The war was raging on and the skies were a dangerous place to be without fighter plane escort. They feared being shot down by enemy planes or encountering the famously harsh weather of the North Atlantic.

The interior of the DC-3 transport plane was cramped and utilitarian. The fuselage was lined with olive drab canvas seats that were bolted to the floor, providing minimal cushioning. The overhead compartments were filled with canvas bags and crates while the floor was littered with equipment and supplies.

The plane's interior was dimly lit by a series of small, circular windows along the sides of the plane which did little to brighten the space. The noise level was deafening as the engines roared and the plane jostled through the air.

The galley was a tight space with barely enough room to turn around. The cockpit was separated from the passenger area by a small door which was usually kept closed during flight. Inside the cockpit, the pilot and co-pilot sat in small, cramped seats surrounded by a complex array of dials and instruments, communicating with the ground crew and air traffic control through static-filled radios.

Despite its Spartan accommodations, the DC-3 was a lifeline for troops and supplies during the war providing a vital link between bases and battlefields across the globe during the war.

But the flight crew was skilled and experienced, and they navigated the skies with precision and they seemed carefree. The hours passed slowly and the men's nerves were stretched thin.

TWENTY-TWO
Life at Bury St Edmunds Air Base

Jimmie and his crew had been on edge for hours as their transport plane flew over the coastline and into the heart of England. The noise and turbulence of the flight had been exhausting and the fear of what lay ahead was almost too much to bear. But as they began their descent into Bury St Edmunds Air Base, the mood in the plane shifted from fear to eager anticipation.

Jimmie peered out the window as the transport plane banked sharply to the left, revealing the green fields and rolling hills of the English countryside. In the distance, he could make out the sprawling airfield with its runways and hangars stretching as far as the eye could see.

As they came in for the landing, the crew felt the jarring impact of the transport plane's wheels hitting the tarmac and they braced themselves for the sudden stop. But to their surprise, the plane taxied smoothly to a stop and the crew quickly disembarked, eager to explore their new home.

Jimmie led the way, his heart pounding with excitement and nerves as they made their way to the control tower. The air was thick with the sound of planes taking off and landing and the smell of fuel and oil hung heavy in the air.

As they approached the tower, a young officer in uniform stepped forward to greet them. "Welcome to Bury St Edmunds," he said with a smile. "You must be the new B-17 crew we've been expecting. We've got a briefing scheduled for you in the mess hall in half an hour. In the meantime, feel free to get settled in and make yourselves at home."

The officer cleared his throat, "Also, what name do you want the ground crew to put on your assigned plane?" he asked, trying to gather Captain Galloway's attention.

Jimmie thought for a moment. "How about *Little Brenda*?" he suggested.

The officer shook his head. "Sorry, we already have a bomber named *Little Brenda*."

Jimmie thought for a moment longer, then said, "How about *Little Helen*?" The officer smiled, "That'll work. I'll give it to the ground crew to start painting *Little Helen* on her."

The crew nodded, grateful for the warm welcome, and made their way to the barracks to get settled in. As they walked, they couldn't help but feel a sense of awe and wonder at the sheer magnitude of the operation they had just become a part of.

For Jimmie and his crew, this was the start of a new chapter in their lives, one that would test their courage and their strength in ways they could never have imagined. But for now, they were content to rest and prepare for the challenges that lay ahead, eager to take on whatever the war had in store for them.

Jimmie and his crew quickly settled into life at Bury St Edmunds Air Base in England. They were stationed there as a part of the Allied war effort during World War II and he was proud to be serving his country. The air base was made up of several Quonset Huts, including the one that served as his barracks. The huts were simple but functional and Jimmie was impressed with their design.

The Quonset Huts were long and narrow with a curved roof that was made of corrugated metal. The walls were made of thin metal sheets that were connected to form a continuous curve with large windows that let in plenty of light during the day. The inside of the huts was a single long room that was filled with bunk beds for the airmen to sleep in. In one corner of the room, there was a small stove that provided heat and there was a simple bathroom with sinks, showers and a line of toilets.

Despite the modest appearance of the Quonset Huts, Jimmie was grateful for the improved living conditions compared to many of the bases he was stationed at during flight schools. The huts provided more privacy in the bathrooms than the previous barracks he had lived in and they were much more comfortable and well-insulated from the weather. The high windows allowed for plenty of natural light to come in, making the room feel less cramped and more open.

At the air base, the sleeping barracks were divided according to military rank. The officers of higher rank, like captains or pilots, had their own separate barracks, while the lower ranks, like 2nd lieutenants or co-pilots, had theirs. This segregation was maintained to ensure that men of similar standing could bond and support each other.

The air base was situated in a rural area of North East of London, surrounded by farmland and dense forests. Despite its location, it was a hub of activity during the war with planes coming and going at all hours of the day and night. However, to avoid being targeted by Nazi bombers, the air base was not lit up at night. The Quonset Huts that served as barracks for the airmen were surrounded by darkness, and the airmen had to navigate the air base using flashlights and lanterns if out at night.

In addition to the huts, there were several large hangars where the planes were kept and maintained. The hangars were positioned near the runway and were also made of metal with large sliding doors that allowed planes to be moved in and out with ease. The air base was also home to a small community of support personnel, including mechanics, cooks, and clerks. The airmen and support personnel worked together to ensure that the planes were in good working order and that the air base was running smoothly.

They spent long hours on the air base, and their hard work and dedication was essential to the war effort. Despite the constant activity, there was a sense of camaraderie among the airmen and support personnel at Bury St Edmunds Air Base. They were all there for a common cause and bonded over their shared experiences and challenges. In their free time, the airmen would gather in the recreation center or attend events put on by the entertainment division of the military. These activities helped to break up the monotony of life on the base and provided a much-needed sense of normalcy in an otherwise uncertain world.

Bury St. Edmonds Ca

Here are the names of the people in the crew picture on the previous page with their positions, written on the back side of the photo:

Taken at Drew Field
RT U #3
Front Row
STAPP - Assistant Radio
FiTE - ENqiNEER
LiVENgood - NAViqAToR

    Middle Row

1. MORSE - WAS TAil gUNNER
    Loot him because operatin
KiMMEl - BoMbARdiER
    BACK Row
SMiTU - ASSiSTANT ENgiNEER
SMiTW - RAdio OPERATOR
CliNE - ARMoRER
BERKEN FiElD - Co-pilOT

TWENTY-THREE
Surprise at Two in the Morning

The U.S. 8th Air Force, which flew daylight missions over Europe, had a death rate of 19%. For those who were lucky enough to survive being shot down, the odds of becoming a prisoner of war were even higher, at 17%. The RAF Bomber Command, who flew the more dangerous night missions, had a staggering death rate of 44.5% with only an 8% chance of becoming a POW. The reality of the situation was that the average bomber crew member was just 22 years old and facing near-impossible odds. Despite the high death toll, the rules of the game remained unchanged.

Before 1944, each crew had to complete 25 grueling combat missions in order to be eligible to return home. Unfortunately, the statistics of the time showed that each crew member only had a 1 in 4 chance of making it to their 25th mission. This meant that, on average, each crew member could only expect to survive for about 12 to 14 missions. The odds were even grimmer for certain positions. A tail gunner, for example, had an average life expectancy of only four missions - a mere two weeks of constant fear and danger. The pressure was intense and each day felt like a test of survival for these brave young men.

One of the most dangerous positions on the bomber was that of the ball turret gunner. Nestled in a small, spherical compartment beneath the aircraft, the gunner was exposed to enemy fire from below and was responsible for protecting the vulnerable underside of the bomber. But the dangers didn't end there. If the plane was hit by enemy fire and the engines were damaged, it could knock out the turret's electrical or hydraulic systems, trapping the gunner inside. If the damage also affected the landing gear, the full weight of the plane would come crashing down on the ball turret gunner and the skid, leaving nothing but scraps of metal and shattered dreams. The bravery and sacrifices of these young men will forever be remembered as a testament to the strength of the human spirit in the face of great adversity.

Jimmie and his crew at Bury St Edmunds saw their fair share of loss. In the midst of war, the rules for sending personal belongings of fallen airmen were different. If an airman was declared dead or missing in action for a long time, his personal belongings would normally be collected and sent to his family during peacetime. However, the scarcity of resources during the war made this process more challenging. When a captain or crewman failed to return from a mission, it was considered almost certain that he had lost his life.

After a week or so had passed, all the surviving airmen of his barracks would gather at the deceased airman's former bunk. They would pay their respects to the fallen hero and remember the good times they had shared. The airmen would raise a toast to their comrade using whatever alcohol they could find and go through all the items in his foot locker. Sometimes, the fallen airman would leave behind written promises to give out specific items to his fellow officers, but if there were no such promises, the items would be distributed to settle any outstanding debts from poker games.

The process of going through a fallen comrade's belongings was a solemn and bittersweet occasion. It was a time for the surviving airmen to honor the memory of their friend and to share their experiences with each other. Despite the hardships and dangers of war, these moments of camaraderie helped the men to keep their spirits up and find comfort in each other. The shared experience of loss and the bond formed by going through their fallen comrade's belongings was a crucial part of maintaining their mental health and resilience during such a trying time

Jimmie had been at Bury Saint Edmund's for almost three weeks, but due to the inclement weather, only three missions had taken off. On the second mission, Jimmie's bottom bunkmate, William Masters, and his plane, never returned. William was a tall man from outside the Dallas/Fort Worth area and was a pilot before the war broke out. He volunteered to be a fighter pilot but was too tall to fit in P-47 Thunderbolts or the British fighter planes, so he was assigned to bomber school.

The loss of William hit Jimmie particularly hard as he was the first fellow officer that Jimmie had grown close to and lost in combat. For a week, Jimmie went to the Red Cross office on base every day to check the list of new American POWs in German camps, but William and his crewmates were never listed. As the days passed, the other captains in the hut noticed Jimmie's distress and decided it was time to clean out William's foot locker. One evening, after lights out, all the captains gathered around William's locker to pay their respects to their fallen comrade. They made a quick toast and went through all of William's belongings. Since Jimmie was William's bunkmate, he was given first choice of the items. He chose William's cigarette lighter, a simple yet meaningful memento of their friendship and the sacrifice William made for their country. The rest of the items were divided among the captains based on size or any outstanding poker debts. The foot locker was then closed and the men dispersed, each lost in their own thoughts, remembering the brave man they had just honored.

As the days went on, the tension in the air base grew thicker with each passing week as more and more men didn't return. The relentless sound of engines roaring to life echoed through the air, a haunting reminder of the constant danger that loomed over the soldiers' heads. The pressure was palpable, each day bringing the possibility of not returning to the mess hall for breakfast the next morning. The thought of becoming a statistic, a mere footnote in the history of the war, weighed heavily on the minds of the airmen. The 5 a.m. breakfast was a solemn affair, with every man lost still fresh in their memories. The once lively chatter had been replaced with quiet whispers and the clinking of silverware against plates. The mission briefings were even more intense, each man carefully studying the maps, searching for any clue that could increase their chances of survival. But despite their preparations, the casualties continued to mount. Thirty percent of their brothers-in-arms were shot down in the skies, never to return. The Red Cross office was always filled with worried airmen, their eyes glued to the list of POWs, searching for any word of their fallen friends. The reality of the war was inescapable and the fear of becoming another statistic haunted them all.

After a few months of terrible missions with heavy losses, Jimmie took some rations back to his captain's barracks to just eat and lay down. But little did he know, the real entertainment for the night was about to begin.

The sudden and forceful opening of the barracks' big metal door was like a thunderbolt in the still of the night, jolting Jimmie and all his fellow airmen from their slumber. As he rubbed the sleep from his eyes and peered out of his bunk, Jimmie's heart raced with fear. Was it an air raid? Where was the alarm siren? But before he could fully comprehend what was happening, the figure of William Masters appeared in the doorway, looking more disheveled and exhausted than Jimmie had ever seen him.

"Boys, you won't believe what happened to me," William yelled, his voice ringing with excitement and urgency. "I got shot down over Northern France and had to hitchhike my ass all the way back here!" Jimmie and the others gaped in disbelief as William strode into the barracks, recounting his harrowing tale of survival and determination. They listened in awe as he described his treacherous journey, dodging enemy patrols and relying on the kindness of strangers to make it back to England.

And then, with a sudden change in tone, William's expression darkened and he announced, "Another thing, I want ALL of MY shit back!" He cast his gaze around the barracks, fixing each of his comrades with a stern look. "I know my personal belongings would have been gobbled up among you fuckers, but I want them all back, now!"

The airmen shifted nervously, realizing that William meant business. They scurried to gather up his possessions, returning them to him with sheepish apologies.

But as they did so, William couldn't help but let out a chuckle real loud. "Relax, boys," he said with a smirk. "I'm just messing with you. I've been gone for months, I'm sure you all needed something to remember me by."

The airmen let out a collective sigh of relief and a few even chuckled along with William. "But seriously, though," he continued, "I'm starving. Any chance one of you guys could rustle up some grub?"

As the night progressed and the homemade hooch started flowing, the mood in the barracks became increasingly light and jovial. William's infectious laughter and devil-may-care attitude had the men in stitches and they eagerly listened as he shared stories of his adventures with the French Resistance. William Masters, after his B-17 was shot down, found himself in a foreign land and separated from his crew, surrounded by the enemy. Fear gripped him as he fled through the dark, winding streets with the sound of Nazi boots pounding the pavement behind him.

The French Underground Resistance had taken him in, risking their own lives to protect him, but it came at a cost. He witnessed the brutal and senseless deaths of many of the Resistance Fighters who aided him in his escape. As William made his way through the treacherous countryside, he saw the devastation wrought by the occupying forces. The smell of death hung heavy in the air and he knew that at any moment, he too could fall victim to the wrath of the Nazis. But he pressed on, driven by the desire to return home to Bury St Edmunds and his comrades in arms. Despite the danger, the Resistance smuggled William across the border and back to England.

As he landed on English soil, he fell to his knees, overcome with emotion and gratitude for those who had risked everything to save him. He looked back across the channel, thinking of the lives lost and the bravery of those who had fought against the Nazi oppressors.

William would never forget the sacrifices made by the Resistance Fighters, who gave everything to protect their fellow man from the horrors of war, but what really got everyone's attention were William's tales of the beautiful French women he had encountered during his time with the Underground Resistance. The men roared with laughter as he regaled them with stories of romantic escapades and close calls, each one more outrageous than the last.

Jimmie couldn't help but smile, feeling grateful for the bond they shared and the memories they created, despite the danger and uncertainty they faced each day.

As the night wore on, the group became more somber as William recounted the harsh realities of war. They mourned the loss of their comrade, Jeb, the tail gunner who had been shot by a Nazi fighter plane before the rest of the crew had bailed out.

They raised a glass in his memory and in that moment, Jimmie was filled with a sense of camaraderie and brotherhood that transcended all else. Despite the horrors they faced each day, they were bonded together by their shared experiences and their unwavering determination to see the mission through.

The night progressed, the laughter and jovial mood in the barracks continued, providing a much-needed reprieve from the stress and danger of war. The airmen traded stories, reliving their experiences and reveling in the bond they shared. It was a reminder of the importance of laughter and camaraderie in even the most trying of circumstances. However, the reality of their situation soon set in as the time for their pilot's meeting approached.

Despite their best efforts to forget the dangers of war, the men knew that the next day could bring them back to the front lines of the air war. As the hour approached 5 a.m., the airmen reluctantly put away their drinks and prepared for the meeting.

The mission for the next day was canceled due to the thick fog that blanketed the airbase. The men breathed a collective sigh of relief, knowing that attempting to fly drunk would have been a suicide mission even before they faced the enemy Nazis fighter planes in the skies.

The following pictures show life at the base.

Jimmie loved bikes and motorcycles

TWENTY-FOUR

Two Colt 45 Pistols in the Small of the Back: OPERATION GOMORRAH

The First Mission Targeting Civilians in Hamburg Germany

Jimmie sat down at the mess hall table telling his fellow bomber pilots, "Something's up boys! They're serving us some real meat tonight!" After about six months of bomber missions, it didn't take long to figure things out. Not all missions are created equal; after a while, bomber crews knew which missions were hell while others were missions *straight TO hell.*

All the crews knew that the night before the straight TO hell missions, the meals tended to be a little better with real meat, even if it was horse meat. Tonight, it was one of Jimmie's favorites, SPAM. Many times, they would even give them a Hershey candy bar for dessert, something very special in wartime. That night all the crews got some real SPAM meat in the stew AND a Hershey Bar for dessert. Something was definitely up!

After a restless sleep, the knock on the pilot's and co-pilot's barracks came around 4 a.m. The meeting at the briefing room started around 5 a.m. after breakfast, and no one was late for this one! General Meade was at this meeting…

something big was going on. The maps were rolled down the front meeting board with the map of the city of Hamburg, Germany in front of them. This week of July 1943, the U.S. Army Air Forces of the 8th Air Force launched a daylight raid on the city of Hamburg in Northern Germany. The mission that day was part of a larger campaign known as Operation Gomorrah, which aimed to disrupt German operations and economic targets in and around Germany.

The briefing room was a buzz with whispers! This was the first military-sanctioned targeting of civilians and civilian assets since Sherman's march to Atlanta during the Civil War which created the term "Total Warfare."

The room was filled with an intense silence as Captain Terry Fitzgerald finally stood up and spoke out against the mission because there was NOT a military complex target at those coordinates.

Major General Ira C. Eaker's expression darkened, his eyes narrowing as he faced off against the dissenting Captain. The tension in the room was thick as everyone held their breath, waiting to see how the situation would unfold.

"Captain Fitzgerald, this isn't a request," General Eaker growled, his voice filled with anger and authority. "This is an order and you will follow it, God Damn It! The Germans have been doing this for almost two fucking years and now it's our turn to return the favor!"

What General Eaker was referring to was the very first mission in World War II to bomb civilian targets on May 14, 1940, when German planes bombed Rotterdam, the second-largest city in the Netherlands. This bombing raid caused widespread destruction and civilian casualties, prompting the Dutch government to surrender to the German invaders the following day. The bombing of Rotterdam is widely regarded as a turning point in the war, as it demonstrated the willingness of the Germans to target civilians and non-military infrastructure and helped to set the stage for the broader strategic bombing campaign that would come to define the war in Europe.

Captain Fitzgerald stood his ground, his jaw set in determination. "I cannot in good conscience follow an order to indiscriminately bomb civilian populations. It goes against everything we stand for in America!"

General Eaker slammed his fist on the table, causing a loud echo throughout the room. "You will follow orders, or you will face the consequences! You think you can just ignore your duty and refuse to do what needs to be done to win this war?"

Captain Fitzgerald met General Eaker's gaze with a steely resolve. "I will not be a party to war crimes, Sir. I would rather face the consequences of my actions than live with the guilt of what I've done."

The room was deathly silent as General Eaker and Captain Fitzgerald locked eyes, the tension between them reaching a boiling point. Then, without warning, two military police officers stepped forward, their hands resting on the holsters of their Colt 45 pistols, pulling them out while pressing them into Fitzgerald's back.

"Captain Fitzgerald, you are under arrest," one of the MPs declared, his voice cold and emotionless.

As the MPs escorted Captain Fitzgerald out of the room, the other pilots looked on in stunned silence, shocked by the turn of events. Some of them were filled with admiration for Captain Fitzgerald's bravery and integrity, while others were filled with fear for what lay ahead for them on the mission to Hamburg. Regardless of their thoughts and feelings, they all knew one thing for certain: their lives would never be the same again.

Jimmie and the rest of the bomber pilots sat in stunned silence as they watched their comrade, Captain Terry Fitzgerald, being escorted out of the room by the MPs with two Colt 45 pistols at the small of his back. The atmosphere in the briefing room was tense as the reality of their mission hit them all. It targeted a civilian population, marking a shift in the war strategy towards a more aggressive, scorched earth policy.

After the briefing, the crews were quiet and somber as they made their way to their planes. The usual pre-flight banter was absent, replaced by a heavy weight of uncertainty and fear. Jimmie, like many of his fellow pilots, was torn between his duty to follow orders and his morality. He admired Terry's bravery, standing up for what he believed in, but at the same time, he was also afraid of the consequences of defying the military's authority. The mission was a grueling one with intense flak and fighter attacks from the Luftwaffe. Despite their best efforts to avoid hitting civilian targets on previous missions, many of the city's residents were caught in the crossfire. The new reality was images of the burning cities and its civilians that would stay with Jimmie and his crew. Many were haunted with nightmares into old age!

As Jimmie laid his head down this particular night, he wondered to himself, after performing a mission that they all knew had killed innocent women and children, if he had indeed lost his eternal soul. He pictured himself meeting his "Maker" on judgment day and the only answer to that day's atrocities would be, "I was just doing my job!" Jimmie went to sleep in the darkness thinking his truthful answer would NOT save his soul. Even a nightmare would have been welcomed, but there was nothing but blackness again.

Days turned into weeks and weeks turned into months and the war raged on. Army intelligence had estimated around 37,000 civilians were killed during Operation Gomorrah. It was only towards the end of the war that they heard the pope of the Catholic Church had intervened to secure Captain Fitzgerald's release from Leavenworth Military Prison. The news was a welcome relief to Jimmie and his fellow bomber crews, a glimmer of hope in the midst of all the destruction and chaos. Operation Gomorrah and the events that followed would leave a lasting impact on Jimmie and all the 8th Air Force. It was a turning point in the war and a reminder of the atrocities that can be committed in the name of victory. The memory of Captain Terry Fitzgerald and his bravery would always serve as a testament to the importance of standing up for one's beliefs, no matter the consequences. Captain Fitzgerald was a brave and honorable man!

Replica of a pilots' briefing room at 8th Air Force Museum

Jimmie going over their mission plans

The tone of this article sounds like the boys were just on a vacation "at rest center… with all the touches of home":

Stone Gap and Appalachia, Virginia, Thursday, March 29, 1945

Capt. Jimmy Galloway At Rest Center After 25 Missions in Air

(Special to The Post)

An Air Service Command Station, Somewhere in England. — Capt. Jimmie G. Galloway, husband of Jean Compton Galloway, of 433 Wood avenue, Big Stone Gap, Va., recently enjoyed a "recess" from aerial warfare at an Air Service Command Rest Center—an English Seaside Resort Hotel where America's airmen who provide aerial cover for the advancing Allied Armies in Germany may relax between missions.

Here, Capt. Galloway lounged in the restful atmosphere of this vacationland hostelry and was provided with every type of recreational facility. American atmosphere, and all the touches of home" are provided by the American Red Cross, copartners with the Air Service Command in the operation of the Rest Center.

After 7 days he went back to his combat station ready to play his part once again in the air battle supporting the Allied march across Germany.

Capt. Galloway has completed 25 missions over Nazi-dominated Europe. Before entering the Army he was employed as a dairyman by the Pet Dairy Products Company.

Pre-Seventh War Loan Drive To Be Launched

Richmond. — James S. Easley, executive manager, Virginia war finance committee, announced an intensive pre-seventh war loan drive during April in every industrial and business establishment in the state to increase participation of employees in payroll savings for the purchase of war bonds.

The announcement followed official notification from the treasury department that the seventh war loan campaign will be conducted from May 14 through June 30.

PUTS A SONG IN YOUR HEART

Thursday, March 29, 1945

Capt. Jimmy Galloway At Rest Center After 25 Missions in Air

(Special to The Post)

An Air Service Command Station, Somewhere in England. — Capt. Jimmie G. Galloway, husband of Jean Compton Galloway, of 433 Wood avenue, Big Stone Gap, Va., recently enjoyed a "recess" from aerial warfare at an Air Service Command Rest Center—an English Seaside Resort Hotel where America's airmen who provide aerial cover for the advancing Allied Armies in Germany may relax between missions.

Here, Capt. Galloway lounged in the restful atmosphere of this vacationland hostelry and was provided with every type of recreational facility. American atmosphere, and all the touches of home" are provided by the American Red Cross, copartners with the Air Service Command in the operation of the Rest Center

After 7 days he went back to his combat station ready to play his part once again in the air battle supporting the Allied march across Germany.

Capt. Galloway has completed 25 missions over Nazi-dominated Europe. Before entering the Army he was employed as a dairyman by the Pet Dairy Products Company.

Pre-Seventh War Loan Drive To Be Launched

Richmond. — James S. Easley, executive manager, Virginia war finance committee, announced an intensive pre-seventh war loan drive during April in every industrial and business establishment in the state to increase participation of employees in payroll savings for the purchase of war bonds.

The announcement followed official notification from the treasury department that the seventh

TWENTY-FIVE

Black Thursday, October 14, 1943, and a Chest Full of Medals

The pre-flight captains' meeting was crowded with late arriving captains having to stand along the walls. Normally, bomber crews were assigned missions on a rotational basis between bomber groups, but this mission was different. The generals had decided to make a big dent in the German military complex by bombing the ball-bearing plants located around Schweinfurt, Bavaria with the full force of all the bomber groups of the 8th Air Force!

What the Military Brass didn't know was that by the summer of 1943, bombing raids in the area by the British Royal Air Force had led the Germans to establish a new early warning radar line of towers along with increasing the number of fighter aircraft and anti-aircraft artillery flak towers around the ball bearing plants. Lying in wait were 300 Luftwaffe fighters with some of the most experienced pilots the Germans had to offer.

At 6 a.m. sharp, 291 B-17 Flying Fortress high-altitude heavy bombers with their 10-man crews started taking off from Bury St Edmunds air base. It took almost an hour to get everyone airborne and up to 30,000 feet. Jimmie was squadron leader of the 332 Squadron of the 94 Bomber Group and had all his planes in formation. Looking out to the side, he saw the bulk of the 291 B-17s of the whole 8th Air Force in flight along with the 100 or so P-47 Thunderbolt fighter planes flying escort to the German border. The P-47 Thunderbolts could only escort the bombers to the German border before they ran out of fuel, leaving the bombers vulnerable to attack from the waiting German fighters. This was the main reason so many bombers never came home.

As the bomber crew watched the P-47s make their turn back toward base, a feeling of unease and vulnerability washed over them. The absence of the protective fighter escorts meant that they were now on their own against the deadly Nazis Luftwaffe. The men exchanged nervous glances, knowing full well the dangers they faced.

Isaac, the tail gunner, summed up the feeling perfectly when he said, "It's like the first day you left your momma to go to school, you know you're on your own to survive the day!"

As the Little Helen crew approached the target, the sky was filled with the deafening sounds of bullets and flak hitting the fuselage and the sharp crack of gunfire from Little Helen's machine gunners.

Jimmie and his crew were on edge, their nerves jangling with anticipation. Suddenly, a burst of anti-aircraft fire exploded just below their plane, shaking them violently. The Luftwaffe fighters swooped down on them with ferocity, their machine guns blazing. Jimmie's bomber was hit multiple times and the plane shuddered under the impact.

The Germans were relentless in their attacks and it seemed like there was no escape from the carnage. But Jimmie refused to give up. He remained focused on his mission and his duty to his crew, despite the chaos and danger. As the attack progressed, it quickly became clear that the German defenses were more formidable than anticipated. The sky was alive with the sound of antiaircraft fire and the Luftwaffe fighters were relentless in their pursuit of the American bombers.

As the B-17s flew over their targets, the ground defenses responded with an intense barrage of fire, and the sky was soon filled with smoke and explosions. Despite the bravery and determination of the American airmen, the losses were staggering. Of the 291 B-17s that made up the attacking force, 80 were lost to enemy fire and another 17 were so heavily damaged that they would never fly again. Most of the remaining planes suffered varying degrees of damage, but were repairable. These losses amounted to a devastating 25 percent of the attacking force.

The Luftwaffe, meanwhile, would only lose 38 fighters, but many of those downed pilots were able to bail out and return to duty. For the Americans, the cost was much higher. A full 20 percent of their aircrew - a total of 650 men - were either killed or taken prisoner, while many others were wounded. The battle had been a brutal and costly one, and the full impact of the losses would be felt for years to come.

Jimmie's plane was hit multiple times, but he was able to keep it in the air and eventually make it to its bombing target, though very damaged.

As the Nazis Luftwaffe took their kills, they suddenly pulled away and all hell broke loose with the anti-aircraft artillery. The plane flying right next to Little Helen was hit dead center by a flak burst. The explosion was so massive that it shook Jimmie's plane violently and sent debris flying everywhere. It was a direct hit and the other bomber was instantly torn apart by the explosion, sending flames and smoke billowing into the sky.

Jimmie and his crew watched in horror as the wreckage of the other bomber rained down to the ground. They could hear the screams over the radio of the crew as they plummeted toward the ground. It was a brutal reminder of the dangers they all faced every day and Jimmie wasn't the only one that couldn't help but wonder if the crew of the Little Helen would eventually suffer the same fate.

The crew members, meanwhile, were filled with fear and uncertainty. The sounds of the flak hitting Little Helen, the explosions of the other bombers, and the fear of death weighed heavily on their minds.

"Oh my God, we're never going to make it out of here alive," cried navigator Saul.

"Keep it together, Saul," replied Bob. "We've got to stay focused and get this bird back home."

"I don't want to die up here," said bomber, Marty, with tears streaming down his face and saying a Jewish prayer over the intercom.

"I acknowledge before You, Adonai, my God, and God of my ancestors, that my healing and my death are in Your hands. May it be Your will to grant me a complete healing. If it be Your will that I am to die of this illness, let my death be atonement for all the wrongs that I have done in my life."

"Amen, none of us want to die, Marty," replied Jimmie. "We're too far into this, so we've no choice now but to get this damn job done and we're going to see it through one way or another!"

Thirty minutes later, Jimmie yelled over the intercom, "Bombs away boys, let's get the hell out of here and turn Little Helen hard starboard!"

The artillery leaving the bomb target wasn't any lighter but the number of Nazi fighters seemed a little less leaving the target area.

After about 45 minutes of flak going off all around the plane, there was a sudden quietness in the air.

Jimmie came over the intercom, "Roll call boys, let me know how are you doing!"

"Gunner one, all good, Sir."

"Radio operator here, no injuries."

"Navigator reporting in, just some bruises Sir."

As the roll call continued, Jimmie breathed a sigh of relief that all of his men were okay.

He then went to inspect the damage to the plane. He noticed that one of the engines was smoking and the left wing was damaged and shot to shit.

He quickly informed the crew of the situation and instructed them to prepare for an emergency landing.

"Listen up boys, we got some damage here. Engine number 3 is smoking, the left wing is hit and the hydraulics aren't working worth a damn. I'm going to try and make it back to base, but I need you all to be ready for anything." "Everyone get your parachutes on and be ready to bail out! And Tex, work on getting Smitty out of that damn belly gun turret!"

"Roger that, Captain!" replied the radio operator.

The crew continued to keep a watchful eye on the damage, hoping that the plane would make it back to base safely. Jimmie skillfully navigated Little Helen through the skies, trying to keep the plane level and steady.

"Captain, this is the navigator, I've got us a new heading that will take us around some of the heavier flak if we're good on fuel."

"Copy that, we're good on fuel, that's the only thing we're good on though," replied Jimmie. "Let's get home, boys."

The journey back was fraught with tension and exhaustion, but the sight of the airbase on the horizon provided a glimmer of hope.

"Almost there, boys. Brace yourselves, this might be a little rough!" Jimmie's words were both a warning and a promise. The landing was indeed rough, the screech of metal against concrete and the thud of impact echoing throughout the plane. But they had made it back, and the crew of Little Helen breathed a collective sigh of relief as they emerged from the battered aircraft. Despite the damage and injuries, they had accomplished their mission and returned home to the cheers of their fellow comrades of the ground crew, their bravery and determination in the face of death and danger an inspiration to all who witnessed it.

Upon landing, the landing crew was shocked by the extent of the damage to Jimmie's plane, Little Helen. The ground and repair crews later reported that the plane had over 300 bullet and flak holes, a testament to the dangerous conditions that Jimmie and his crew had faced on their mission. A few days after Little Helen had been patched up, Tex made the comment, "Gosh I haven't seen so many patches since I was back home sleeping under one of my patch quilts!"

That night was difficult, to say the least. Jimmie had to sleep alone in his barracks. None of the other pilots from his barracks had made it back from "Black Thursday"… none from his 332nd Squadron. That night Jimmie realized he was not going to live through this. Surprisingly, he was at peace with this realization.

The next morning, Colonel Jessee came by to check on Jimmie. He couldn't imagine having to sleep in a whole barracks by himself. He had news that Jimmie was being promoted from his 332nd Squadron Leader to the larger 94 Bomber Group Leader, combining survivors of three other squadrons into the 332nd. New B-17 bomber crews were arriving state side the following week fresh out of flight school to fill out the other squadrons.

Jimmie looked at Colonel Jessee, "Hard to take a promotion when all you did was survive."

Colonel Jessee replied, "In any case, you deserve it!"

Despite the difficulty and cost of the raid, Jimmie and his crew's bravery and determination earned them a chest full of medals, a proud recognition of their heroic efforts during the raid on the ball bearing plants in Schweinfurt, Bavaria.

The raid on the ball bearing plants in Schweinfurt, Bavaria, was a turning point in the air war over Europe. Despite their best efforts, the American bomber crews faced overwhelming opposition from the German air defenses. The loss of 60 bombers, with many others heavily damaged, was a devastating blow to the 8th Air Force. The high loss of aircrew, with 650 killed or taken prisoner, was a sobering reminder of the dangers of flying over enemy territory without adequate escort. The mission's outcome was a wake-up call for military leaders, who now realized that bomber raids into Germany could no longer be conducted without fighter escorts. The P-47 Thunderbolts that flew escort during the raid were limited by their range and could not provide the needed protection against huge losses. Deep bombing missions into Germany were halted until the arrival of the P-51 Mustang long-range fighters in January 1943.

It was rumored that General Meade told his assistant, "If the American public knew what had happened today, they would hang me!" A lot of the 8th Air Force was killed and sent home injured from this mission.

General Meade gathered all the pilots together at the air traffic control tower for a big announcement the next morning, "The crew of Little Helen and the other surviving planes are going to be honored and receive medals of bravery from the 'Fat Man' himself, Winston Churchill, this upcoming week."

Despite their initial feelings of shame for surviving when so many of their comrades had died, the personal recognition from such a revered leader as Churchill made the award feel even more significant. The crews were proud to have served their country in such a dangerous and demanding role and the medal was a symbol of their dedication and sacrifice. As they looked into Churchill's eyes and shook his hand, taking in the scent of his cigar, they felt a sense of validation for all the hardships they had endured during their time as bomber pilots and crew.

After all the medals had been pinned on the men, General Arnold, Commanding General Army Air Forces, stepped in front of the men. The general, who had come all the way from London, cleared his throat and began to speak.

"Gentlemen," he said, addressing the crews, "you have all performed above and beyond the call of duty. Your bravery and selflessness have inspired us all and I am honored to be able to present you with this Distinguished Flying Cross medal. I hope it serves as a reminder of the sacrifices you have made for our country and the world. Keep up the good work."

The crew members stood at attention, their chests swelling with pride and guilt as General Arnold continued his speech remembering their fallen airmen. Still, they were filled with a sense of purpose and were ready to continue their mission, despite the dangers that lay ahead

His voice got very solemn and he said he wanted to leave us with these thoughts: "He lived to bear his country's arms. He died to save its honor. He was a soldier...and he knew a soldier's duty. His sacrifice will help to keep aglow the flaming torch that lights our lives...that millions yet unborn may know the priceless job of liberty, and we who pay him homage, and revere his memory, in pride, rededicate ourselves to a complete fulfillment of the task for which he so gallantly has placed his life upon the altar of man's freedom."

Example of what flak can do to a plane. This plane still landed.
These birds were tough!

TWENTY-SIX
Magic Planes WITHOUT Propellers:
Messerschmitt ME 262s

Jimmie and his fellow bomber captains had become accustomed to the light targets and minimal resistance they faced on their recent missions. After the devastating loss on the Black Thursday mission, they were grateful for the reprieve. But every morning, Major Phillips would show up to their pre-flight meetings with his intelligence reports reminding them of the ever-present danger they faced from new planes, radar, and new Luftwaffe fighter tactics.

As they sat in the pilots' briefing room, eating some stale mess hall biscuits, and listening to Major Phillips' briefing, they would roll their eyes and smirk when he mentioned the new German fighter: the Messerschmitt ME 262. It was a plane without propellers, powered by a rocket engine. To the bomber pilots, it sounded like fantasy, nothing more than war talk designed to scare them into paying attention during their boring pre-flight meetings.

"Gentlemen, the enemy is developing a new weapon that could change the course of the war. The Messerschmitt ME 262 is a rocket-propelled fighter capable of reaching speeds over 500 miles per hour, speeds never seen before," Major Phillips would say, his glasses slipping down his nose as he leaned over the table to emphasize his point.

But the bomber crew would just laugh, yelling out, "500 miles per hour… my ass!" "Hell, Spitfire Fighters could only go up to 375 mph!" trying to brush off the fear that threatened to grip them. They knew that war was a serious matter, but this "magic" plane seemed too far-fetched to be real.

"Come on, Major," one of the captains would say with a smirk. "A plane without propellers? How could it possibly fly? That's crazy talk!"

The others would chime in, making jokes and teasing each other. They were all seasoned pilots, having flown countless missions, and the idea of a plane without propellers seemed ridiculous. But deep down, they couldn't help but feel a twinge of fear at the thought of facing such a weapon. Little did they know, the Messerschmitt ME 262 was more than just war talk. It was a real and deadly weapon and they would soon have to face it head-on.

This was THE mission! As Jimmie and his crew of Little Helen were flying over Schweinfurt Germany, they suddenly noticed something different in the skies. The Messerschmitt ME 262, sleek and silver with its revolutionary design, had arrived on the scene. These planes were unlike anything they had seen before; with no propellers in sight, they seemed to be defying the laws of physics.

Jimmie and the other bomber pilots watched in awe as the ME 262s zoomed past their planes, their powerful jet engines leaving behind a trail of smoke. The feeling of dread in Jimmie's stomach grew with each passing moment as he realized that their missions would never be the same again. The air war had changed and they were no longer flying against equal equipment.

It was chaos and mayhem with the sound of the high-pitched engines piercing the sky, and the sight of the sleek, aerodynamic fighters zipping past their bomber group. The Messerschmitt ME 262s were everywhere, leaving a trail of destruction in their wake. Every pilot in the group was now fully aware of just how real the war talk was. The reality of their existence was now hitting hard.

Jimmie's heart was pounding as he tried to maneuver his bomber and avoid the relentless barrage of gunfire from the enemy fighters. Tex was frantically trying to take out the enemy planes, but the speed advantage the Germans had was too great. The B-17s were simply no match for these machines. In what felt like an eternity, but was only a matter of minutes, Jimmie saw several bombers in his group get shot down one after the other. The explosions and crashes were like a scene out of a nightmare. This was no longer war talk; it was a deadly game of survival.

But, despite their bravery, the Nazis 262s were relentless. They swooped in, their machine guns blazing, raining down a hail of bullets onto the bombers. The sound of metal hitting metal echoed through the cabin causing the men to duck for cover.

"You don't scare me, you Sons of Bitches!" Tex yelled, his voice filled with determination as he reached for both of his trusty Colt 45s and began firing both pistols out the side window since the German jet fighters were too fast to even swing his Browning 50 caliber machine gun to fire at them. Instead, he turned to unloading his Colt 45s out the side gunner's window and then grabbing another clip of ammunition from his shoulder holster!

Jimmie, who was at the controls of the bomber, was struggling to keep the plane steady. The enemy fire had shaken him to his core and his hands were trembling uncontrollably.

"They sure do scare the shit out of me!" he shouted over the intercom, his voice betraying his fear. "I can't believe a plane can fly that fast!" "How in the hell can they do that, Bob!?"

Bob, in an unsteady voice, replied back, "I don't know but we're in some fucking trouble, Capt.!"

Despite their efforts, the ME 262s were too fast and too agile. They could weave in and out of the bomber's defensive fire, their machine guns blazing away. The airmen could hear the telltale whiz of bullets as they flew past their heads.

"We need to get the hell out of here!" shouted Jimmie, his voice tinged with desperation. "I'm going to try to make a run for the cloud bank!"

"You do that, Jimmie!" yelled Tex, still firing away with his Colt 45. "I'll keep these fuckers busy!"

With a Herculean effort, Jimmie pushed the bomber to its limits trying to reach a large cloud bank below them, pushing Little Helen into a steep dive. The enemy fighter planes followed, their machine gun fire never letting up. But just when it seemed like all was lost, the plane made it to the thick cloud bank at around 15,000 feet, enveloping the bomber and providing it with a chance to escape. Isaac, the tail gunner, yelled on the intercom, "The Nazis are pulling back, refusing to follow in the thick clouds!"

"We did it!" Jimmie shouted over the intercom; relief evident in his voice, "We're out of here!"

Then Jimmie yelled over the intercom, "Did anyone see how many other bombers had made it to the cloud bank safely?"

Isaac responded, "I couldn't see much through the clouds, but I think a couple of them made it in. Looks like at least we won't be alone up here."

Tex, who had just holstered his weapons, added, "Good thing we made it to the clouds, otherwise we'd be shit out of luck fucking with those Nazi jet fighters."

"Yeah," Jimmie agreed, "And we'd better stay in the cloud bank as long as we can until we hit the channel, just in case they decide to come after us. Let's keep a watchful eye out, everyone." The crew of the Little Helen knew Nazis fighters would hesitate to venture towards the channel where American P-47s and British Spitfire fighters would be waiting to escort them back to base.

The crew sat in silence for a few moments, taking deep breaths and calming their nerves. They knew they weren't out of danger yet, but the cloud bank had given them a reprieve from the enemy's fire and allowed them to regroup. They checked on each other and made sure everyone was okay.

Jimmie spoke again, "Okay, let's see if we can make our way back to base. Everyone, keep your eyes peeled and let's stay sharp."

The crew of Jimmie's plane returned to base with a very damaged Little Helen and a heavy heart. They had lost many of their comrades in arms that day and the reality of the war had set in. The "magic" plane without propellers was no longer a joke, but a deadly threat that they would have to face again and again.

Jimmie finally brought Little Helen to a stop, looked over to Bob, his co-pilot, and tried to lighten the mood by saying, "Well, at least we won't have to dodge those flying brooms anymore!"

Bob gave a weak smile and replied, "Yeah, but I heard Hitler is developing a flying unicorn next, so brace yourself." They both chuckled, grateful for the moment of levity in the midst of the grim reality of war.

That night in the captains' barracks, Jimmie was deep in thought about the day's mission and experienced his very first notion of the Allies actually losing this war!

He whispered to himself, "Damn, those German fighter planes were fast!"

Expecting some nightmares of jet fighters, the continued "blackness" of sleep was a welcomed event that night.

Luckily for Jimmie, the crew of the Little Helen, the 8th Air Force, and all the Allies, Hitler and Germany were not able to mass produce the Messerschmitt ME 262. Resources and factory production had been dwindling from the bombardment of the bombing campaigns of the Allies, so Hitler's Magic Plane was too few and too late.

Messerschmitt Me 262 Nazi Jet Fighter

TWENTY-SEVEN
The Americans are Coming!

"Get the damn landing gear down!" yelled Bob over the intercom. While Jimmie and Bob were struggling to hold the yoke back, both men's arms were shaking.

"We're working on it!" Isaac yelled back.

"What about getting Smitty out of the damn ball turret, he'll get crushed if we belly land without the landing gear!" Tex yelled.

Not only were the main hydraulics shot out that operated the landing gear, the lack of hydraulic pressure had locked up the belly ball turret gun with Smitty in it. It wouldn't swivel around to allow the hatch to open to exit the turret into the main fuselage.

The fuselage of Little Helen was cramped and filled with a maze of wires and piping that snaked their way through. The floor was now littered with spent ammunition casings, tools, and bits of shrapnel that flew around the aircraft during the intense barrage of enemy fire. The heat was unbearable and sweat poured down the crew's faces, mingling with the soot and grime. The air was thick with acrid smoke which made it nearly impossible to see anything beyond the flickering red glow of the instruments. The pungent smell of burning oil and metal permeated the air along with the metallic tang of fear. Despite the chaos, the crew worked with fierce determination, sweat pouring from their brows as they desperately tried to repair the damage and save their own lives.

Seven hours earlier, the crew had been complaining about how damn cold it was at 33,000 feet. The crew of the B-17 Flying Fortress knew all too well the biting cold that awaited them at high altitudes. In preparation, they donned layers upon layers of clothing, making sure to bundle up from head to toe. First, came the standard-issue olive drab flight suit followed by thick woolen socks and boots. Over that, they put on a thick electric flying suit complete with plug-ins that would keep them warm and toasty. The flying suit was like a second skin, hugging their bodies tightly to retain body heat. On top of all that, they wore a thick wool-lined leather jacket, gloves, and a fur-lined helmet to protect against the freezing winds that could easily numb the skin and impair one's judgment.

Despite the warm clothing, there was always the risk of frostbite and hypothermia and the crew knew they had to be vigilant to stay warm and healthy. So, they huddled close together, sharing body heat, and kept moving as much as possible to keep the blood flowing. It was a constant battle against the elements. You seemed to be either burning up or freezing to death!

The crew of Little Helen was now sweltering in that same cramped fuselage. Jimmie and James had leveled the plane out at about 10,000 feet after an anti-aircraft artillery round exploded right below them causing the plane to nose dive and the temperature to rise by 50 degrees or more with the decrease in altitude alone.

The air was thick with smoke and the smell of burning wires and metal and the heat was unbearable. The crew was drenched in sweat and shedding their heavy leather jackets and liners in an attempt to stay cool. The electric flying suits, once a source of warmth in the freezing cold, were now adding to the oppressive heat.

"I don't know if we're going to make it back this time, Captain!" Bob said over the intercom.

The sound of metal creaking and groaning under the strain of the wind was deafening as they frantically cranked the landing gear by hand, sweat pouring down their faces. With every rotation of the crank of the manual jack of the landing gear, their hearts beat faster and their breaths came quicker with eyes flicking back and forth between the landing gear crank and the earth below the plane. With the landing gear crank finally coming to a stop, the crew held their breath as they anxiously peered down through the fuselage, searching for any sign of the gear being in place. But alas, the gauge that indicates whether the landing gear was locked in place was broken, leaving the crew in a state of uncertainty. They had no idea if they were out of danger yet or if their worst fears were still to come.

The crew sat in fear as Smitty remained trapped in the belly ball turret with his fate uncertain. No one wanted to say a word about what everyone knew, afraid they would jinx him! There was no way to free him, no way to ease his fear or give him comfort. All they could do was hope and pray that the landing gear was indeed down and locked and that the plane would make it safely to the ground.

The possibility of a catastrophic crash was always looming with every mission, but the thought of Smitty being crushed inside the belly ball turret if the landing gear failed was most terrifying. The crew's hearts were heavy with worry and each man was lost in his own thoughts, hoping and praying that somehow, by some miracle, they would all make it out alive and Smitty wouldn't be crushed to death.

Nathan, the navigator, broke the silence over the intercom, "Hey boys, if we hold the plane together a little longer, we'll hit the English Coast in thirty minutes and another fifteen minutes or so until Bury St. Edmunds."

Jimmie thought to himself, *that had to be the longest and shortest 45 minutes in Smitty's life*!

Cline, the radio operator, chimed in, "I got more bad news, Captain. Bury St Edmunds just radioed and said the air base is fogged in and they have diverted us to the Royal Air Force Base at Mildenhall." "Smitty, you'll have to wait a little longer!"

Nathan replied back, "Here are the new coordinates, Captain. It's only fifteen minutes further away and we look good on fuel on my gauges."

Smitty let out a relieved sigh, "I don't mind an extra 15 minutes before finding out about that damn landing gear!"

As Little Helen approached Mildenhall with two of its four engines smoking something fierce, Jimmie started to nose her down with everyone praying about the landing gear.

Closer, closer, then the screech of the tires hitting the tarmac!

"Thank God! the landing gear held up!" Jimmie exclaimed.

Smitty, "Great job fellas! Great job! I thought I was going to be a flat pancake there for a while! I owe all of you a drink tonight! Thought I was going to buy the farm this time!"

After shutting down the engines and opening the hatch, they were greeted by a group of British ground crew who helped them secure the plane and unload their equipment. Jimmie and his crew exchanged pleasantries with the Brits, but they couldn't help feeling a little out of place in this English airbase with all the pomp and circumstance of the Brits.

"Welcome to Britain, boys!" one of the ground crew shouted as he helped them off the plane. "You'll find a hot meal and a warm bed waiting for you at the barracks."

As they walked through the British airfield, they noticed the different types of planes parked nearby. There were Spitfires, Hurricanes, and other planes that they had never seen before. The sound of unfamiliar accents filled the air, making Jimmie and his crew feel like they were in a different world instead of another airbase in England.

As they made their way to the base operations building, they were introduced to the British commanding officer. He welcomed and thanked them for their service, but Jimmie couldn't help feeling a little uneasy. He was used to taking orders from his American superiors and the thought of taking orders from a foreign officer was a bit unsettling and just odd.

"Sir, if you don't mind, can you point us to the mess hall? It's been 14 hours since we had breakfast. We sure could use some grub." Jimmie asked.

The British officer complied, "The dining hall is the last building past the barracks, go help yourselves, by all means!"

The crew of the Little Helen had NO IDEA that even in wartime, dinner was a formal affair for the British. Back at the American air base, when crews landed, they would often grab meals at the mess hall wearing their flight suits and side arms straight off the plane; it was no big deal to eat first and then go shower for the night.

Brits did the exact opposite! British bomber crews would immediately shower and change into formal dress uniforms before stepping foot into a dining hall while American crews might go weeks or months and not touch their dress uniforms; only for visits by high-ranking military brass or the press would they get dressed up.

When Jimmie and the crew stepped into the dining hall, the whole place got quiet with tables and tables of British in their fine dress uniforms staring right at them. What they saw was ten men, dirty and gritty from head to toe in filthy flight uniforms. All but Jimmie had a shoulder harness carrying the famous American Colt 45 pistol under their arms. Hell, Tex had a double holster carrying two Colt 45s, with one being the gift Jimmie had blessed him with!

The nearest British Officer shouted, "Watch out boys, the Americans are coming, like cowboys off a cattle drive with their six-shooters!!!"

Laughter erupted! And the English food was terrible.

Typical side gunner, where Tex was posted

A postcard that Jimmie sent home

TWENTY-EIGHT
Shell Shock Hotel / Red Cross Center

Jimmie and his crew had been through many grueling missions over the past fourteen months and they had seen their fair share of destruction and loss. The 94th Bomber Group had suffered great losses along with the whole 8th Air Force. It had taken a toll on their physical and mental health and that was why General Meade decided to give them some time off by sending them to the Red Cross Center outside of London.

During World War II, the Red Cross Center, located at a country club outside of London, England, was an important hub of support and care for soldiers and civilians alike. The center provided medical attention, nourishing meals, and other essential supplies to those in need. It was staffed by dedicated Red Cross volunteers who worked tirelessly to assist those impacted by the war. The center served as a beacon of hope and compassion in a time of conflict, offering much-needed aid to those suffering and bringing comfort to the wounded and traumatized. Despite the challenges posed by the war, the Red Cross Center was unwavering in its commitment to its mission of providing help and support to those in need

When Jimmie and his crew arrived at the center, they were greeted by the compassionate staff of Red Cross volunteers, who were dedicated to helping those affected by the war. The first rule of the Shell Shock Hotel, as it was affectionately known, was that military uniforms were not allowed. This was to help the men heal from the trauma of war and to ideally enjoy a long weekend as civilians. No ranks and no salutes were allowed either!

Jimmie and his crew arrived at the Shell Shock Hotel with a mix of excitement and trepidation. They were eager to take a break from the stress of combat but were also wary of the change of scenery and the sudden peace.

"Boys, welcome to the R&R Headquarters!" said Jimmie, with a sly grin. "Looks like we'll finally get to sleep in a real bed for a change."

"You mean we won't have to share a bunk with the bombs for once?" quipped Tex, with a laugh. (Side gunners' barracks were located right beside the bomb depot on base.)

"Ha! I could get used to this," added David, as he looked around the luxurious lobby. "Where's the bar and the nurses?" Isaac, who was always the quiet one, simply smiled and nodded in agreement.

Jimmie and his crew enjoyed a variety of games and activities arranged for the men, providing them with a much-needed break from the constant stress of combat. Some members of the crew, such as Tex, David, and Isaac, who were single and unattached, were especially eager to take part in these activities and were rarely seen once taken under the wings of some attentive and attractive nurses.

At the center, they were able to escape the horrors of war and find some respite, but the tranquility of the center was shattered in less than 24 hours when a V2 missile struck nearby. The V2 missiles were feared by all because of their sudden and devastating impact which had caused widespread panic and destruction throughout London.

The German V2 missiles, also known as the A-4 rockets, were the first long-range ballistic missiles used in warfare. Developed by the Germans towards the end of World War II, these missiles were capable of reaching high altitudes and delivering a large payload with incredible speed and precision. The V2 missiles were particularly dangerous because of their unpredictability, as they traveled at such a high velocity that they could not be tracked or intercepted by conventional means.

England was one of the primary targets of the V2 missiles during the war, as the Germans aimed to disrupt British morale and weaken their military capabilities. The V2 missiles were launched from sites in occupied Europe, mainly from the Netherlands, and caused widespread panic and destruction as they rained down on the cities and towns of England. The sudden and devastating impact of the V2 missiles left many people feeling helpless and afraid and their use was seen as a ruthless and inhumane tactic of the German war effort. Despite efforts by British authorities to counter the V2 threat through anti-aircraft defenses and the bombing of the launch sites, the missiles continued to cause significant damage and loss of life throughout the war. The V2 missiles left a lasting impact on the people of England, and their use remains one of the most controversial and devastating elements of the war.

Jimmie was asleep in his room, surrounded by luxury linens and pillows when the explosion occurred. The loud detonation shattered his window, sending glass flying everywhere and knocking him out of bed. The sudden and violent impact was a stark reminder of the war and Jimmie was suddenly overcome with fear and helplessness. The once peaceful and tranquil Red Cross Center was now a testament to the dangers and uncertainties of war, and Jimmie and his crew were again acutely aware of the fragility of life.

The V2 missiles were a terrifying reminder that no one was immune to the effects of war, not even those who had flown above the clouds and dropped bombs. The crew was now grappling with the reality that they were not invincible on the ground and that the war was affecting them in ways they never thought possible. The experience of the Red Cross Center and the V2 missile strike was a humbling reminder of the need for compassion and support during times of conflict.

Despite the traumatic event, Jimmie and his crew remained at the Red Cross Center for the rest of their time off. The experience of being on the receiving end of the violence and destruction that they had inflicted on others for so long had a profound effect on them. They spent much of their time reflecting on the consequences of their actions and the impact that war had on civilians and soldiers alike.

On the last night, as they sat around a fireplace, they discussed their experiences and the lessons they had learned. They realized that they were not so different from the people they had bombed and that the war had touched everyone's lives, leaving a trail of destruction and heartache in its wake.

Jimmie and Little Smitty

TWENTY-NINE
Fox & Hounds Pub

After about six months of being stationed at Bury St Edmunds, Jimmie and the other airmen of Little Helen's crew developed a routine. They were part of Squadron 332 of the 94th Bomb Group, one of the many sub-divisions of the 8th Air Force. On their "rest days," when they had a little bit of time off as Little Helen underwent some much-needed maintenance and repair, Jimmie and some of his airmen would venture into the nearby village and frequent the Fox & Hounds.

The Fox & Hounds was a bustling pub located in a small village in Edmonton, England. It was a popular gathering place for local residents, servicemen, and airmen who were stationed nearby. The pub was built from brick and stone and had a traditional wooden sign hanging above the entrance that depicted a Hound hunting a Fox.

Inside, the pub was dimly lit with a warm yellow glow that spilled from lanterns and the fireplace. The walls were lined with dark wooden panels and there were a few small tables scattered throughout the sitting room. The bar was located at the far end and was made from rich, dark wood. The bartenders were always busy pouring pints of warm ale and whisky for the patrons.

The pub was filled with worn and weathered wooden tables and stools in the main hall with a bar that ran along one wall. The walls were adorned with faded newspaper clippings and black and white photographs of soldiers who had left to fight in overseas battlegrounds, who were not coming back.

One of the most notable features of the Fox & Hounds was the large fireplace located in the center of the room. Always roaring, people would gather around it on chilly nights to warm their hands and swap stories. The pub was known for its lively atmosphere and you could always hear the sounds of laughter, clinking glasses, and animated chatter.

At the side of the pub was a small stage where local musicians would perform for the patrons. The music was an important part of the atmosphere and people would dance and sing along with the musicians. The music was typically performed by a small band, consisting of a pianist, a guitarist, and a drummer. The band played a mix of popular songs from the era as well as traditional folk tunes. As the night went on and the drinks flowed, the patrons of the Fox & Hounds would often join in on the singing. The pub was always lively and the music provided a welcome distraction from the stress and worries of the war as patrons would dance, laugh, and sing together, forgetting their troubles for a little while.

One particular night, a group of British soldiers came into the pub, fresh from the front line. They were eager to let loose and have some fun after the hardships they had faced. The band struck up an energetic tune and the soldiers began to dance and sing with gusto, their voices ringing out in harmony with the others in the pub. The song was an old favorite, and as they sang, they were transported back to a time before the war when life was simpler and happier.

As the night wore on, the music slowed and the band played a mournful ballad. The soldiers and patrons stood in silent reverence, paying homage to the friends and loved ones they had lost. The music was a reminder of the sacrifices they had all made, but it was also a celebration of the hope and resilience that carried them through the dark days of the war.

The regular customers of the Fox & Hounds were a mix of working-class people, soldiers on leave, and those who had been left behind. The war had taken a toll on all of them and the exhaustion was evident in their worn and weary faces. Many of them had lost loved ones, either to the fighting or the bombings, and the weight of the loss was etched into their expressions. The men in the pub were dressed in tattered and stained uniforms while the women were dressed in clothes that had seen better days. Despite their tired and poor appearance, the customers of the Fox & Hounds had a sense of camaraderie and shared experiences that brought them together.

As they drank the pints, the customers talked about their experiences during the war, exchanging stories of the battles they had fought, the friends they had lost, and the hope they held for the future. The sounds of laughter and conversation mixed with the clinking of glasses and the occasional singing of a war-time ballad. Despite the horrors they had faced, the Fox & Hounds was a place where they could find comfort and solace in each other's company, and it was a symbol of their resilience and determination in the face of adversity.

For Jimmie, the Fox & Hounds had become a sanctuary, a place where he could decompress after each mission and let his guard down. He would sit at the bar, drink a cold beer, and listen to the tales of his fellow bomber pilots. Over time, he came to cherish the relationships he built there and the Fox & Hounds became a second home to him. Despite the horrors of war, he always felt a sense of comfort and belonging within those four walls. The war was taking its toll on Jimmie, but the Fox & Hounds was a place where he could recharge, find solace, and feel a sense of normalcy amidst the chaos.

On one visit, Jimmie walked into the Fox & Hounds feeling exhausted after a long day of flying a bombing mission. He took a seat at the bar and ordered his regular ale which was always a welcome respite after the horrors of war. The barkeep, a gruff and experienced man, took notice of Jimmie and called over to the kitchen, "Liam! Come on out here; I've got someone I want you to meet!"

Moments later, a young boy emerged from the kitchen. He was maybe 8 or 9 years old with a head of messy red hair and bright, curious eyes. The barkeep ordered him to run to the kitchen and bring back a clean mug for Jimmie. The young boy obediently ran back and forth, bringing a mug to the barkeep who filled it with ale and handed it to Jimmie.

"You sure got some good help there," Jimmie said, taking a sip of his ale.

The barkeep smiled; pride evident in his eyes. "Yep, he sure is. This is my grandson, Liam. He's been helping me out since he was old enough to carry a mug."

Jimmie took another swig of his ale and looked at the young boy with a smile. Despite the war and all the tragedy it brought, moments like these reminded him of the goodness and innocence that still existed in the world.

Jimmie reached into his inside bomber jacket pocket and pulled out a Hershey candy bar he had saved from his recent Red Cross package. With a smile, he offered the treat to the young Liam. "Come over here, Liam. I've got something for you," Jimmie said. Liam approached him, his eyes lighting up when he saw the chocolate bar. He looked up at his grandfather with a hopeful expression. "Can I, Papaw?" he asked, and without hesitation, his grandfather nodded in agreement. The little boy eagerly took the candy bar from Jimmie's outstretched hand and broke into a wide grin. "Thank you, Sir!" he said, before running back to his grandfather's side to show him his treat.

Jimmie had just finished the last sip of his ale and set his mug down with a satisfied sigh. That's when Liam came around the bar with something hidden in a napkin and handed it to Captain Galloway. Intrigued, Jimmie opened the napkin and was surprised to find two brown eggs. He hadn't seen real eggs since basic flight school days back in Florida.

"Liam, this is too much," Jimmie said with a smile, "You don't have to give me anything for that candy bar."

Liam looked up at Jimmie with big, innocent eyes and replied, "This is all I have to give you. I wanted to show my appreciation."

Jimmie started thinking about how good those eggs would taste for tomorrow's breakfast and had an idea. "I tell you what Liam, I get one of those candy bars every week, how about I trade you my weekly candy bar for some eggs? That way we both win."

Liam's eyes lit up with excitement and he smiled from ear to ear. "That's a DEAL!" he exclaimed, and the two shook hands, sealing the deal.

Later in January of 1944, the crew of the Little Helen had made it back down to the pub to kick off a 3-day weekend break. The barkeeper, Terry, poured Jimmie and his men some ale and when Jimmie asked about the lady and child at the end of the bar, Terry filled him in on her story. Mrs. Lewis was a widow who did laundry for the village to make ends meet. Her husband had been missing for over a year, fighting in North Africa, and the war had only made their already difficult circumstances worse. Despite the hardships, the people in the village tried to help Mrs. Lewis and her son as much as they could.

Feeling moved by her story, Jimmie reached into his jacket pocket and pulled out an orange from his recent Red Cross package. He walked over to Mrs. Lewis and her son and offered the fruit to the young boy, who looked at it in confusion. Mrs. Lewis explained to him what an orange was and both she and her son expressed their gratitude. It dawned on Jimmie that the reason the young boy didn't know what an orange was, is that all the boy has ever known is wartime scarcity!

A few weeks later, Jimmie returned to the Fox & Hounds with another orange for Mrs. Lewis and her son. However, when he entered the pub, he didn't see them there. Jimmie asked the barkeeper, Terry, if he could leave the orange for them, but Terry had some sad news. Mrs. Lewis had passed away from the flu and her son had been taken to an orphanage in Scotland to keep him safe from the bombings. The village doctor had tried his best to treat Mrs. Lewis, but all the medicine he had to treat her was some aspirin. Being frail and malnourished didn't help. Medicine was hard to get during wartime.

Jimmie was overcome with anger and frustration at the senseless ways the war had taken yet another life. The war was never-ending and it seemed like it was always finding new ways to kill and destroy lives.

Heading to the Fox & Hounds, Edmonton, England

THIRTY
One in a Million Shot

As Jimmie climbed into the cockpit of his B-17 bomber, Little Helen, he was greeted by his co-pilot, Bob, who was already examining the replacement instrument panel.

The cockpit of a B-17 Flying Fortress is a cramped and busy space, filled with dials, switches, and gauges. The pilot sits in the left seat and has control over the yoke, throttles, and flaps. To the right of the pilot is the co-pilot who has similar controls. In front of both seats is the instrument panel which houses the altimeter, airspeed indicator, turn coordinator, heading indicator, and other essential flight instruments. The pilot has access to a map table which is located just behind the instrument panel.

Directly in front of the pilot and co-pilot are the control wheels which are used to direct the ailerons, rudder, and elevators. Above the control wheels are the engine control panels which allow the crew to manage the four engines. On the left side of the cockpit is the electrical panel which provides power to the various systems on the plane. On the right side is the fuel system panel which allows the crew to oversee the fuel system and monitor fuel levels.

Behind the cockpit is the upper gun turret which is manned by the top turret gunner, Benjamin. This position provides a 360-degree view of the sky and the gunner has control over the two .50 caliber machine guns that are mounted in the turret.

The previous mission had been a close call with a Nazi fighter plane shooting and narrowly missing the pilots, hitting the control panel in front of James. Luckily for the crew, none of the destroyed control panels were essential to landing that day.

The other crews of B-17 bombers were always talking about their lucky charms and rituals, convinced that they would somehow protect them from the dangers of war. Some believed that carrying a rabbit's foot or wearing a particular article of clothing would bring them good luck while others insisted on sitting in the same seat or saying a certain prayer before every mission.

But the crew of Little Helen, well, they didn't quite buy into any of it. They were a different breed, with a majority of the crew members being Jewish. They didn't put much faith in superstitions or lucky charms, believing that their survival depended more on skill and strategy than on chance.

Jimmie, as the captain of Little Helen, would scoff at the other crews' antics. He knew that the only way to make it through the war was not going to be with trinkets or charms. Tex, the side gunner, would often join in on the ridicule, pointing out the absurdity of relying on something as trivial as a lucky charm to protect oneself from the horrors of war. Instead, he put his trust in his pair of Colt 45s, right or wrong.

It was a tense time, as the war raged on and the stakes grew higher with each mission. The crew of Little Helen was feeling the mounting tension, wondering if their "Good Luck" would run out before long.

Jimmie put on his headset and was about to conduct his pre-flight checks when a thought suddenly crossed his mind. He turned to Bob and asked, "Bob, do you ever think about dying over here?" Jimmie's own words echoed in his ears and he quickly glanced over his shoulder to see if any other members of the crew had boarded the plane. He knew it was considered bad luck to talk about death, let alone for a captain to bring it up and he hoped that his impulsive question wouldn't jinx the mission.

Bob gave Jimmie a slight grin, recognizing Jimmie's concerned scan for the crew as an acknowledgment of bad luck to even broach the topic, and said, "Don't worry, remember I'm Jewish, I don't believe in luck! To answer your question, the first several weeks I was over here, that's all I could think about! I went to bed every night certain our next mission was going to be my last! We've been over here 14 months now and I've had four different bunk mates and there might be three guys left alive in my barracks that were here when we got here. The way I figure, we're probably not going to live through this. Hate to say it!"

Jimmie continued routinely going through his pre-flight checklist and replied back, "I know the feeling! But what I'm really scared of is how I used to be so scared and had nightmares of getting shot down and dying in a fiery crash, BUT now I don't dream at all! I mean, I never remember a dream and I hardly ever think of anything except some practical joke Tex or someone pulled playing cards at night. I used to dream of getting back to my wife, Jean, and my daughter, Brenda Helen; now it just seems like THAT life was just a dream. What scares me now is, what if I survive? What kind of a person is my family getting back?"

With a chuckle, Bob replied, "Well, Jimmie, I've got a plan. If we do make it out of here alive, we'll open up a bar in Texas and call it 'The Lucky Bastards.' We'll serve up cold beers and tall tales about our adventures over here. And the best part? We'll never have to worry about death again because we'll have outsmarted the Grim Reaper himself."

Jimmie laughed, "Bob, you're a genius! That's the best plan I've heard yet. We'll be living the good life and telling stories for years to come. But let's just make sure we actually survive this mission first." The two of them continued their pre-flight checks, their spirits lifted by the thought of a brighter future and a cold beer waiting for them at the end of this war.

Jimmie took a deep breath and smiled at Bob, trying to lighten the mood. "Well, let's hope the fighters are busy elsewhere today. It would be a shame if they ruin our 'routine' mission."

Bob chuckled and added, "Yeah, let's just focus on keeping Little Helen in one piece and bombing those German Sons of Bitches. We can worry about the rest later."

Jimmie laughed and went back to his pre-flight checks. He always tried to make light of the situation, but deep down he knew the danger they faced every time they went on a mission. As the rest of the crew boarded the plane, Jimmie felt a sense of camaraderie with his fellow airmen. They were all in this together, facing the same dangers, relying on each other to make it back home safely. The engines roared to life and the B-17 bomber began to taxi down the runway.

Jimmie could feel the adrenaline pumping through his veins as they lifted off the ground and climbed higher into the sky. Even after all he had been through, he still loved flying!

It was a sunny day in England and the sky was dotted with B-17 Flying Fortress bombers of the 94th Bomb Group flying over the English Channel. The pilots and their crews were on their way to their next mission in Germany, but for now, they were taking in the breathtaking views from the cockpit and gunners' windows.

As they flew over the Channel, the sun was shining on the water below, creating a shimmering reflection that seemed to go on forever. The water was a deep blue and the white clouds above looked like fluffy pillows. The bombers flew in formation, their wings almost touching as they headed toward their destination.

The sound of the powerful engines filled the air and the crew members were consumed with a sense of pride and awe at the spectacle of the day. The pilots were in complete control, navigating the massive bombers through the skies with ease. The flight engineer was monitoring the systems, making sure everything was running smoothly while the rest of the crew was on alert, ready to take action if necessary, against Nazi fighters.

As they flew over the coast of France, they caught a glimpse of the small towns and villages below. The homes were like dots on the landscape and the roads were thin lines that snaked through the countryside. The pilots could see the lush green fields dotted with sheep and cows. The flight over the English Channel was one of the most beautiful moments of the mission. Despite the danger and the stress of their assignment, the crew members took a moment to appreciate the beauty of the world around them. They were flying high in the skies, seeing things that few others had seen and experiencing a sense of freedom and excitement that was hard to describe.

As they reached the coast of France, the pilots and crew members had a moment of reflection. They were on their way to war, but for now, they were flying over some of the most beautiful landscapes in the world.

The 94th Bomber Group was in luck TODAY! Marty, their bombardier, yelled over the intercom, "Five minutes until the target!" Jimmie could see the Nazi airfield on the horizon and not a fighter was in sight in the air or on the ground. The best thing about bombing Nazi airfields was, if the fighters were gone, the

Germans didn't protect them with anti-aircraft artillery. That was reserved for more valuable installations like military factories.

Jimmie looked over to Bob, "Hot damn, the Nazi fighters must be over London today; they'll have a surprise waiting for them when they get back!"

The crew let out a collective sigh of relief and settled in for the bombing run. The plane had been loaded with a full complement of bombs and was ready to unleash its payload on the airfield.

Jimmie and Bob double-checked the coordinates and gave the signal to Marty to drop the bombs. There was a sudden jolt as they were released and the plane rose a few feet in the air as the weight was lifted.

The crew cheered, "Eat that you Nazi fuckers!" Tex yelled over the intercom, as they watched the bombs explode on the airfield below leaving a trail of smoke and fire in their wake. Turning the plane around to head back to base, Jimmie couldn't help but feel a sense of pride and satisfaction. This mission was a success, and the airfield was no longer a threat to the Allies, for a few days anyway. The crew relaxed and took a moment to enjoy their victory, laughing and joking as they flew back to base.

About an hour and a half later, Little Helen crossed over to Northern France to make their run-up to the English Channel. Suddenly, over the intercom, Marty yelled, "Oh SHIT, Captain, we got a problem, a huge fucking problem!"

Jimmie yelled back, "Fighters?"

"NO, one of the bombs in the payload didn't release and is still hanging there, ARMED!" Marty exclaimed.

Marty was the bombardier of the plane and besides being in charge of navigating the bomb runs and dropping the bombs, he had the assignment of checking to see if all the payload was released out of the plane.

Jimmie immediately opened the radio channel to the other bombers in the 94th Bomber Group, "Boys you all are going to have to go on without us; we got a stuck bomb!"

Some of the other captains replied back, "Good Luck Little Helen, Godspeed! See you later at the Fox & Hounds!"

You could hear in their tone; this was serious business because you couldn't land the plane with an armed bomb inside. Normal procedure was to contact aircraft control and try to schedule a bail out and parachute out of the plane somewhere in the English Channel off the coast of Bury St Edmunds, hopefully with an English patrol boat waiting.

The dangerous problem with that was this was February 1944 and if you didn't get picked up and out of the water within five minutes, the cold water would cause severe hypothermia and you would die!

Isaac, the tail gunner, interrupted, "We gotta get that bomb out of here! I can't parachute into any damn water. I can't swim!"

Jimmie replied, "Can't swim?! How in the hell did you make it out of basic flight school? You have to take a swim test to pass!"

Isaac, sounding really nervous, responded, "I paid one of my poker buddies to take the test for me to write off his markers to me! Don't give me no shit, Captain, I know how Tex goes down with your Military I.D. card to the shooting range every month to qualify you with your side arm! For a man that doesn't like guns and can't shoot worth shit, you have a perfect marksman grade and medals with the 8th Air Force!"

With a quick chuckle Jimmie admitted, "You got me there Isaac! Marty, I'm going to drop down to around 10,000 into some warmer air and open the bomb doors, see what you guys can do to get that bomb to drop!"

Not seeing any fighter planes, Isaac had already made it up through the fuselage to David and the bomb bays. Bob hit the switch and the bomb doors started to open up with David putting on the safety harness in case he accidently slipped, he wouldn't fall out of the fracking plane. Below David's feet was a 10,000-foot drop to the French countryside.

Isaac handed David the big rubber hammer to beat on the bomb harness housing to see if the vibrations would cause it to release. By this time, Tex and Cline, the radio operator, had left their posts to come down and see how things were going.

Tex said, "What the hell?!" and grabbed a safety harness, lowering himself down on the other side of the bomb bay from David and started kicking the bomb itself!

David let out a huge yell, "What the fuck are you doing Tex? That's a live bomb! You're going to kill us before the cold waters of the North Atlantic get a chance!"

Jimmie and Bob were up in the cockpit listening to the intermittent comments over the intercom. Jimmie told Bob that they had better contact Bury St Edmunds to arrange a boat for them to ditch Little Helen in the Channel.

Jimmie had just grabbed the microphone when the whole intercom lit up with "There goes the bastard!" The bomb had just been released, dropping down towards the French Countryside.

Isaac got back to his tail gunner post just in time to see the single bomb hit the ground. All of a sudden, Isaac yelled on the intercom, "Captain, you gotta see this, swing around and take a look at this shit!!!"

Jimmie said "What the hell are you talking about, swing back around?!"

Isaac, "You got to swing around, you won't believe this shit!"

Jimmie turned the plane and brought Little Helen around to take a look.

Isaac was laughing and yelling, "I told ya Sons of Bitches you wouldn't believe me unless you saw it yourselves; the bomb went down the fucking chimney of that big ass French castle sitting in the middle of the countryside!"

Going down the chimney, the single bomb had leveled a whole castle! Normally the men would be worried about killing civilians, but all the crew knew that the Germans had confiscated every nice house in the French countryside to house upper ranking Nazis officers for R&R.

Tex let out a yelp on the intercom, "I hope you fucking Nazis enjoy our little American present!" The whole crew burst out laughing.

Jimmie and Bob smiled at each other in the cockpit and Jimmie said, "If it wasn't for all the killing and getting killed, this shit ain't half bad! That was a one in a million shot!"

Bob replied back, "If it weren't for the killing and dying!"

A typical B-17 bomber in flight

B-17 bomb bay

B-17 pilot's cabin

THIRTY-ONE
Marksman Medal
Without Ever Shooting a Pistol

Jimmie couldn't help but feel like a bit of an outsider in his hometown community of Crackers Neck. Maybe it was his lack of interest in guns or maybe it was his dream of becoming a pilot, but he never quite fit in with the other boys as far as hobbies go. While they spent their afternoons hunting or shooting old cans, Jimmie could usually be found with his nose buried in a library book or magazine about aviation, if he wasn't doing chores around the farm.

Growing up in the 1920s and 1930s, there were plenty of reasons for having guns and even liking guns for the protection they gave. Heck, Ma was always packing her pistol day and night with Paw keeping one in his church desk, his Harley motorcycle saddlebags, or in his truck nearby. Violence was just common in those days and guns were the only law around, but Jimmie was never one who desired a gun.

As Jimmie grew older and the threat of war loomed, he knew that he had to do his part and so he had joined the Army Air Corps and was sent to basic training where he found himself surrounded by guys who lived and breathed guns. Jimmie tried to fit in, but he just couldn't seem to shake his disinterest in firearms.

Despite his lack of enthusiasm, Jimmie managed to get through basic training thanks to a combination of bribes and luck. He always figured if his plane was ever shot down and he was fortunate enough to parachute out, he would hit the ground with his hands held high to surrender. *No commando stuff behind enemy lines for me*, he thought. But when he was finally sent overseas, he found himself facing a new set of challenges.

Jimmie was a skilled pilot, but flying over enemy territory was a far cry from the peaceful skies he was used to. That is why the Army Air Corp was committed to a lot of basic survival training and marksman training even at their post at Bury St Edmunds in England. Every month, the Air Corps would have all crew members of military planes pass a marksman training test.

Jimmie never failed to utter a silent prayer of gratitude whenever he handed his military I.D. to Tex Smith to take his monthly marksmanship testing for him. He was convinced that God had sent Tex to their crew for a reason and that reason was to shoot guns which had earned him a marksman medal without ever shooting a pistol! Heck, Jimmie had even given Tex his Colt 45 sidearm to carry which motivated Tex to fashion himself a double shoulder holster to carry a pistol under each arm.

Tex Smith was a living embodiment of the quintessential Texan. The Lone Star State has long been known for producing men of incredible and outrageous character and Tex was no exception. He had a humble beginning - abandoned as a newborn in front of the biggest whorehouse in Texarkana. Fortunately, the madame of the house took him in and christened him "Tex" since he was found on the Texas side of the state border. Not knowing anything about his origin, she gave him the last name of Smith. And thus, Tex Smith came into the world.

Tex Smith had been raised in the brothel and had always been a bit of a mystery. He never knew his actual birthday or where he was born which left his official identity in question. But, despite his lack of formal education, the ladies of the house made sure Tex was well-educated in reading, writing, and math. And, as he got older, they entrusted him with the important responsibility of handling the house's money and banking chores.

To protect the ladies and their money, Tex was given a pistol at a young age before he could even ride a bicycle and quickly became a natural-born marksman. He spent hours practicing in the back alley, shooting at old cans with all kinds of pistols. He became so good that he could shoot the wings off a fly at a hundred yards, or so he claimed.

When Tex enlisted in the Army after the bombing of Pearl Harbor, it was the first time he was officially recognized as a citizen of the United States of America. But, for Jimmie and his crew, Tex was a godsend and Jimmie knew that God had sent him to their team for a reason - to shoot guns.

As Tex entered the Army and volunteered for the Army Air Corps, he quickly found out he had another valuable talent… becoming the unofficial procurement officer for contraband or other hard-to-get items on military bases. He guessed that years of living in a whorehouse had given him the ability to size up human nature and he was a natural-born horse trader. At every base from basic training all the way to being a crewmember of the Little Helen, he ended up being "The Man" who could get you something if you could pay!

Even at Bury St Edmunds, it was rumored that General Meade would, on occasion, ask Tex to acquire some silk stockings for a gift to send to his wife. Of course, everyone knew stockings were not that hard to get stateside, so the most logical need may have been to give his girlfriend down in London, or at least that was the rumor. But, for the crew of the Little Helen, the most important procurement Tex ever did for them happened after their second mission flying over enemy territory.

The first flight of Little Helen and her crew over Northern France had gone off without a hitch. The Nazis' Juvincourt Airbase was the target and due to its close proximity to Bury St Edmunds, the American P-47 Thunderbolt fighter planes could escort the 94th Bomber Group all the way to the target, minimizing enemy resistance from Nazi fighters. It was a smooth operation, but everyone knew that luck could only last for so long in the brutal skies of World War II.

The second mission of Little Helen's crew was the memorable one. They were assigned to bomb the Nazi Valentin Submarine Pens at Rekum, Germany. During the mission briefing, they were warned about the large anti-aircraft artillery they would face. As Little Helen took off from Bury St. Edmunds, Jimmie noticed his co-pilot, Bob, taking off his flak jacket and folding it. Bob then put it underneath his butt like a seat cushion.

Jimmie was confused and asked, "What in the world are you doing, Bob? Aren't you afraid of the flak killing you, or can't you see out?"

Bob replied, "Hell no, I can see fine! But did you hear what happened to Craig, the co-pilot of the Bronx Bomber?"

Jimmie shook his head, indicating he hadn't heard.

Bob continued, "We heard that they were flying over this same target a few weeks ago and a flak shell exploded right below the fuselage that Craig was co-piloting and it blew his balls off… you know, the family jewels!"

Jimmie exclaimed, "Hell, did he live?"

Bob nodded, "Yeah, but he got his ticket punched for back home and he's missing his family jewels! What's the point of going back home without the family jewels? I'd rather just die over here!"

Jimmie sat there in amazement for a few seconds before he said, "Hold the yoke, Bob!"

Jimmie then took off his own flak jacket and sat on it. "Yeah, what's the point of going home like that!"

The whole crew heard the conversation over the intercom and within minutes they were all sitting on their flak jackets.

Jimmie yelled, "Hey, Tex! I got an order for *my-man-who-can-get-anything*!"

Tex replied, "I already read you, Captain. Extra flight jackets for the whole crew!" He laughed over the intercom.

By the next mission, Tex had delivered the extra flak jackets, but no one asked him where or how he got them. The crew had gotten inventive with some old horse tack snaps and fashioned what looked to be large baggy adult diapers out of the extra jackets, walking around bow-legged with them.

Smitty let out, "Tex, you're the man! We might be the oddest-looking bomber crew in the whole 8th, but we're going home with our family jewels or not coming home at all!"

Pistol Qualification Badges

THIRTY-TWO
V.I.P. Passenger

For a B-17 crew in the European theater during WWII, a mission was defined as a sortie where the aircraft took off with the intention of attacking an enemy target. A mission would count towards the total number required for a tour of duty if the aircraft crossed into enemy territory and hit its intended target. Misses for various reasons, didn't count towards one tour of duty.

However, the exact criteria for what constituted a mission could vary somewhat. For instance, if a plane had to turn back due to mechanical problems or bad weather before reaching the target, it might not count as a mission. Sometimes, but rarely, the rules were modified to count sorties that did not reach the intended target but still encountered heavy enemy action, such as anti-aircraft fire or enemy fighters. At the end of the day, a B-17 crew prepped and took off many times, faced the stresses of war, and due to circumstances out of their control, the mission would not count towards their tour of duty.

The requirement of 25 missions for a tour of duty was initially set when the loss rates were very high (more than 60% of crews of the 8th Air Force did not survive to complete their 25 missions in 1943 and the first eight months of 1944).

Given the fact that so few flight crews were reaching the 25-tour completion, the War Department brought in *"The"* Major General Doolittle to command the 8th Air Force to tighten things up and reduce casualty rates of the bomber groups.

At a January 1944 mission briefing, General Doolittle himself was in attendance with a fiery speech about how his 8th Air Force was going to tighten things up, "get back to combat basics" to increase survival rates. Major Collins got up to go over what the Top Brass thought was the problem and how to fix them. They had determined that it was to get back to the Combat Box formations. In fact, they were so sure that this was the big problem that General Doolittle himself was going up with the 94 Bomber Group as an observer on Jimmie's Little Helen.

Jimmie raised his hand to address this "getting back to basics" solution in order to explain why his group and all the other groups had modified the Combat Box formation for "real-life" situations that the Brass weren't considering. Major Collins told Jimmie to put his hand down, that this was not up for discussion. Major General Doolittle himself was going on this mission to see *FOR HIMSELF* what was going on with these casualty rates.

In the early stages of World War II, the U.S. Army Air Forces developed a formation known as the "Combat Box" for their B-17 Flying Fortress bombers. This was a defensive formation intended to concentrate the firepower of the bombers' machine guns, making it more difficult for enemy fighters to attack any single aircraft.

A Combat Box formation was typically made up of three squadron-sized elements stacked vertically, with each squadron flying in a tight "V" formation. This resulted in a box-like pattern when viewed from above or below, hence the name "Combat Box." The idea behind the Combat Box was that it allowed every B-17 in the formation to provide overlapping fields of fire, protecting not only themselves but their fellow bombers as well. In theory, this would make it very costly for enemy fighters to attack the formation.

However, the Combat Box was not without its problems over German occupied territory. The tight formations required for the Combat Box made it harder for individual pilots to take evasive action, and the formation, as a whole, was a large target that was easier to spot and track. Moreover, losses from flak could be severe as flak gunners could concentrate their fire on the predictably straight-and-level flying box formations.

As Jimmie and the crew of Little Helen boarded their plane, there was a noticeable addition besides the VIP passenger of General Doolittle; overnight, Doolittle's staff had instructed the ground crew to bolt a metal office chair to the floor right in the middle and behind the pilot and co-pilot's chairs in the cabin. Jimmie's first thought was, *Wow, this doesn't help our escape route if we're trying to parachute out of our bird today!*

As the General hopped aboard, the crew snapped to attention, each man nailing his salute and military greetings to General Doolittle, nonchalant as if he'd done this a hundred times, Doolittle clambered up front, easing into his bare-bones metal seat.

Bob threw a glance around, then turned to the General, "You want me to get the boys to rustle up some rope or straps, General? Seems this chair's missing a seat belt. This mission's gonna be a rough ride. Flak's gonna be hell— we've bombed these German factories before."

Doolittle shot back, a hint of a grin playing on his lips, "Son, I've had a front-row seat to enemy anti-aircraft fire more than a few times. Trust me, the Japs have given me their best shots!" The dismissive edge in his voice said it all — this might've been a new horse, but it sure as hell wasn't his first rodeo.

The General was famous throughout the U.S. Military for his "Doolittle Raid" that bombed Tokyo, Japan. The Doolittle Raid, his most daring rodeo yet, was one to remember. Sixteen bombers, each crewed by five brave men, slipped through the early morning haze and headed straight for the Land of the Rising Sun. The mission was as risky as they came - the B-25s had been modified for the job, their bomb bays crammed with extra fuel tanks to give 'em just enough range.

The plan was simple, in theory. Take off from the USS Hornet, fly low and fast over the Pacific, then rise up to drop their bombs on Tokyo and other key targets. After that, they'd head for the safety of Allied controlled territory in China. But everyone aboard knew the stakes. If they were spotted before reaching their targets, or if their fuel ran low, or if they ran into heavy flak, their chances of making it back were slim to none. Still, they flew on, guided by Doolittle's unwavering resolve. On April 18, 1942, they struck the first American blow to the Japanese homeland, proving that even the mighty Empire was within their reach.

Bob and all the crew had respect for the General's war resume, but under his breath, he mouthed, "You haven't faced Nazi fighters and anti-aircraft artillery before…" Jimmie couldn't quite make out what Bob was saying, but was thinking exactly the same thing!

As the P-47s began turning back, the Bomber Group had clear skies for about twenty minutes before they crossed into Germany. As soon as the General put his radio headset on and tuned into the open channel, Little Helen's machine guns started to fire; Tex was first with his side gun, yelling, "Fighters, 3 o'clock!"

Smitty wasn't far behind with his belly guns; all guns were blazing from Little Helen!

Over the radio, the General could hear:

"Big Easy to Lucky Seven, we've got a wave of Nazis fighters coming in!" Johnson's voice was filled with urgency as more Nazi fighters swarmed into view.

"Copy, Big Easy. Hellcat, can you assist with visuals?" Harris responded, his B-17 shuddering under a hail of bullets.

"Roger, Lucky Seven. We've got our own –" Riley's voice cut off as a loud explosion echoed over the radio. "Damn, direct hit on the nose! We're going down, I repeat, Hellcat is going down!"

"Mayday, Mayday! This is Big Easy! We've lost an engine! We're losing altitude!" Johnson's voice was desperate. The radio filled with the sound of alarms, shouting, and the roar of engines struggling to keep airborne.

"Lucky Seven to Hellcat, Big Easy, do you copy?" Harris shouted into the radio; his voice drowned out by the cacophony of chaos around him.

"Lucky Seven, we're hit! We're hit!" Thompson's voice was barely audible above the roar of fire and the groaning metal.

"Keep it together, boys! We've got a job to do!" Jimmie's voice rang out from Little Helen; his voice trying to cut through the chaos, steadying his crew and the other squadrons.

"Damn it, more fighters coming in! Five o'clock!" Kowalski's warning was followed by the chatter of his guns as he engaged the enemy.

The sky was filled with tracers, smoke, and the darting forms of enemy fighters. The radio chatter was a symphony of chaos, the voices of the bomber crews echoing over the radio their struggle against an overwhelming enemy force for over thirty minutes.

Then with nothing but silence, Doolittle said, "Where did they go?"

Jimmie came back on the intercom, "Wait for it!"

"Jesus, that was close!" Tex hollered as a piece of flak tore through the fuselage, missing him by inches.

"Hold on boys!" Bob shot back; his voice suddenly tense. The B-17 lurched as another explosion rocked them.

The radio crackled to life with Johnson's panicked voice, "Black Jack is hit! Starboard wing on fire! We're going down!"

"Black Jack, do you copy? Bail out!" Bob shouted into the radio.

"Susan Ruth, we've got flak at six o'clock!" Kowalski's voice was shrill with fear. The rookie had never faced this much flak before.

"Flak's getting thicker!" Riley's voice came through, filled with dread. "All-American hit! Losing altitude!"

The radio was filled with the sounds of chaos: shouting, alarms, the deafening roar of engines and exploding flak. The skies had become a fiery hell, each crew fighting their own private war amidst the storm of German anti-aircraft fire. Fear was a live-wire running through each man, but there wasn't even something to shoot back at, the flak was like "Russian Roulette!"

Finally, over the radio, "Group Leader, do you copy? This is Squadron Leader Mi Amigo."

Jimmie replied, "Group Leader copies!"

Mi Amigo added, "Flak explosion just knocked the Nashville into the Lone Star hard, both are going down; no visible chutes, I repeat, no visible chutes! Tell the MAJOR GENERAL he can kiss my ass with his tight Combat Box formation, I'm telling the rest of my squadron to spread out! He can arrest me back at base!"

Jimmie made a quick look back at Doolittle, who, while gripping his seat, said, "Tell the boys to do what they have to do to get through this. Jesus, if you can get us back alive, I'll give everyone R&R passes for a long weekend!"

Jimmie yelled over the radio, "Group Leader to all squadrons, SPREAD OUT, SPREAD OUT, per General's orders!"

After his observatory flight with the 94th Bomber Group in the Little Helen, Major General Doolittle did indeed lower casualty rates of B-17 crews, but it wasn't through any Combat Box formations or with changing any bombing techniques at all.

In the dying months of '43, the P-51B Mustang hit the scene over Europe, under the banner of the USAAF. Fuel-wise, it could match the P-47's range, even with the latter all decked out with drop tanks. But when the Mustang first rolled out in November '43, it was stamped a tactical fighter not an escort. So, the Brass handed the first batch over to the 9th Air Force, leaving the boys in the 8th Air Force Bomber Command in the lurch.

Then, with the 8th Air Force, he wasn't shy about shaking things up. Doolittle tossed out the old playbook after experiencing Nazis combat first-hand with the crew of the Little Helen and said escorting fighters had to stick to the bombers like glue. With Doolittle's go-ahead, American fighters were sent out front, sweeping the skies clear of any Luftwaffe fighters. Those Messerschmitt 109s and the twin-engine Zerstörergeschwader and their replacements, the Fw-190As didn't stand a chance. By late '44, the Allies had the German skies pretty much to themselves.

But Doolittle's fighter boys weren't done. After the bombers made their runs, the fighters were free to pepper German artillery fortifications, airfields, and transport on the way home. It was a one-two punch that had the Luftwaffe and German anti-aircraft artillery reeling and cleared the skies for the 8th.

The Mustangs, acting as the top dogs of the sky, had the German planes on the ropes in no time. Post D-Day, the Luftwaffe was a rare sight over Europe. Sure, they could still launch a sortie or two against the Allied bombers, but they were taking a beating from the swarms of B-17s and B-24s.

By the middle of '44, the 8th Air Force had swelled to a force of over 200,000 strong. They had forty heavy bomber groups, fifteen fighter groups, and a handful of specialized support crews. They could, and often did, send out over 2,000 four-engine bombers and more than a thousand fighters on a single mission. By '45, the P-51 Mustangs controlled the skies as the top birds of prey!

THIRTY-THREE
Hillbilly Reunion in Southampton

Jimmie had been called Captain since flight school by his crew and fellow comrades, but it wasn't quite official yet. Like other fellow B-17 pilots, the pilot was always referred to as "Captain" due to his job responsibilities and not necessarily due to his rank. He was a Second Lieutenant just like Bob, his co-pilot, and most other pilots in the 94th Bomb Group.

This all changed on Little Helen's 20th mission. After that mission of dropping supplies to the "Big Red One" regiment after their Battle of the Bulge, as they were making their last big push on to Berlin, the crew noticed a large group of military brass near the landing strip over towards the hangar bay. Upon landing, the ground crew motioned for Jimmie to taxi Little Helen over to the crowd.

Jimmie looked over at Bob, "Wonder what that's all about?" as he pointed to the group. "You reckon Tex or one of the other boys are in trouble again?"

With a slight smile, Bob answered, "I think I have some idea; you'll find out shortly. Don't worry, it's a good thing. I promise!"

Jimmie was the customary last of the crew to climb the ladder down out of Little Helen. Without warning, Tex and Smitty started to shower him with the spray of some champagne and the crew all patted Jimmie on the back.

Colonel Jessup stepped up to the crew with a small box in his hand, "Second Lieutenant Jimmie Galloway, I proudly give you the field commission of 'Captain Jimmie Galloway of the 8th Air Force!"

About this time, some of the other bomber crews of the 94 Bomb Group had made their way over to start singing, "For He's a Jolly Good Fellow!"

Jimmie, feeling overwhelmed, looked at Bob and said, "This is crazy, Bob! I'm just a farm boy from Crackers Neck! I'm not sure I can handle all this."

Bob put his hand on Jimmie's shoulder and replied, "Don't worry, Jimmie. You'll get used to it. Just enjoy the moment and let the champagne flow!"

The crew erupted in cheers as Jimmie received his official captain's bars and commission. It was a moment that he would never forget, a symbol of his hard work, dedication, and bravery in the face of danger with his men.

In the wake of all the awards and accolades, the most welcome recognition for the crew of Little Helen was a seven-day R&R pass.

Tex, always quick with a quip, let out a boisterous, "Hot damn, a whole week to chase some beautiful British women! But count me out of London; I heard they still get the occasional V2 bomb there. I don't want any part of that, no Sir. Remember what happened at the Red Cross Center?"

The crew laughed, exchanging good-natured jabs and ribbing each other. Despite the horrors of war, moments like these reminded them of the joys of life and they savored them all the more for the danger that surrounded them.

Colonel Jessup had a mischievous glint in his eye as he spoke, "How about I make you boys some reservations down in Southampton? It's been quite some time since they've had any bombings down there. You all can enjoy some well-earned rest and little fun."

Jimmie looked around at the crew and they all nodded enthusiastically, "Sounds good to me, Colonel!"

The next morning, the crew of Little Helen was up and packed, ready to go. As they piled into four different jeeps, Cline, the radio operator, had an idea, "Why don't we fly a transport plane down to Southampton instead of driving? It'll save a day of traveling there and another one coming back."

Jimmie scratched his chin. "That's not a bad idea, but where are we going to get a plane?"

Bob grinned. "Don't worry, Captain. I've got it covered."

Jimmie looked at Bob in confusion, but then it dawned on him. Bob was referring to the officer in charge of plane assignments at Bury St. Edmunds air tower, 2nd Lieutenant Wilson.

Jimmie and Bob marched confidently into the air traffic office, both wearing their dress uniforms.

Jimmie cleared his throat. "Lieutenant Wilson, I'm taking the C-47 parked outside Hangar 4 down to Southampton."

Wilson looked up from his paperwork, "The hell you are! I don't have you down for any transport flights today or any other day."

Bob stepped forward, his voice rising, "Lieutenant Wilson, I don't think you know who you're speaking to. This is Captain Jimmie Galloway!"

Jimmie deepened his voice, "That's an order, Lieutenant!" A few minutes later, Jimmie and Bob walked out of the office with the necessary paperwork. Jimmie had a big grin on his face, "I could get used to this Captain stuff!"

Southampton, England was a hub of military operations in late 1944 during World War II. The city was a major port for Allied Forces and the activity was non-stop. In fact, it was one of the most significant locations for the Allied Forces in Europe.

It was from here that the majority of American GIs would arrive and depart; the city served as a crucial transportation center for troops, supplies, and equipment. As Jimmie and the crew of Little Helen approached, the airfield outside of town was bustling with activity. Transport planes were taking off and landing constantly and the sight of aircraft could be seen all over the skies.

The city was in a constant state of flux with soldiers and supplies coming and going at all hours of the day and night. The docks were filled with ships of all sizes, with cargo being unloaded and loaded onto transport vehicles. Soldiers could be seen marching through the streets and the sound of jeeps and trucks could be heard constantly.

As the war raged on, Southampton became a key location for military operations. The city was home to several large military bases including the 9th Air Force and the 2nd Tactical Air Force. The city was also home to many important military hospitals and was a vital location for the evacuation of wounded soldiers.

At the Army bases, soldiers were being trained and prepared for deployment to the front lines. Every day, new recruits arrived, eager to do their part in the war effort. They were greeted by a city full of military operations where every man and woman was working hard to help bring an end to the war.

Despite the constant activity, the people of Southampton welcomed the American troops with open arms. They knew the sacrifices that these young men were making and were determined to do all they could to support them. The city was filled with friendly faces and the soldiers were often invited into homes for meals and rest.

For the American troops, Southampton was a brief respite from the horrors of war. It was a place to rest, recover, and prepare for the battles that lay ahead. And while the city may have been a temporary home for these young men, the memories of Southampton and the kindness of its people would stay with them forever.

Jimmie and Bob glided their C-47 into a smooth landing at the Southampton Army Air Base where the rest of the crew had already started their R&R, passing around a couple of bottles of whisky in the back of the plane.

As Jimmie stepped out onto the tarmac, he was struck by the sheer size of the terminal that had been constructed just before the D-Day invasion. Hundreds of GIs were lounging around, some getting ready to ship out over the Channel to the German front lines, while others had earned enough points or had been injured and had received that coveted "magic" ticket home.

The terminal was a hive of activity with military personnel scurrying about, trying to keep things organized amidst the chaos. Everywhere Jimmie looked, he saw American soldiers coming and going, some looking haggard and worn, others relieved and overjoyed to be heading home. The air was thick with the sounds of chatter, laughter, and the occasional shout of a commanding officer trying to restore order.

As Jimmie and Bob made their way through the terminal, they were greeted by countless familiar uniforms and new ones alike. There were soldiers from every branch of the military with different uniforms and different accents, but all were united by their shared experience of serving their country during the war.

Despite the hustle and bustle of the terminal, there was an unmistakable sense of camaraderie and brotherhood among the soldiers. Everyone was eager to share stories and experiences, to bond over the trials and tribulations of war.

For Jimmie, it was a reminder of just how much he had come to rely on the support of his fellow soldiers throughout his time in Europe. As they made their way towards the exit, Jimmie turned to Bob with a sense of awe, "Can you believe it?" he said, gesturing towards the throngs of soldiers around them. "All of us coming through here, heading out to war or back home to our families. It's incredible."

Over the sound of the chaos, Jimmie heard a very familiar accent he hadn't heard since before the war, coming from the huge man in an Army uniform smoking a big ole cigar!

Jimmie, "I recognize that accent anywhere, Bob, you go ahead with the men and I'll catch up. I need to check something out."

Jimmie made it over to the hulking sergeant with his name tag showing Stallard. "May I bother you for a second, Sergeant, and ask where you are from? You sound like you're from back home."

Sergeant Stallard took a long drag of his cigar and looked Jimmie up and down, "Well, I'm from a little coal mining town in Southwest Virginia. I'm pretty sure you've never heard of it: Coeburn, Virginia."

Jimmie smiled from ear to ear, "Never heard of it! I'm from East Stone Gap, in an area called Crackers Neck to be specific."

Sergeant Stallard let out a horse laugh and choked a little on his cigar smoke, "Well ain't that some shit; never thought I'd run into someone from so close to home over here in England. What brings you here?"

Jimmie replied, "I'm a pilot with the 8th Air Force, flying B-17s over Germany. Just got back from a mission and we're here for some R&R before we head back out."

Sergeant Slew Stallard nodded, "I was with the 9th Air Force and 442nd Troop Carrier Group, landed on Normandy Beach on D-Day, and been fighting our way through France and the Low Country all the way to the Rhine River in Germany ever since. It's been one hell of a ride." Jimmie listened intently as Sergeant

Stallard told him about his experiences in the war, sharing stories of battles and close calls.

Jimmie was more than a little curious about Sergeant Stallard's experiences during D-Day. "Hey Sergeant, was D-Day as bad as I've heard around base?" he asked. "I flew cover missions before and during D-Day making bombing raids on Nazis airfields."

Sergeant Stallard took a deep breath and said, "I guess it was probably worse than anything you've heard: men getting all shot up; hell, saw some get blown up! Absolutely terrible shit! Hell, I'll tell you what, the only thing I know is the day after, I was sitting in a foxhole eating all kinds of Army rations and had new boots on, new clothes, shit that's better than starving to death eating rotten apples! If it wasn't for all the shooting and killing, I'd say it's not that bad!"

Sergeant Stallard grew up as Burchell "Slew" Stallard on an apple orchard atop Coeburn Mountain. The Great Depression had been harsh and hunger was a constant companion. Burchell attended Coeburn High School even though he lived in the Wise High School District. Slew was always quick to say they didn't want "Po Folks from Coeburn Mountain" coming to school with those "High & Mighty" rich coal company and lawyer kids at the County Seat.

The one thing Burchell made clear was that he despised apples while growing up in an apple orchard. He grew up eating them every day, especially when he and his siblings had nothing else to eat, and the kids got stuck with the old, rotten cull apples while Ma and Paw tried to sell the good ones at their apple house along the main road. Slew was a scrawny, hungry kid, making it all the more remarkable that he had grown to be 6-foot-4 during his high school years.

Burchell had a mean streak and excelled in high school football which gave him the opportunity to attend Milligan College, just outside Johnson City, Tennessee.

As the story goes, after Slew graduated high school in the spring, the football coach for Milligan College pulled up to the Stallard Orchard to recruit the young man to play football. Coach found Slew pruning suckers off apple trees, barefoot, wearing overalls with no undershirt and a single strap over his shoulder secured with baler twine. He was a sight to behold, looking like a 6-foot-4-inch scarecrow.

Coach Stacy approached the young man pruning trees, "Are you Burchell Stallard?" knowing full well he was.

Burchell replied, "I am, what of it to you, city slicker?"

Coach said, "Well, I'm the head football coach for the Milligan College Pioneers and I'm here to see if you would be interested in a scholarship to play football for me and attend college."

Burchell, now with great interest, said, "That sounds fine with me, but we have to go down to the apple house where Ma and Paw are selling apples along the highway and talk to them."

Coach responded, "Fine, you can hop in the car with me, and we'll drive down to the apple house."

As they drove, Burchell was impressed with the clothes Coach was wearing, and this was the nicest car he had ever sat in before. Coach even offered him some beef jerky to eat on the short ride.

As they pulled up and Coach set the park brake, Burchell said, "Wait right here, Coach, I'll be right back."

Coach sat there quietly and a little confused as Burchell hopped out of the car and walked up to the front door of the apple house.

Burchell opened the door, bent over slightly, and stuck his head in, yelling with a booming voice, "Ma, Paw, I'm leaving to play football for this coach down at that Milligan College; I'll see ya later!"

Then he closed the door, walked fast-paced to the car almost skipping, opened the door, sat down, and closed it, looking at Coach Stacy he firmly said, "All done, now get me the hell off this apple orchard!"

Coach asked, "What about your parents? Don't I need to see them? What about your stuff and some clothes? Football practice doesn't even start for a couple of months and the college dormitory and cafeteria is closed until then too."

Burchell replied, "I'm 18 and I don't have a damn thing or clothes to take anyway. If you want me to play football, you better take me home with you right now!"

So Burchell stayed with Coach and his wife for the summer. She remarked that she never thought she would be adopting a 6-foot-4 inch 18-year-old "man-child" as their first kid, who was a 160 lb. scarecrow when he got there.

Burchell had just finished up a stellar sophomore football season for Milligan in which they had gone undefeated and won the Burley Bowl. He had also put on some impressive weight, now standing 6-foot-4 inches and weighing 225 pounds, thanks to the college cafeteria, gaining almost 55 pounds since that day Coach found him almost starved to death in that apple orchard.

The week after the Japanese bombed Pearl Harbor, Burchell Stallard walked into the Army recruiting office in Johnson City, Tennessee to enlist and soon became Sergeant Stallard.

After two and a half years of killing Nazis all the way from Normandy Beach to the Rhine River in Germany, and eating as many Army rations as he could get a hold of (heck he even ate German rations if he found them), Sergeant Stallard now weighed 250 pounds of pure Paul Bunyan muscle!

As Jimmie stood there in awe, he thought to himself *If we had a thousand Sergeant Stallards, we could win the damn war without any other help!* Years later in life, when Jimmie first saw a HULK comic book, he picked it up and thought to himself, *Take away the green and put a big ole cigar in his mouth, this is Sergeant Burchell "Slew" Stallard.*

Right then, the curiosity was getting the better of him, so Jimmie asked, "What are you getting shipped home for? Did you get hurt or just mustered out on points?"

The Sergeant smiled, "Awe, I had enough points to muster out months ago, but I reenlisted. Hell, this shit ain't that bad. I'm getting shipped home because my newbie 2nd lieutenant that hadn't been in combat two months filed a report and said I was too damn rough on the fucking Nazi prisoners we've been transporting! Can you believe that? These Nazi SS and Gestapo soldiers kill women and children… children Jimmie! How in the hell can you be too ROUGH on these Nazi fuckers?!"

Sergeant continued, "Nah, getting sent home will be okay. I'm going to finish up college on my GI Bill, maybe finish my degrees and be a high school football coach or something. Might as well ship back stateside now, the last month or so we ain't killed nothing but young boys and old men German soldiers. Hell, there's no honor in killing boys and old folks even if they are dressed in German uniforms. This shooting match is going to be over shortly! Germany is out of men!"

As much as Jimmie wanted to stay and chat more, he knew he had to catch up to his men on Little Helen.

"Sergeant, it was great to meet you! Maybe if I live through my tour and get home, I'll look you up!"

Sergeant replied, "That sounds wonderful; you better!"

Sergeant Burchell Stallard did exactly what he told Jimmie he would do. He came back home, finished his college degrees, and went onto graduate school with the GI Bill to become a local high school teacher and legendary football coach.

When he inherited the family's apple orchard after both of his parents passed, the first thing he did was pull up every damn apple tree on the place. He planted grass, bought some cows, and became a part-time gentleman cattleman. No more rotten apples in his life!

A whole army of "Superior Race" Nazis never scared Sergeant Burchell Stallard, his only fear was having to eat rotten apples again. Damn, he was a Nazi fighting machine!

The Art of the Haggle

In the mountains, the art of the haggle is as natural as the flow of the Clinch River. It's a skill passed down from generation to generation, honed and perfected by the Greatest Generation. Unlike the city slickers and their "Art of the Deal," haggling is not just about arguing over price, it's a friendly, intimate interaction. Outsiders might perceive the theatrics of haggling as confrontational, but refusing to haggle could be seen as unfriendly and uppity.

Haggling is not just about getting a good price; it's about feeling like you're getting a little something extra out of the deal. In farming, for example, deals worth thousands of dollars for equipment like tractors have been closed over a simple offer and acceptance of a ten-dollar John Deere hat or something similar. Farmers and country folk wear their "Haggle Prizes" with pride, the symbol of a successful negotiation.

But haggling is not just a mountain tradition, it's a way of life in the country that embodies the spirit of hard work, respect, and community. It's a reminder that a fair deal is not just about the price, but the relationship between buyer and seller.

My "haggle dance" with Coach Burchell "Slew" Stallard had been a long-standing tradition. It was a dance we both knew well and enjoyed. Our latest performance had begun a few weeks before when Slew had dropped by our farm store to inquire about the price of fertilizer per ton.

We exchanged some pleasantries and caught up on family news before the dance began in earnest. I gave him our listed price, fully aware that it would be too high for his liking no matter the price. And, of course, he didn't disappoint. He launched into a theatrical monologue about the high cost of farming and his fixed retirement income, complete with stories about the first commercial fertilizers he'd ever bought after the war.

But I was ready for him. I countered his arguments with my own, reminding him of the high freight costs of getting fertilizer to Big Stone Gap nowadays. Then I offered a discount for buying more than one ton. Slew was still not satisfied and suggested he needed to think it over and would call me back. As he left, slapping me on the back and grinning, he declared, "You're a good boy, need to work on your thinking about that fertilizer price tho!" And with that, our "haggle dance" continued.

In the art of the haggle, it's not uncommon for negotiations to stretch out over weeks. Such was the case with Coach Slew Stallard and his attempt to secure the best price on fertilizer for his hay fields. Each call ended with the same phrase, "I'll think it over and call you back."

But finally, a chance presented itself. A local coal company needed a delivery of grass seed and straw from the farm for which they were paying handsomely and the route ran right by Coach Stallard's farm on Coeburn Mountain. I knew I could make that delivery to the reclamation site and still have plenty of room for Coach's fertilizer on the trailer to deliver it on the way back.

When Coach called, I knew it was time to act. His last offer was still too low, but I had a card up my sleeve, "How about we agree on my last price per ton of fertilizer, Coach, and I'll throw in FREE delivery? I'll come up and put it right in your barn this Friday. You can finish telling me your stories about coaching in the legendary Bear Bryant Football Camps down at the University of Alabama."

Coach was thrilled, "NOW you're thinking right, Sonny! I'll see ya Friday!" And just before he hung up, I could hear him hollering to his wife Illo, "Hey Honey, the Old Coach did good. I got Ole Johnny Boy to throw in FREE delivery!" The phone clicked off and the deal was done.

A month had passed when Coach Stallard gave me a call at the farm. The conversation started with an apology, much to my confusion.

"Why are you apologizing, Coach?" I asked.

"I need to apologize for giving you a hard time about your fertilizer prices," said Coach. "Guess what I'm looking at right now?"

"I have no idea," I replied back. "And you don't need to apologize to me. We made a fair deal."

Coach sighed, "I'm looking at a veterinarian bill for this old mutt cat I got that's over $400 dollars! Four hundred dollars, Son! I must be losing my mind to pay that much on an old mutt cat that just showed up here one day!"

I tried to console him. "That's a lot of money, but you like that cat. I bet if you're in your recliner right now, that cat is in your lap as we speak!" I chuckled a little.

Coach laughed too. "You're right, Son. It's in my lap right now. Damn, it better be in my lap. I just spent $400 dollars on it! I must be losing my mind. If I keep doing foolish things like this, we'll go bankrupt and end up on the poor farm! Next time I do something this foolish, you just bring up that cattle trailer of yours and load me up in the back and take me off to the nut house! You'll have to haul me off because, at this rate, I won't be able to pay for an ambulance ride!"

Later that year, Coach Burchell "Slew" Stallard passed away. I was very honored to be a pallbearer at his funeral! Even in the afterlife, the Old Coach haggled me into doing a little "Extra!"

After Coach died, his widow Illo Stallard donated the money to build the new baseball field at UVA's College at Wise. It's located just right down the road from Coach's farm (the old apple orchard). Stallard Field held its first game on February 20, 2004 with Uva-Wise winning over Bluefield College 7-3. The infield is meticulously manicured and soft with smooth bluegrass in the outfield.

Coach Burchell "Slew" Stallard

Stallard Field

THIRTY-FOUR
Lucky Bastard Club

Jimmie couldn't understand what was happening to him. As Little Helen approached the landing strip, he was suddenly hit with a panic attack. He considered asking Bob to take over, but his pride held him back. *What's wrong with me*? Jimmie wondered.

It had been only six hours ago when the crew of Little Helen was on their last bombing mission, dropping bombs on Hitler himself on March 15th, 1945. The last few missions had targeted Berlin and there was hardly any anti-aircraft resistance. Even the once-feared Nazi Luftwaffe was scarce, due to a lack of pilots and planes. When they did manage to get planes in the air, the P-51 Mustangs, the new American fighter planes, made quick work of them.

As the P-51 Mustangs arrived at Bury St Edmunds in the late summer and fall of 1944, everything changed for the 8th Air Force Bombers. They were no longer sitting ducks waiting for German Messerschmitt 109s to swoop in for the kill. With the Mustangs as their escort, they could fly all the way to Berlin and beyond with confidence.

But this improved reality presented a new challenge for Marty, the bombardier on board the Little Helen. With so much of Germany already in ruins, he struggled to find targets that were still standing. Despite the bomber's advanced Norden bombsight, accurate targeting was useless if there was nothing left to target. The device used gyroscopes to stabilize the sight while the operator entered altitude, airspeed, and wind speed data to calculate the correct release point for the bombs. But with the devastation of war all over the ground, even the most advanced technology couldn't guarantee finding a target that day.

Finally, Marty shouted out, "Bombs away!" and the aircraft lurched up as the bombs fell out of the belly of the plane.

Jimmie came over the intercom, "Let's go home for good this time fellas!" As he turned starboard, they could hear all the other squadrons of the 94 Bomber Group over the radio yelling one after another, "Bombs away!" Bob started contacting all the squadron leaders for a status update. Today was a good day, no lost planes, no casualties, and no injuries were reported.

As the crew was jubilant and all over the intercom talking about the first thing they were going to do when they got stateside, Jimmie reminded everyone that they weren't back to base yet. "Let's not 'Screw the Pooch' this late in the game!" he warned.

But right then, Jimmie had a personal problem and was thinking, *Hell, I'm going to be the one to Screw the Pooch!* As many times as he had landed Little Helen and the countless times, he had landed other planes, he felt nerves like his first solo flight, having to think about every move he made. Finally, he said to himself, *Screw it!* and nosed the bomber down as the plane's wheels hit the tarmac hard with a few small bounces down the runway.

Tex came over the intercom, "What the hell, Capt'! That was more than a little rough! That was the most excitement we've had in weeks!" all the while laughing.

Jimmie gathered his wits and came back with, "Shit, Tex, I caught a bad cross wind at the last second, 'bout took us out!"

The whole crew, almost in unison, responded, "Sure, Capt'!" while laughing loudly at his expense.

It was a fateful night in '43 when the Lucky Bastard Club first took shape, born from the smoke and stories of B-17 bomber crews huddled around a makeshift table in the Bury St Edmunds' canteen. Their faces spoke of war's weariness, but their eyes danced with the knowledge of the odds they'd beaten. As they swapped tales and toasted their glasses, the weight of their shared experiences drew 'em in like a moth to a flame.

Jimmy "Rascal" O'Shea, a charismatic pilot, rallied the founding members, recognizing the need for a joint where survivors could find comfort and kinship, celebrating victories and mourning the fallen before shipping back home. And so, the *Lucky Bastard Club* was conceived.

With Eddie "Wrench" Turner, a mechanic who could turn a wrench like nobody's business, they turned a forgotten nook of the airbase into the club's first digs. Word spread like wildfire among bomber crews and the joint became a symbol of hope and grit.

A tradition was set: when a crew member wrapped up their required combat missions, Rascal himself would welcome 'em into the fold. Handing over a certificate with a devilish, grinning cartoon and the words "Lucky Bastard," their exclusive membership was sealed.

Over the years, the club grew, its walls filling up with photos of lost comrades, frayed flags, and relics of battles hard-won. The Lucky Bastard Club stood as a living testament to the courage and perseverance of the B-17 crews who braved the European skies to secure freedom for the many.

For these flyboys, joining the Lucky Bastard Club was more than just a badge of honor; it was a reminder of life's fragility and the unbreakable bonds forged in the heat of war.

That night, the boys from Little Helen weren't just swigging at the Lucky Bastard Club as guests; they were knockin' 'em back as bona fide members. Rascal had mustered out stateside late in 1944, so the honor of passin' Jimmie his Lucky Bastard certificate fell to Captain Mitchell Swinney, the fella who had kept Lady Luck flyin' high in the 333rd Bomber Squadron. The crew collected their certificates, each bringing along a personal trinket to grace the club's storied walls.

It was to be the last hurrah for the whole crew of Little Helen, a last drink together, not knowing it'd be the last time they'd be together as a unit. The joint was buzzing with fellas from different squadrons, all hoisting glasses and doing what men do when they are celebrating. As the wee hours rolled in and the crowd thinned, Jimmie found himself shooting the shit with Captain Mitchell Swinney, an "Old Guard" Lucky Bastard himself.

Swinney drawled, "So, Jimmie, what's the plan now that your combat tour is done? Headin' home?"

Jimmie replied, "Been thinkin' that over. My crew's all set to hightail it home soon as their paperwork's squared away. Mitchell, when you're alone, really alone, alone with your thoughts, do you ever think about all the innocent women and children that we've killed over here? People that didn't have nothin' to do with nothin'? I'm scared to death I'll go home and my wife won't recognize me and my innocent baby girl WILL recognize me for what I've done over here."

Swinney looked solemnly into his mug of English ale. After a long, long thought, he finally snapped out of it. "Hell, Jimmie, we gotta quit thinking and start drinking! Tonight is about celebrating you all making it to the Lucky Bastard Club." As he held up his mug.

Jimmie held his mug up and started smiling, "Anyway, Major Collins asked me to stick around, flying some supply and transport gigs around Europe in them shiny new C-47s. Be like driving a bus around town, if you ask me!" he chuckled.

Swinney grinned, "Well, looks like I just found the fella to hand out them Lucky Bastard certificates!" He slapped his knee. "I'm shipping out next week. Been ferryin' brand spankin' new B-17s back stateside the past couple months since my tour ended. From there, they're haulin' 'em off to some airplane boneyard in Arizona. Seems we got more bombers than missions; not much left worth bombing, I reckon." He leaned in, "Between you and me, with what you boys have been telling me 'bout Berlin and the rest of them German cities, this war's just 'bout run its course."

Swinney took a deep breath, "Time for me to head home. Ain't much room for us Old Guard fellas from '43 and '44. I look around and all I see is these 'Guys from '45'." He snorted, "These young pups fly a single mission over Germany and reckon they've seen combat just 'cause they spot a few Nazis Luftwaffe planes and let their guns bark!"

> The Old Guard crews, those battle-hardened vets who had survived 1943 and 44, had a term for the greenhorns who'd come in as replacements: "Guys from '45." It was a nod to the fact that most of these fresh-faced rookies had arrived at the start of 1945.

Jimmie scoffed, "You ain't kidding! I was chewin' the fat with one of them 'Guys from '45' pilots in the mess hall, told him about being' attacked by 300 Nazi Luftwaffe fighters and he gawked at me like I was spinnin' a tall tale!" He shook his head, "Hell, I told him back in '43, a mission with just 60 Nazis fighter planes buzzing around would've been considered a light day!"

As the night wound down, the crew of Little Helen said their farewells, jawin' 'bout gettin' their families together for summer vacations and seeing each other at veterans' reunions. Their words rang true in the moment, but Jimmie couldn't help but wonder if everyone else had that same naggin' thought at the back of their minds, that such things would never come to pass. Veterans' reunions and get-together vacations, well, those were for the 'Guys from '45', not for the likes of the Old Guard fellas who lived through 1943 and 44.

... ay *Man* nnteen hundred and forty five, the ... finger of Fate finds it expedient to trace on the roll of the

LUCKY BASTARD CLUB

The Name of

Captain Jimmie G. Galloway
Pilot on "Little Helen"

Who on this date achieved the remarkable record of having sallied forth, and returned, no fewer than 30 risky times, bearing tons and tons of H.E. Goodwill to the Feuhrer and would-be Feuhrers, thru the courtesy of Eighth Bomber Command, who sponsors these programs in the interest of Government, "of the people, by the people and for the people."

COMMANDING OFFICER

AIR EXECUTIVE

SQUADRON C.O.

Captain Jimmie Galloway

In the cauldron of World War II, over 50,000 Airmen disappeared into the abyss of sacrifice. Among the heaviest casualties, the skies above Nazi Germany bore witness to the staggering toll inflicted upon the brave crews of B-17s and B-24s. With youth in their eyes and hearts aflame with ambition, these valiant souls took flight, their average age barely exceeding 25.

Within the fuselage of the B-17s, a fellowship of warriors embarked on their perilous odyssey. Four officers guided the mighty machine through the tumultuous heavens. Alongside them, six enlisted Airmen manned their posts with unwavering dedication, forming the backbone of this airborne fortress. United by purpose and mission, they forged an unbreakable bond amidst the roar of engines and the chaos of war.

Yet, their path was fraught with danger, their chances of survival a precarious gamble. The whims of fate cast a dark shadow over their hopes, leaving their odds of returning home, weighed down by uncertainty, at less than 50 percent. Each mission undertaken was a high-stakes gamble, where bravery and resilience clashed with the unforgiving winds of fortune.

During World War II, the U.S. Army grappled with the unsettling reality that even the strongest among its soldiers had a breaking point. They discovered that the human spirit could only endure the relentless storm of combat for a finite period. The duration varied, ranging from 60 to 240 days, contingent upon the intensity and frequency of engagement.

This affliction, known by various names in previous conflicts such as "Nostalgia," "Old Sergeant's Disease," or "Shell Shock," had now been aptly labeled "Combat Fatigue." Military medicine made significant strides in unraveling the mysteries of this malady, gaining a deeper understanding of its underlying causes.

In bygone eras, the War Department clung to the notion that soldiers suffering from Combat Fatigue harbored pre-existing mental conditions. Prospective recruits underwent psychological evaluations and those deemed vulnerable or displaying signs of mental deficiencies were deemed unfit for service, their potential for breakdown in combat considered to be too great. However, a seminal moment arrived during the arduous Guadalcanal Campaign when the U.S. military confronted a sobering truth. The ability to endure the psychological rigors of combat eluded prediction. This revelation struck with full force in 1943 when over 500 Marines returning from Guadalcanal exhibited symptoms that defied comprehension — tremors, sensitivity to loud noises, and episodes of amnesia. This affliction was christened "Guadalcanal Disorder," leaving an indelible mark on the annals of military medicine.

As the number of American servicemen thrust into the crucible of battle swelled, the toll of psychological casualties climbed ever higher. During the Normandy Campaign, Army psychologists observed a sharp decline in combat effectiveness after 30 days of sustained engagement. Beyond 45 days, troops teetered on the precipice of a near vegetative state, their spirits dimmed, and their resilience all but shattered. Psychiatrist John Appel, who diligently studied Combat Exhaustion cases during the Battle of Monte Cassino and the Anzio Campaign, arrived at a disheartening conclusion, "Practically all men in rifle battalions who are not otherwise disabled ultimately became psychiatric casualties."

Jimmie's mailbox got its fair share of invitations: veteran reunions and VFW meetups. Folks wanted to hear from a real, live member of the Lucky Bastard Club. But as Jimmie would sit there, thumbing through the invites, he'd find himself wrestling with an old, gnawing question. Looking back on all the death and guilt of '43 and '44, he'd wonder, *Do I deserve to be a Lucky Bastard*?

THIRTY-FIVE
Back Home During the War

Jean found herself alone in their new little house with a young daughter, Brenda Helen, after Jimmie went off to war with his brothers. She understood Jimmie's desire to defend their country and protect their family, but she couldn't help thinking that he could have found other ways to contribute to the war effort; after all, his brothers Graham and John had no family to take care of. Jean believed that Jimmie's job at Pet Dairy would have been deemed essential to feeding the fighting G.I.s and the coal miners who produced steel for the tanks and war machines needed in the war effort.

Despite all of this, Jimmie decided to volunteer even though he could have been exempted from the war draft due to his job downtown at Pet Dairy or by signing up as an essential worker with Mr. D. Terpstra at Clinch Haven Farms. Mr. Terpstra owned a large dairy farm and milk processing facility up the road from their little house in Crackers Neck.

Mr. Terpstra had even tried to recruit Jimmie to manage his processing plant just weeks before the bombing of Pearl Harbor, offering a stock option as a deferred benefit because his hourly wage was lower than what he currently earned at Pet Dairy.

But at the end of the day, Jimmie made his decision to serve his country, leaving Jean to tend to their newborn daughter and manage their young family on her own with much help from her Compton family downtown.

Life in Crackers Neck and at Clinch Haven Farms continued despite the ongoing global conflict and so many young men being absent. Mr. Terpstra, the owner of the farm and milk processing facility, had established the farm in 1922 as both a tax write-off and a hobby. His love for farming stemmed from his childhood on a Dutch dairy farm, but he left to pursue an education in math and engineering at Erasmus University Rotterdam.

Terpstra was a brilliant engineer and graduated at the top of his class which landed him a job with a Dutch engineering firm. He worked on projects around the world building dams on the Nile River as well as the preliminary engineering work for the Autobahn Road system in Germany. This was years before Hitler and the Nazis rose to power and the Autobahn project was still just an idea. (Hitler later used slave labor to make it a reality as a military project.)

After his work on the Autobahn, Terpstra was hired by the Stonega Coke and Coal Company in the United States in 1914. He moved to a little farm near Castlewood, Virginia, just outside Abingdon, VA, and his first project was to build an electrical power plant in 1914-1915 to provide power to the Dorchester section of Wise County. After the completion of this job, he moved to Crackers Neck full time as he bought parcels of land and pieced them together to make up the current Clinch Haven Farms. This was all while providing engineering services to Stonega Coke and Coal.

This man, a true mastermind of his craft, had made many savvy financial decisions throughout his long and illustrious engineering career. However, the one mistake that would haunt him for decades to come was accepting a significant portion of his compensation throughout his career in stock options rather than cold hard cash. It all seemed like a stroke of genius at the time, but as fate would have it, that was a decision that would bring him to his knees.

A fateful day in October of 1929, "Black Tuesday," would forever be etched in his memory, as well as the country's. It was the day when the stock market crashed, taking with it the life savings and financial futures of countless Americans. And this man, Mr. Terpstra, with all his brilliance and ingenuity, was not immune to the devastation. His once valuable stock options were now worthless, leaving him with nothing to show for his years of hard work and dedication but what he physically owned at Clinch Haven Farms.

Terpstra, his workers, and his cows somehow survived the worst of the Great Depression. By some measure, he had even excelled during these trying times, expanding the dairy farm into milk processing and even offering store and home delivery of milk products throughout the coal camps of the coalfields.

When World War II broke out, Terpstra and every other business owner in the U.S. were facing challenges and obstacles never seen before in American history. On one hand, you had government officials wanting PRODUCTION, PRODUCTION, PRODUCTION to meet wartime demand. On the other hand, there were labor shortages of young, strong men and local government ration boards that limited the input of raw materials needed by those same businesses to produce their given product.

During World War II, ration stamps were issued by the government to control the distribution of certain goods that were in short supply due to the war effort. These items included food, gasoline, tires, building supplies, and other commodities that were needed for the war effort.

Ration stamps were typically distributed through local offices known as ration boards which were established by the government to oversee the distribution of goods in each area. These boards would assess the needs of the community and determine how much of each item should be distributed, and to whom.

The ration stamps themselves were often printed on small pieces of paper or cardboard with a series of letters or numbers that indicated the specific item and the amount that could be purchased. For example, a ration stamp for sugar might be labeled "Stamp No. 10," and would allow the holder to purchase one pound of sugar.

Ration stamps were distributed to individuals, families, and businesses such as Clinch Haven Farms based on their needs and circumstances. For example, families with young children or special medical needs might receive more stamps for certain medical items than others.

Ration stamps were issued by the government as part of the war effort in order to ensure that critical resources were distributed fairly and efficiently. They played an important role in conserving resources and supporting the war effort and are still remembered today as a symbol of the sacrifices made by Americans during World War II.

By the fall of 1944, Clinch Haven's milking herd of cows had outgrown its loafing barn, and a larger one was needed before winter set in. Terpstra, being the engineer, had already drawn up the plans and his men had started grading the land for construction. But Bobby Poole, the farm manager, had a grave concern. As the men set the first poles for the new barn, Poole approached Terpstra with a worried look on his face.

"Mr. Terpstra, we've got plenty of timber for the boards, but there ain't no way the ration board gonna give us any stamps for metal roofing for new construction," Poole said, his voice heavy with concern. "What are we gonna do when it's time to put a roof on the barn?"

Terpstra was fully aware that the ration board would not grant any request for metal roofing for new construction during wartime. Such materials were reserved for the production of war machines. "Poole, let me worry about that and keep the men building," he said.

As the new loafing barn construction was ending, the day came when the final nail was hammered into the last rafter. Terpstra arrived in his car shortly after. "We finished all that we can do without metal roofing, what do you want us to do now?" Poole asked.

Terpstra replied without hesitation, "I want you to take the men and pull the existing roofing off of every old barn on the farm and start putting it on the new barn. If you need to, take some off my house if you still need some to finish the job."

When the job was done, Terpstra waited patiently for the ration board manager to arrive early that fall morning. As the manager approached, he couldn't believe his eyes at the sight of the bare-naked old barns. Terpstra explained that he was in dire need of ration stamps to repair the existing structures on his farm, including all the old barns, all within the ration board's rules of roof repair.

The manager just smiled and pulled out his briefcase while laughing to himself, "That must have been one hell of a windstorm to rip off all the metal on these old barns and it all landed on the new barn!"

"I heard you immigrated from Europe, Mr. Terpstra," he said. "But it seems you've learned the Hillbilly Hustle real well. How many metal roofing stamps do you need?"

A few weeks later, the new barn stood tall with its patchwork of old roofing while every old barn on the farm had brand new metal roofing on it. It was an odd sight for everyone driving through Crackers Neck, but one that was a symbol of "Doing whatever it takes to get the job done!" Terpstra was proud of it.

The military draft in America is a tale of the late 19th Century and the 20th Century. It's the story of Uncle Sam calling on every able-bodied young man to serve his country in its time of need.

The first draft in America was during the Civil War, but it was the World Wars that really made the draft a household name. The Selective Service Act of 1917 authorized the draft of young men for service in the First World War. It was a controversial move, but one that was deemed necessary to ensure America's victory.

During World War II, the draft was expanded to include men aged 18 to 45 and it was an important part of the war effort. Many young men were drafted into service, but some were exempted for various reasons, such as medical conditions or essential jobs. The draft continued during the Korean War and the Vietnam War, but it was met with much more resistance. Many people saw it as an unfair burden on the poor and working class who were more likely to be drafted while the wealthy and well-connected could avoid it.

In 1973, the draft was ended and the all-volunteer military was established, but the legacy of the draft lives on and it remains a symbol of America's willingness to call on its citizens to defend its freedom and ideals.

Here are the numbers of men drafted for military service throughout America's history:

1. American Revolution (1775-1783): No official draft, but many colonies had quotas for men to serve in the Continental Army.

2. War of 1812 (1812-1815): No official draft, but many states had quotas for men to serve in the militia.

3. American Civil War (1861-1865): Approximately 2.7 million men drafted.

4. Spanish-American War (1898): Approximately 107,000 men drafted.

5. World War I (1914-1918): Approximately 2.8 million men drafted.

6. World War II (1939-1945): Approximately 10 million men drafted.

7. Korean War (1950-1953): Approximately 1.5 million men drafted.

8. Vietnam War (1955-1975): Approximately 1.8 million men drafted.

During World War II and other wars, several groups were exempted from being drafted into military service in the United States. Here are some examples:

1. Men who were physically or mentally unfit for military service.

2. Men who were already in essential civilian occupations, such as farmers, miners, railroad workers, and certain factory workers.

3. Men who had dependents or were the sole breadwinners in their families.

4. Men who were enrolled in college or other educational programs.

5. Men who were ministers or other religious workers.

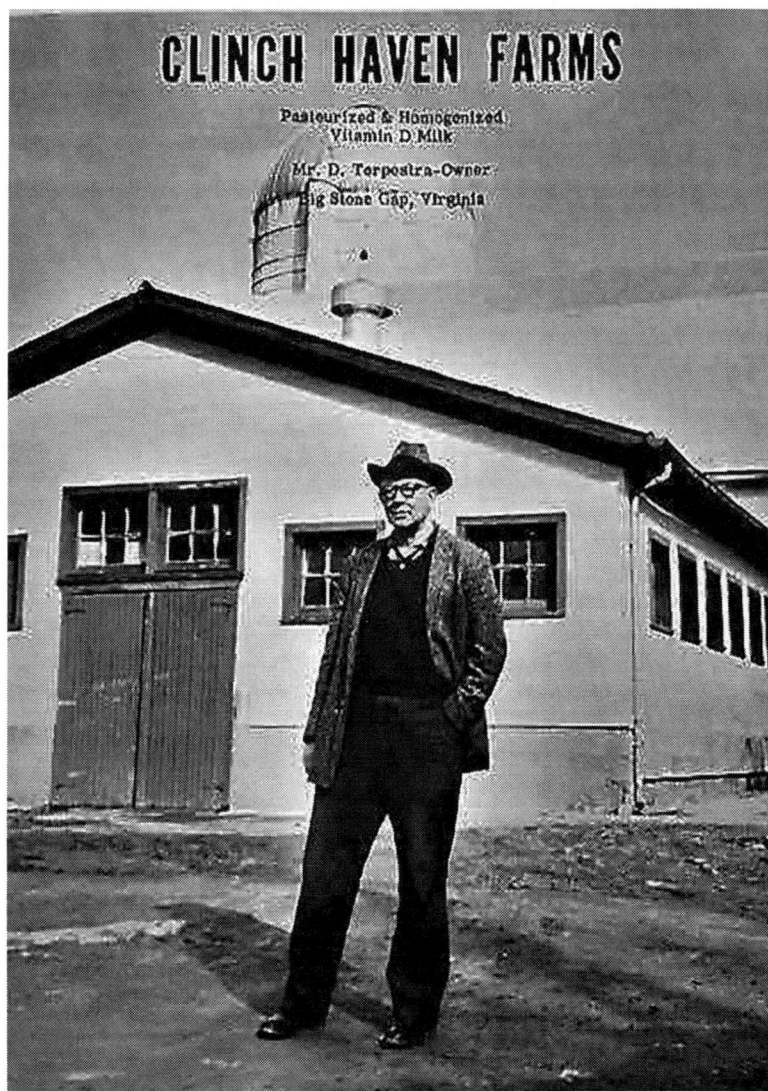

D. Terpstra in front of the Clinch Haven Farms barn

Clinch Haven Farms

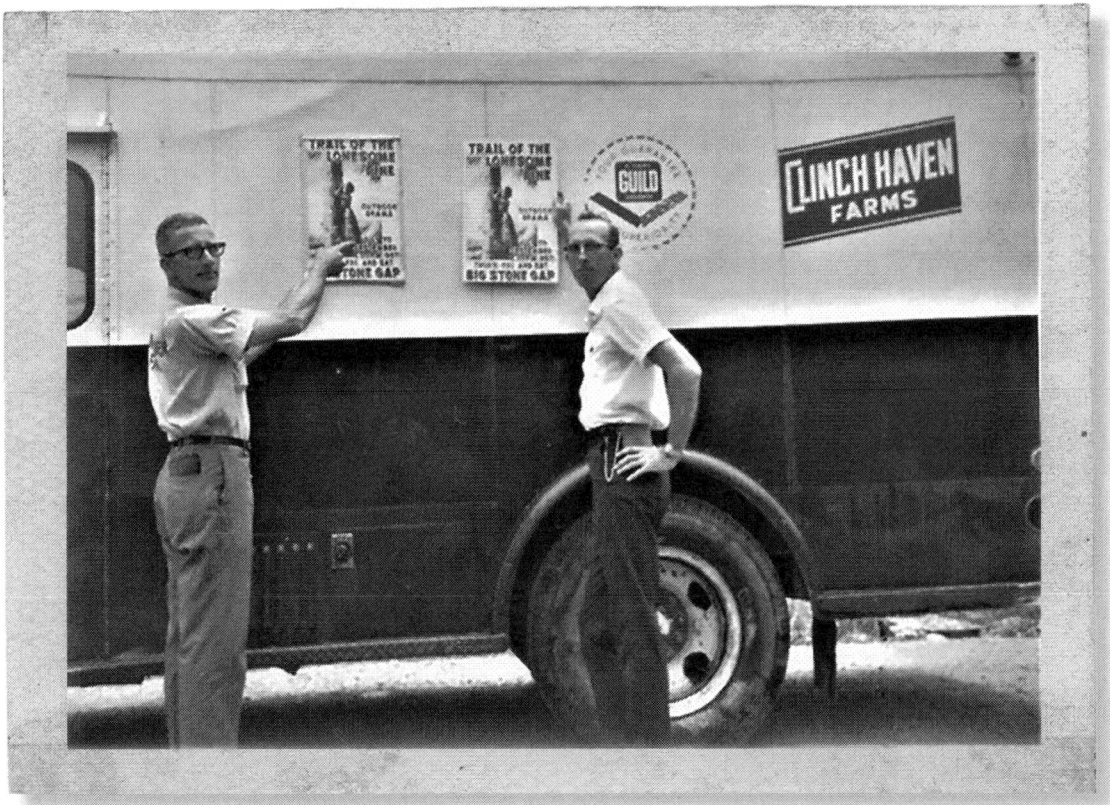

The Clinch Haven Farms Milkmen

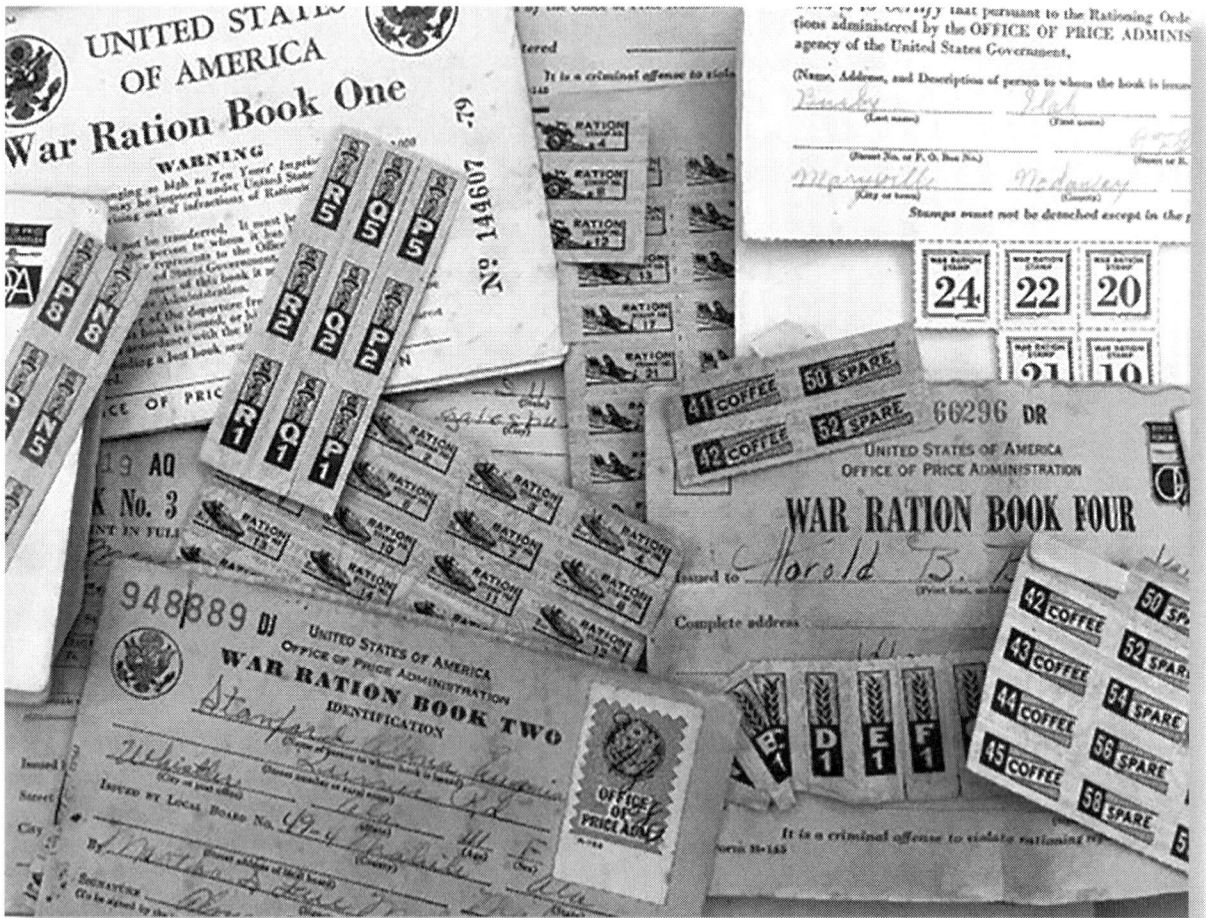

War ration books

THIRTY-SIX
Life Flashing Before Your Eyes?

The United States had over seven million G.I.s stationed overseas during WWII, many of whom had been away from home for several years. As the war ended and the troops began to come home, the focus quickly shifted to reintegrating them into civilian life. One of the biggest challenges for returning G.I.s was finding employment. With millions of veterans returning at once, the job market was incredibly competitive. Some veterans had difficulty transitioning from military life to the civilian workforce and many found themselves struggling to make ends meet.

For those who had not been wounded or disabled during the war, finding a job was seen as a crucial first step toward reclaiming their place in society. Some G.I.s returned to their pre-war careers, but many found that their jobs had been filled by others in their absence. The rapid influx of returning veterans created a surge in unemployment which was felt acutely by those who had given so much to their country.

Despite these challenges, many veterans were able to find work through their own determination and hard work. They leveraged their skills and experiences from the military to secure jobs in fields like construction, manufacturing, and transportation. Some started their own businesses, using their G.I. benefits to help finance their ventures. Overall, the end of the war marked the beginning of a new chapter for millions of G.I.s. While finding a job was a top priority, they also had to readjust to life back home and rebuild relationships with friends and family.

Jimmie was thrilled to finally be home after serving overseas during World War II. However, being a pilot, job opportunities were limited in his hometown of Southwest Virginia. With a young daughter to care for and a baby on the way, he was determined to find a steady source of income.

After some searching, Jimmie landed a job as a crop duster in the Carolinas for an agricultural company. He would fly his small open cockpit bi-plane to work during the week and return home for the weekends to be with his family. The job allowed him to keep his flying skills sharp and provided a steady income for his growing family. Despite the long hours and long-distance commuting, Jimmie was grateful for the job and took pride in using his flying skills for something positive versus his wartime duties.

As Jimmie checked into the foreman's office one morning, he noticed the bright sunshine and crisp air. It was going to be a great day for flying. The foreman greeted him with a nod and handed him the coordinates and instructions for his next job. It was a recently plowed and planted sweet potato field located about 14 miles east of Raleigh, North Carolina. The foreman explained that the field was in dire need of some fungicide spray to help them grow and flourish. Jimmie nodded; he knew how important it was to keep the crops healthy. He made his way to his bi-plane, eager to get up in the air and go to work.

Jimmie was an experienced and skilled pilot, but on this day, he was faced with a new challenge he had never met before. His usual plane was undergoing maintenance, so he was assigned a surplus Boeing Kaydet dual-wing converted crop duster. As he climbed into the cockpit and started the engine, he immediately noticed something off. The engine was running roughly, making a loud and uneven sound. Jimmie quickly shut it down and removed his flying goggles.

"Something doesn't sound right with this one, good buddy!" Jimmie yelled over to the airport mechanic, Joe, who was working on the planes in the hangar.

Joe, looking more than a little bit annoyed, replied, "Nothing wrong with her; she just takes a while to warm up and then she'll smooth right out."

Jimmie wasn't quite convinced, but with a field of sweet potatoes waiting to be sprayed, he decided to give the plane another try. He climbed back into the cockpit, adjusted his flying goggles, and hit the starter button again. The engine started up, rough at first, but after a few minutes, it did exactly what the mechanic said it would do, settling down and running smoothly. Jimmie taxied the plane out to the airstrip and took off. He circled the airfield once, got his compass bearing, and flew off towards the sweet potato field.

As Jimmie located the designated field and made his way over it, he lined the plane up to nose her down for his first pass with the fungicide spray. Jimmie's hand had just pushed the stick forward so the nose went down... and then it happened.

The engine locked up and the propeller froze right in front of him as still as the needle on the fuel gauge. Pulling back on the stick did nothing. The plane was nose down at a 45-degree angle with a full load of fuel and chemical spray. Jimmie had a "dead stick" on his hands!

Frantic seconds passed in slow motion. Jimmie hit the starting button repeatedly as the plane plunged straight down. The only thought that came to his mind was how he had survived 30 combat missions over occupied war territory and been shot at by countless Nazis and now, he was going to die in a sweet potato field in North Carolina. There wasn't even time for feeling fear as Jimmie struggled to regain control of the plane. His heart was pounding in his chest and he knew that he had to act quickly. The ground was getting closer and closer and he could see the rows of sweet potatoes rushing up to meet him.

Boom!

As Jimmie regained consciousness, the pain in his body became more and more evident. He tried to lift himself up, but the hurt was all over his body. He realized that he was lying on his back in the middle of the sweet potato field. He couldn't remember how he got there, just lying in the dirt, but the loud boom still echoed in his head. He struggled to sit up and his eyes slowly adjusted to the bright sunshine. He saw his bi-plane, a crumpled mess, lying about 40 yards away from him. As he started to remember the events that led up to the crash, he realized that he had miraculously survived. He couldn't believe his luck. He started to check his body for injuries and found that he was covered in blood and dirt. He groaned in pain as he tried to move his arms and legs, but he knew that he was lucky to be alive.

As he stood up, Jimmie's adrenaline began to wear off and the pain in his body was becoming more apparent. He groaned and winced, but he was relieved that everything seemed to be working, from his feet to his arms. The crash had left him scraped up and bloodied from head to toe and his flight suit had been torn to shreds, barely hanging on his body. Looking around, Jimmie realized that he had crashed at the edge of the sweet potato field and, somehow, he was almost in the middle. The crop duster was in pieces all around the field, the wings and the propeller scattered like broken toys. He couldn't believe that he had survived such a terrible accident; he couldn't believe anyone could survive!

As Jimmie got up and started to assess his situation, he realized what had just saved his life. The fact that the plane had nose-dived and hit the ground at such a steep angle caused the tail of the plane to whiplash at impact, throwing himself straight out of the cockpit. His body rolled down the freshly plowed and softened dirt, which helped to absorb some of the impact.

In addition, the seat belt on the old replacement plane was so old and worn that it snapped as soon as the plane hit the ground. If Jimmie had been flying his usual newer model plane with a more secure seat belt, the impact would have been much more severe and could have resulted in his head smashing into the plane's instrument panel. In the end, it was a combination of factors that came together to save Jimmie's life. The steep angle of the crash, the softer dirt of the freshly plowed field, and the old and worn seat belt all played a role in protecting Jimmie from more serious harm. Years later, after being baptized as an adult, he realized it might have been Ma's prayers that protected him that day and countless days before.

The pain was excruciating as Jimmie made his way to the dirt road to hitchhike back to the airport. Luckily, he didn't have to wait long before a local farmer named Tom pulled up in his truck, loaded with fresh produce.

"Good God, boy! What the hell happened to you?" Tom exclaimed. "You look like you got caught in a meat grinder down at the barbeque joint!"

Jimmie managed a weak smile and replied, "Just had a bit of a run-in with a crop duster plane. It didn't end well."

Tom raised his eyebrows in surprise. "A crop duster plane, you say? Well, that's a new one! Did you forget to duck or something?" Tom shook his head in disbelief. "Banged up? Boy, you look like you went a few rounds with that boxer, Joe Lewis!"

Jimmie let out a small chuckle, "Something like that. I guess I should stick to flying my usual plane from now on."

Tom laughed, "Yeah, probably a good idea. But hey, at least you've got one hell of a story to tell now. You can tell everyone how you survived a crop duster crash and lived to tell the tale!"

Jimmie slowly slid out of the truck passenger seat, wincing at the pain in his back and all over his body. He gingerly closed the truck door and turned to thank Tom for the ride, "Thanks a lot, Tom. I really appreciate it."

Tom nodded, "No problem, Son. You take care now and make sure you see a doctor about those cuts before they get infected."

Jimmie nodded and started to hobble towards the hangar, his anger starting to replace the shock and pain. He was itching to have a little talk with Joe the mechanic.

As the hangar office door swung open, Jimmie limped in, bloodied, and scraped. He gasped for breath and shouted, "Where the hell is Joe?"

Joe, who was working on a plane engine, looked up at Jimmie in shock. He dropped the wrench in his hand and his face drained of color as he said, "Oh, Shit!" before taking off running for his life.

If Jimmie had been able to run, he would have killed that mechanic that day!

Jimmie screamed at Joe, "It just needs to warm up some and it will smooth right out… *You Son of a Bitch!*"

In the quiet of the hangar barracks, with only the sound of the crickets outside to keep him company, Jimmie lay on his bed and took stock of his life. He had pushed his luck too far, flying planes and cheating death, and he knew it was time to call it quits. He missed his wife and kids terribly and the thought of them waiting for him at home made his heart ache. As the dawn light crept through the windows, he made the decision to quit his job and leave the flying life behind for good.

He strode into the foreman's office with a newfound confidence and asked for his final paycheck. The foreman didn't say much, knowing that Jimmie was a good worker and a better pilot, but he could see the determination in his eyes. The paycheck in hand, Jimmie walked into town and found a payphone to call Jean.

"Jean, it's me. I'm coming home for good; this time on the bus," he said, his voice ringing with a newfound sense of purpose.

And with those words, the chapter on Captain Jimmie's life of flying planes came to a close as he boarded the bus that would take him back to the life and loved ones he had at home.

1940s crop duster

Jean Compton Galloway, Brenda Helen Galloway,
and Jimmie Galloway

THIRTY-SEVEN
Governments are Terrible

———— ∼ ————

Terpstra, a shrewd businessman, knew that Jimmie was the right man for the job. Having flown crop dusters for a couple of years, Jimmie was used to working long hours and being away from home, but with a growing family, he was ready for a change and finally took Terpstra's job offer to manage the dairy processing plant at Clinch Haven Farms. The one thing that brought him joy, about as much as flying, was making ice cream and with the ice cream business booming at Clinch Haven Farms, it was time to upgrade the equipment to meet the growing demand.

In 1954, Terpstra ordered new Lekkerkerker Dairy & Food Processing and Packing machines which were shipped all the way from West Germany. The equipment was rated as some of the best in the industry, but after installation, the men and others hired to install the equipment couldn't get it to work quite right. As soon as they fixed one problem, it seemed another one would arise.

Jimmie was perplexed. As the newly appointed processing plant manager, this was the first major upgrade to the facilities under his watch and he was determined to get the equipment up and running. He spent long hours studying the machinery and experimenting with different approaches, determined to find a solution.

Finally, after all efforts failed, Terpstra decided to call the manufacturer and let them know what was going on. The manager of the plant could hear Terpstra's frustration and declared, "I'm going to send over my best engineer, Hans Smidt, who lives here near our manufacturing plant in West Berlin. He could be over there in about a week." Terpstra agreed to the assistance and informed Jimmie that he had help on the way.

A week later, Jimmie received a Western Union wire at the milk processing plant office stating, "Arrive March 18, will be expected at Big Stone Gap Bus Station around 4 pm." The message was from Hans Smidt, the engineer from West Germany who was sent to help fix the malfunctioning equipment.

As Hans made his way through the lobby, he spotted Jimmie waiting for him near the entrance. Jimmie's rugged appearance and no-nonsense demeanor reminded Hans of the farmers he had grown up around in his hometown of Bielefeld, Germany. He approached Jimmie, introduced himself, and the two men exchanged a firm handshake.

As they made their way to the car, Jimmie asked Hans about his journey and if he needed anything. Hans explained that he was impressed with the bus station's architecture, particularly the glass brick exterior wall, and commented on how much nicer it was than the one he had endured in Knoxville, TN. Jimmie chuckled and explained that Big Stone Gap was a small town, but they took pride in what they had. He offered to take Hans to a local diner for a bite to eat before heading to the processing plant and Hans gratefully accepted.

Jimmie looked at Hans, "How about an American hamburger and a beer for dinner?"

Hans replied, "That sounds wonderful; I just had a small sandwich for dinner and nothing for breakfast."

Jimmie said, "I know just the place! It's a local joint with some of the best hamburgers in the area; it's called Carmine's."

Hans nodded appreciatively, "I look forward to trying it out. I've heard that Americans make the best hamburgers."

As they drove to Carmine's, Jimmie pointed out some of the landmarks in the small town including the local movie theater and the town square. Hans was amazed by the simplicity and charm of the place and he could feel himself relaxing after the long journey.

The streets were lined with small brick buildings, many of them family-owned businesses. The town had a cozy, inviting feel to it and people were out and about, going about their day. The sidewalks were filled with people walking, chatting, and window shopping. Cars were parked along the sides of the road and a few were driving through town. There were no stoplights and the only signs were hand-painted ones that hung over the doorways of the businesses.

The air was fresh and crisp, and the sound of birds singing filled the air. There was a sense of community and pride that radiated from the town and it was clear that the people who lived there cherished their little corner of the world. As they made their way through the downtown area, Jimmie pointed out more of the landmarks, including the local UMWA Union Hall and the town's library. Hans was impressed with its charm and commented on how different all this was from the bustling city of West Berlin.

As they entered the diner, the smell of sizzling burgers and fries filled the air. Carmine's was housed in a two-story brick building in the middle of town with a neon sign that read "Carmine's" in bold red letters. The first floor was occupied by the diner while the second floor was where the owners, Carmine and his wife, Marie, lived with their children.

Inside the diner, the walls were lined with red vinyl booths, and the tables were topped with red and white checkered tablecloths. A jukebox sat in the corner filled with the latest hits from Elvis Presley and Chuck Berry. The aroma of sizzling burgers and fried onions wafted through the air making patrons' mouths water.

Behind the counter, a row of stainless-steel stools welcomed customers to sit and chat with the friendly waitstaff. The menu offered classic diner fare, from hot dogs and milkshakes to burgers and fries. The burgers were thick and juicy, cooked to order, and served on a fresh bun with all the fixings.

Carmine himself was often found at the grill, flipping burgers, and chatting with his regular customers. He took pride in his diner and treated everyone like family, often staying open late into the night to accommodate those who needed a good meal after a long day's work. The atmosphere of Carmine's was cozy and inviting, with the sounds of conversation and the clatter of dishes mixing with the music from the jukebox. It was the kind of place where locals gathered to catch up on the latest news and gossip while savoring a hot meal and a cold drink

The owner, Carmine Murphy, greeted them warmly and pointed to a booth by the window. Hans marveled at the colorful jukebox in the corner and the old-fashioned Coca-Cola signs on the walls. As they perused the menu, Hans noticed that the burgers were described as *100% Angus beef.* "What does that mean?" he asked Jimmie.

"It means that the beef comes from a specific breed of cattle that's known for its high-quality meat," Jimmie explained. "And it's all sourced locally, from the farms around here." Hans nodded appreciatively, impressed by the attention to detail. When the burgers arrived, they were hot and juicy, and the fries were perfectly crisp.

As they sipped on their milkshakes for dessert, Jimmie shared the story of how the ice cream in their milkshakes had come from Clinch Haven Farms. He explained that the milk used in the ice cream came from the dairy cows that they raised on the farm and that they processed the milk at the plant where he worked as the processing plant manager.

Jimmie's eyes lit up as he talked about how he loved making ice cream, experimenting with new flavors, and perfecting the process. Hans could sense Jimmie's passion for his work and admired the dedication and hard work that it took to produce such high-quality ice cream.

Hans took a deep breath and his eyes glimmered with a hint of nostalgia as he reminisced about the days before the war. Jimmie could sense a certain melancholy in his voice and he listened attentively as Hans spoke of his childhood on a small farm near the Austrian border.

As Hans finished his milkshake, Jimmie noticed a sudden change in his demeanor. Hans' face looked sad and Jimmie couldn't help but ask if he had said something wrong.

Hans shook his head and replied, "Oh no, I was just remembering some good days before the war. Before I enlisted..."

Curious, Jimmie asked Hans about his experiences during the war. With a hint of sadness in his voice, Hans revealed that he was a pilot - a Messerschmitt Bf 109 fighter plane pilot, to be exact. He explained that he flew in the Jagdgeschwader or Fighter Wing, the primary fighter unit of the Luftwaffe. Their mission was to engage in air-to-air combat and protect military manufacturing during the war against enemy bombers.

Jimmie shared how he was the 94 Bomber Group Leader in the 8th Air Force flying B-17 Flying Fortresses out of Bury St Edmunds Air Base in England.

Now, this was remarkable for Jimmie, for he hadn't spoken of the war in any detail or length to anyone, not even family, for almost a decade. He wouldn't speak of his wartime experiences again for 30 years.

"Man, we lost a lot of good men. Too many to remember; that's sad. I should be able to remember more names." Jimmie said while staring down at his milkshake.

Hans looked at Jimmie with a newfound respect. He could sense the weight of the war in Jimmie's words and he knew that they had both been through something that would stay with them for the rest of their lives, something no man should have ever experienced.

"I can only imagine what it must have been like," Hans said softly. "The bravery and sacrifice of the men who flew those missions is something that will never be forgotten."

Jimmie nodded in agreement, his eyes flickering with a mix of pride and pain. "So many missions ended with empty bunks in the barracks. Of my graduating class at flight school, only three of us survived… how about you?" he said, raising his eyes to look at Hans.

Hans, now in deep thought, "I am the only survivor of my flight school class. The last year of the war really took us out. 'Fliege, bis du stirbst,' which means 'Fly until you die' in English, was our motto. On my last mission, they only loaded the plane with 72 rounds of ammunition in my left gun and 100 rounds in the right because we didn't have any more left. Normally, I would have 1000 rounds total. My commander told me to make them count before I took off. We were out of aircraft fuel, so my plane was running on what we called 'potato fuel,' which cut the horsepower in half; it was hard to even get my fighter to take off. I survived the mission, but when I landed, my front tire on the landing gear had been patched so many times, it exploded on contact with the ground and my plane went flipping over and over."

Hans took a deep breath, "I woke up from my coma in an American POW hospital about three weeks after crashing. Thank God you American Yanks captured us first; you all gave me medical attention. The Russians would have given me a bullet to the head!"

"It's something that I'll never forget," Hans said. "But we did what we had to do, what we were told to do by our governments. And in the end, do you think we made any difference? All our friends dying, did it make a difference?"

Jimmie pondered, "The only thing I know is, here are two men that both grew up on small farms out in the country, who love flying planes and who both answered the call to arms by their governments. For all we know, ten years ago we could have been shooting at each other for no other reasons than our governments told us to!"

Hans said, "Governments are terrible; mine was the worst! Our family, countrymen and comrades paid the price!"

Both men sat there for a while…

In the silence that followed, the weight of their experiences seemed to hang heavy in the air. Both had lost so much… and for what? The whims of politicians and the machinations of governments and evil tyrants like Hitler? It was a bitter pill to swallow, but it was the truth.

Jimmie finally broke the silence, "I suppose all we can do now is try to live the best lives we can. Honor the memory of those we lost and, maybe, just maybe, make a small difference in the world in our own way."

Hans nodded in agreement, raised his milkshake, and toasted Jimmie's, "To my new friend, Jimmie Galloway!"

Jimmie in the 1950's

*A Messerschmitt Bf 109, the plane
Hans Smidt would have flown*

Bus Terminal- Big Stone Gap, Va.

Carmine's

THIRTEY-EIGHT
All Politics is Local

———————~———————

The phrase "all politics is local" echoed through the halls of United States politics, a timeless sentiment that had its roots dating back to 1932. But for Jimmie, following in the footsteps of his Paw, the significance of this phrase went far beyond mere rhetoric. It was a guiding principle that fueled his ambition to make a difference in his community, to roll up his sleeves and dive headfirst into the world of local politics.

In 1972, armed with determination and a large loan from Farm Credit down in Gate City, Jimmie embarked on a new chapter of his life. Fresh off his acquisition of Clinch Haven Farms and armed with his hard-earned stock options with D. Terpstra, he set his sights on the Wise County Board of Supervisors. This was his chance to turn his passion for community improvement and helping people into tangible action.

The coal industry in the 1970s was caught in a storm of change, where the winds of environmental consciousness and labor rights blew with equal force. The Clean Air Act of 1970 brought a fresh gust of regulations to combat industrial pollution and protect the air we breathe. While the intention was noble, the coal industry found itself in the crosshairs of stricter guidelines and heightened scrutiny.

Coal, with its pollution, became a target for environmental concerns. It was a necessary evil, a fuel that powered the nation but also cast a shadow of pollution. Compliance with the Clean Air Act meant electric power companies had to invest in expensive technologies to reduce emissions and meet the new standards.

As the winds of change blew through the coal industry, the labor landscape experienced its own transformation. New laws emerged, designed to protect the rights and well-being of coal miners who toiled deep in the earth's belly. Hazardous working conditions, inadequate compensation, and limited healthcare were addressed head-on. The Federal Coal Mine Health and Safety Act of 1969 brought hope and much-needed protection to those who risked their lives below the surface.

But with every stride towards progress, new burdens emerged. Compliance with the labor laws required coal companies to dig deeper into their pockets, investing in equipment, training, and infrastructure to ensure the safety of their workers. The weight of these expenses burdened smaller players who struggled to keep their heads above water. Mergers and closures became the grim reality for some, casualties of an industry in flux.

The 1970s marked a defining period for the coal industry as it grappled with the demands of environmental regulations and evolving labor standards. It was a time of adaptation and innovation, of navigating treacherous waters. Those who embraced the changing tides and invested in cleaner technologies, while also improving working conditions, found themselves better positioned to weather the storm.

With the birth of stricter environmental regulations, an unexpected twist of fate awaited the coal industry in the hollers of Southwest Virginia and the rolling hills of Eastern Kentucky. As the country sought cleaner emissions, the demand for coal with lower sulfur content skyrocketed and it was these very regions that held the key to such "cleaner" coal deposits. Companies like Westmoreland Coal Company, once known as Stonega Coal and Coke, found themselves swept up in a tidal wave of sales and surging revenues.

Flush with success, Westmoreland embarked on a magnificent spending spree, transforming the mining landscape with state-of-the-art equipment and cutting-edge technology. The pride of their arsenal was the mighty Long-Wall Miners, behemoth machines that seemed to devour the earth itself. These colossal contraptions boasted fearsome efficiency, able to extract coal with unprecedented speed and precision. They were the future of mining, a testament to the relentless march of progress.

With their newly acquired arsenal, Westmoreland's mines became a scene of remarkable activity. The rhythmic hum of machinery filled the air as the Long-Wall Miners gnawed their way through the rich Bullitt Mine coal seams, leaving behind a trail of loaded coal trains in their wake.

The arrival of the Chinese delegation to the United Nations in Appalachia and Big Stone Gap, Virginia, was a momentous occasion in 1975. The seeds of this extraordinary visit were sown during President Richard Nixon's historic trade trip to China which paved the way for improved government relations and cultural exchange between the two nations. Eager to reciprocate the hospitality, the Chinese were invited to tour various industries in the United States, with a particular interest in energy and agriculture. Westmoreland's Long-Wall Miner was the main attraction of the trip followed by their agricultural stop.

Among the farming stops on their ambitious itinerary was Jimmie Galloway's very own Clinch Haven Farms, a shining example of modern agricultural operations of the day. Jimmie, a member of the Board of Supervisors, took great pride in showcasing the advancements of his dairy farm to the esteemed delegation. The farm boasted modern farming practices and a state-of-the-art milking parlor, a testament to the farm's commitment to embracing cutting-edge technology.

With its modern facilities and efficient milking process, Clinch Haven Farms was a marvel to behold. The delegation wondered at the productivity achieved with a herd of 100 to 120 cows, all thanks to Terpstra's exceptional milking parlor design. In fact, the reputation of the milking parlor had spread far and wide, catching the attention of the agricultural experts at Virginia Tech. They were so impressed that they decided to replicate the exact design on their own university dairy farm in Blacksburg.

As the Chinese ambassador concluded the tour, he couldn't help but express his amazement at the level of efficiency achieved at Clinch Haven Farms. Comparing it to the dairy farms in China, he marveled at how a farm of similar size could produce the same amount of milk with only 3 or 4 full-time employees, whereas in China, it would require over a hundred workers. The stark contrast highlighted the transformative impact of modern technology and streamlined processes.

As the sun began its descent, casting a golden hue over Jimmie's front porch, he sat there with his young grandson, John William, by his side. The porch had witnessed countless stories, many from Jimmie and many more from visiting veterans.

Looking at the lightning bugs dotting the evening sky, Jimmie reflected on the incredible journey his life had taken. "You know, John William," he began, a hint of pride in his voice, "I never would've imagined that I'd live through the war and have tales to tell about meeting Winston Churchill in person and now, I can add meeting a Chinese ambassador to that list. Not too bad for a Crackers Neck boy like me."

Jimmie (far right in the hat) conducting the tour of

Clinch Haven Farms with the Chinese ambassadors
Jimmie (far left) walking with the ambassadors and John William Peace II
(author of this book) tagging along at seven years old (far right)

In the year 2003, I made the decision to follow in my Papaw's footsteps and run for the same seat on the Wise County Board of Supervisors that he had held back in the 1970s. It was an endeavor fueled by both a sense of community and a desire to continue the legacy of public service that ran deep in our family's history.

As I delved into the trove of campaign materials left behind by Papaw, a peculiar realization dawned upon me. Amidst the fervor of political slogans, there was a notable absence of any mention of his extraordinary wartime exploits or the numerous medals of honor he had earned during World War II. No trace of the Distinguished Flying Cross, no inkling of the decorated valor that had coursed through his veins in the face of danger.

Puzzled, I mustered the courage to approach Papaw and pose the question that had been gnawing at my curiosity. Why had he chosen not to emphasize his heroic wartime achievements in his political campaigns? In a modern era where politicians flaunted their accolades at every turn, it seemed inconceivable that he would keep such a trove of honors hidden away from the public.

With a hint of wisdom twinkling in his eyes, Papaw offered a simple yet profound response that resonated deep within me. "Son," he began, his voice brimming with quiet confidence, "a real man doesn't need to boast about doing his job. And doing your job, well, that's what a real man does. Fighting in WWII was our duty and our job" His words hung in the air, carrying the weight of integrity and humility.

THIRTY-NINE
The Power of Prayer

———————~———————

O n a mundane Thursday in December of 1985, I found myself craving a break. So, I checked myself out of school and headed over to the farm to see what was stirring. As I pulled up to the milking parlor, Papaw came bounding down the steps, hollering, "Boy, I'm glad to see you. Give me a ride over to your Little Granny's so I can fetch back the John Deere and the silage wagon we left over there while chopping corn behind her house."

He clambered into my maroon color 1979 Jeep CJ and we set off down Clinch Haven Road, taking a left onto East Stone Gap Road to make our way to Little Granny's. Upon arrival, Papaw shouted through the door, "Ma, we're just here to grab the tractor and wagon."

Little Granny emerged from the kitchen, hollering back, "Y'all come grab something to eat before you go." We both knew that you never left her house hungry and, besides, we hadn't had lunch yet. As we bellied up to the kitchen table, she promptly heated up some salt-cured ham that she had already prepared and began to gather bread and sides.

"Granny, I can't stick around too long. I gotta check back into school before the day's out so I can make it to football practice this afternoon. We got our state championship game coming up this Saturday. Big game!" I informed her.

Granny responded, "I was just reading about that in The Post (local newspaper). I plan on praying tonight that y'all win that game."

Papaw couldn't resist a sly chuckle, "Now, Ma! You know the Lord's got more pressing concerns than a high school football game down at Bullitt Park this Saturday."

Granny sternly retorted. "Well, bless your heart, haven't you just outgrown your upbringing?!" she said as she dropped the pan on the hot plate with the sizzling meat in the center of the kitchen table. "For all we know, someone from the other team might be praying for them to win instead of us. I might not be able to play football, but I can sure do my part!" She then strolled out of the kitchen, quoting scripture along the way. "Bring ALL your worries and concerns to the Lord in prayer!" she recited as she marched down the hallway to pray in her bedroom.

I glanced over at Papaw and jested, "Looks like you just stepped in it!" as I picked up a slice of salt-cured ham to place on my bread.

Papaw simply replied, "Son, I knew it was coming the second the words left my lips. I just couldn't rope them back in. Pass me that bread. Might as well make myself a sandwich."

Do I believe in the power of prayer? Well, let me tell you what I do know. During that state championship game, I was blessed enough to be part of one of the final plays of the game that prevented our opponent from scoring a two-point conversion and we clinched the victory, 28 to 27.

Years later, I attended Virginia Tech on an academic scholarship for economics and statistics. In one of my statistics classes, I wrote a term paper analyzing the statistical improbability of my Papaw and his two brothers all surviving their perilous combat tours in World War II without any injuries or fatalities. I cross-referenced their personal service records against government statistics on the likelihood of death and injury during their respective tours. The analysis revealed that it was statistically impossible for all three brothers to remain unscathed. But they were!

FOURTY

We Could Have Won the War by Ourselves!

On January 17, 1991, Operation Desert Storm, or the Gulf War as it's more commonly known, officially began. For weeks, Coalition Forces had been massing on the borders of Kuwait and Iraq in preparation for a full-scale military invasion. The operation was sparked by Iraq's invasion and occupation of Kuwait in August of 1990.

The fighting was intense and lasted for over a month with Coalition Forces launching a massive air campaign against Iraqi military targets before beginning a ground invasion on February 24, 1991. The ground assault was swift and decisive, with Coalition Forces quickly driving Iraqi troops out of Kuwait.

On February 28, 1991, a ceasefire was declared, officially bringing an end to the Gulf War.

As far as wars that the United States had been involved in, this one was over and done within a blink of an eye compared to so many others in our history.

But back in 1991, Operation Desert Storm was different from any other war before. It was the first war that was being watched by Americans on TV with live CNN updates. Back in the 1960s and 1970s, there was TV reporting from Vietnam, but all that footage was taped and viewed later, after editing. In the 90s, people were glued to their screens trying to get a glimpse of what was happening in the Middle East.

The sound of the bombs exploding echoed throughout the living rooms of America. Families huddled together, trying to make sense of the images they were seeing on their screens. It was like nothing they had ever seen before.

The reporters on the ground were the eyes and ears of America, bringing the war to life in a way that had never been done before. They were in the midst of the action and Americans felt like they were right there with them. For the first time, people could watch a war unfold in real-time from the comfort of their own homes. It was a surreal experience that would forever change the way we view war and the media.

I remember visiting my Papaw one weekend home from college in early February 1991 and we sat in his living room, glued to the television set. That day, General Colin Powell and General Norman Schwarzkopf, Jr appeared on CNN, showing live footage of American bombers dropping "smart bombs" or bunker busters from tens of thousands of feet in the air. We watched in awe as these bombs penetrated small air vents and obliterated seemingly "bomb-proof" bunkers. It was a moment that left an indelible impression on me and made me realize the power and precision of American military technology.

The black and white live video on the TV screen depicted the smart bomb being released and tracked all the way down through impact and explosion. And just like that, my 72-year-old grandfather leaped up from his Lazy Boy recliner in excitement, as though he'd just watched his favorite football team score the winning touchdown.

Papaw practically yelled, "Hot damn Son, if we had some of these smart bombs back in WWII, me and the boys could have won the war by ourselves! We could have taken out that bastard Hitler with one bomb!"

It was as if Papaw had just discovered the eighth wonder of the world. And the way he was carrying on, one might have thought that the war was being fought right there in his living room. Sitting back down, he said, "Being able to see that live and to see what they can do now, that's some kind of technology, Son!"

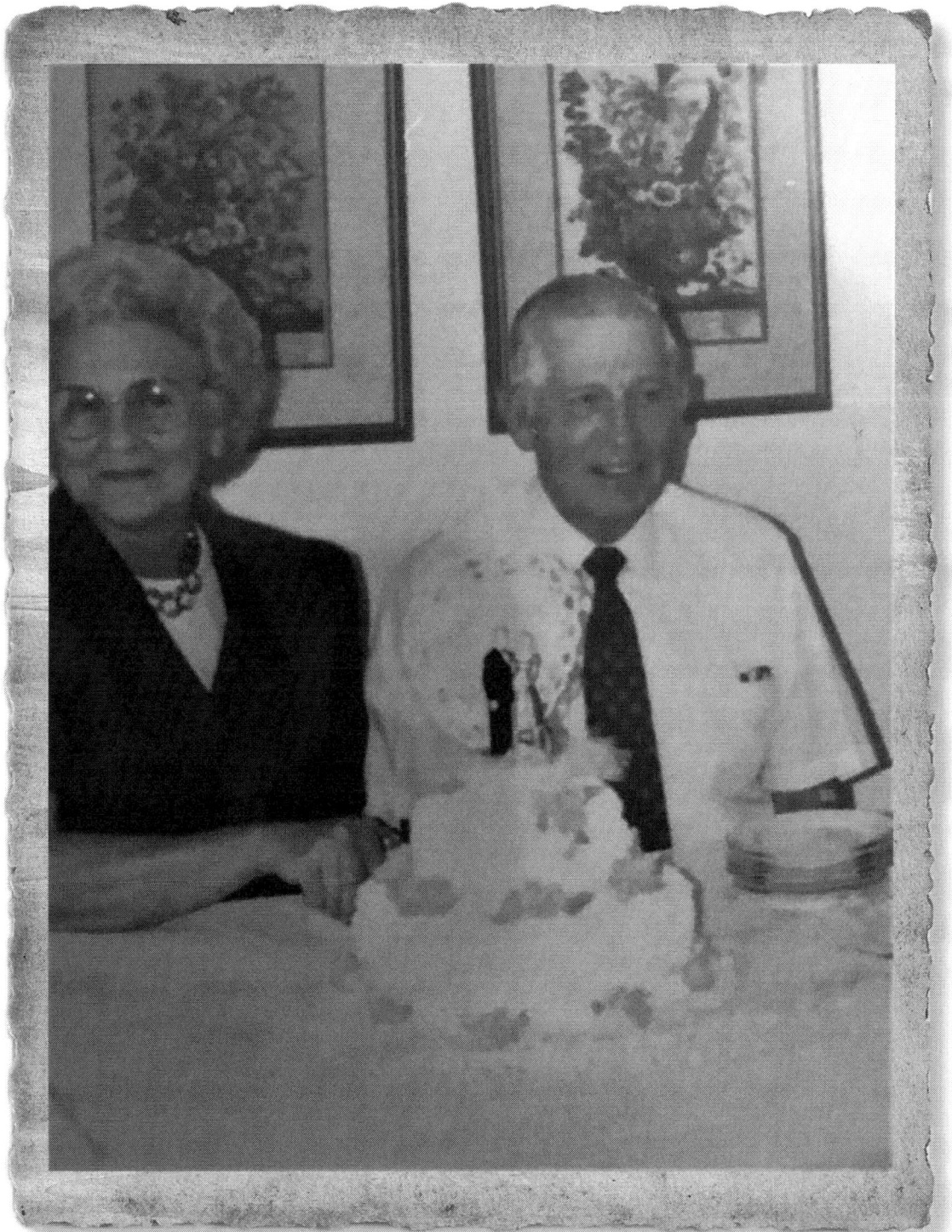

Jimmie and Jean's 50th Wedding Anniversary

Jimmie in the late 1970s

FORTY-TWO

WWII Veterans Who Visited Clinch Haven

———————~———————

The visits from war veterans to Clinch Haven were a regular reminder of the brutality of war that Papaw had himself experienced. While I yearned for more stories from these men about their time in WWII, Papaw would often caution me that "war broke many a good man" and they were hesitant to share many details. You could sense the melancholy that engulfed them if they spoke too much about the war. They would never cross certain lines in their stories and you knew better than to push.

Ed Dickenson

One of the regular visitors was Ed Dickenson from Big Stone Gap. He would come and sit with Papaw for hours between milkings and then, later, when we started the supply store on the farm. Ed was a lanky man with a constant chew of tobacco and a fondness for whiskey which probably accounted for his thin frame. He was always amiable and seemed grateful for the attention.

Ed's personal war story was harsh, to say the least. He was a POW in Germany after being captured in North Africa in late 1942. During the North African Campaign, almost 6,500 American G.I.s were seized and sent throughout

Germany to POW camps. As Ed would tell my Papaw, life as a POW in the early years was better than towards the end, but he was quick to point out that things were harsh and never like what was depicted in the TV show Hogan's Heroes.

In the early years of the war, Germany was winning and life as a POW was brutal, but tolerable. The prisoners were given limited amounts of food, but at least they were fed. Red Cross packages would also be distributed to the G.I.s after the German guards confiscated the candy bars and cigarettes. According to Ed, American cigarettes were highly valued by German soldiers and were even used as currency. He would laugh as he told us that if a prisoner could get their hands on a fair number of American cigarettes, they could have bought their way back to New York City.

As the war dragged on and Germany's fortunes began to dwindle, life for the prisoners only got worse. Ed recounted how hunger and disease ravaged the camps with many POWs falling ill and dying. But it wasn't just the physical conditions that were brutal - the emotional toll was just as harsh. When German guards received news of a setback on the battlefield or the death of a family member, they would take out their frustration and anger on the POWs. It was a constant cycle of fear, uncertainty, and brutality.

It was clear to Papaw and me that Ed's time as a POW had left a lasting impact on him, as it did on so many others who had experienced the horrors of war firsthand. The scars of their experiences would never fully heal and they would carry the weight of those memories with them for the rest of their lives.

Every time Ed visited Papaw at Clinch Haven, he would share a war POW story with him. And without fail, he would end it the same way, looking at me and asking, "Son, did I ever tell you about how your Papaw here almost killed me when one of his bombs hit our POW camp?" The two of them would then share a big laugh, knowing that there was no way of knowing which B-17 bomber had dropped that bomb.

Still, no matter how bleak the stories got, Ed and Papaw always managed to find a way to joke and laugh before parting and their ongoing joke about the bomb was a testament to their unbreakable bond.

"Ed, I was aiming at the front gate trying to liberate you!" Papaw would reply, playing along with their personal joke.

Carlisle Clark

The first time I laid eyes on Carlisle Clark was when I was but a ten-year-old boy, eager to purchase a little rabbit beagle dog to start my hunting escapades. Mr. Clark, who ran the family gas station and local grocery known as Clark's Grocery along Highway 23 in the Jasper section of Lee County, was our go-to guy for this.

We parked our Jeep truck to the side of the gas station so as not to obstruct any paying customers from getting good parking spaces at the store. Papaw waved at Carlisle, who was finishing up pumping gas for a customer back in the days when gas stations provided full service.

As he made his way over to us, Carlisle exclaimed, "Jim Galloway, how are you doing? I haven't seen you in a month of moons!"

Papaw replied, "You know how it is, Carlisle. Dairy farming is not just a job, it's a lifelong commitment… like marriage. How's the family? This here is my grandson, John, and he's in the market for a beagle puppy. I heard through the grapevine that you might have some for sale."

Carlisle grinned and said, "Well, I might just be able to help you out. Come on, let's take a look."

Papaw gave me a pat on the back, "This is your deal, John. See if Mr. Clark has what you're looking for and work out a fair agreement. I'm going inside to grab some Prince Edward cigars. Carlisle, is your wife running the register?"

"She sure is. We'll take care of it, Jim." So, Mr. Clark and I headed over to his kennels and I immediately found the pup I wanted. I asked Mr. Clark how much he wanted for it, and he said, "Normally, I sell pups for $10."

I pulled out the cash and was about to hand it over when Mr. Clark stopped me. "Is that money you earned yourself, Son?"

I nodded. "Yes, Sir."

"Well, then you put that money back in your pocket. I'm going to give you that pup. I can see it really likes you and I know you'll take good care of it."

I hesitated. "Mr. Clark, I don't know if my Papaw will let me take the dog as a gift."

Mr. Clark thought for a moment, "Tell you what, you take that ten dollars and come on down to my store. You can buy your pup some food and a collar. How's that sound?"

I grinned from ear to ear, "Deal!"

From then on, Mr. Carlisle Clark would occasionally drop by the farm to visit Papaw and check in on how I was doing with that pup and swap stories about the "Old Days." A few years later, Mr. Clark shut down the gas station and was doing lawn mowing service for people. One day, he stopped by with his truck and trailer full of mowers as Burchell "Slew" Stallard was already there in "Full Swing" telling stories.

The day's topic was who had the roughest and toughest drill sergeant during basic training for WWII. Unfortunately, I missed a lot of story-trading that day since the milk truck had picked up milk, so I was busy running the sanitary cleaning system to prepare for the afternoon milking.

I did catch the ending when Mr. Clark finished his story of having a drill sergeant from South Alabama that won the day. That sergeant kept a huge chew of tobacco in his mouth and every time he chewed your ass out, the tobacco spit would go flying in your eyes until you were crying like a baby. Then he would get even madder about that. Carlisle suddenly looked at his watch and said he had to go before it got too late.

After he pulled out his truck and trailer, I spoke to Papaw and Mr. Stallard, "I hadn't really heard any war stories from Mr. Clark before. I did hear plenty of stories from the Old Days tho."

Slew Stallard replied, "Son, I've heard from good people down at the VFW that Ole Carlisle there was a heck of a soldier, tough as they come. I heard he was with the 4th Armored Division; he saw some terrible shit!"

I inquired with a little confusion, "Terrible shit?"

Papaw spoke up this time, "Yeah, Son, you know how we recite the Apostles' Creed in church and it says Jesus suffered under Pontius Pilate, was crucified, died, and was buried; he descended to hell and on the third day he rose from the dead. Well, Ole Carlisle there has seen and been to hell just like Jesus!"

Slew finished, "Carlisle was the G.I. that cut the lock and chain off of the front gate of Ohrdruf concentration camp back in '45. He's seen hell, so you're not going to hear many war stories from him, Son! I'm a little surprised he even talked about basic training today."

When the soldiers of the 4th Armored Division rolled into the Ohrdruf concentration camp on April 4, 1945, they were met with a harrowing sight. Piles upon piles of bodies, some covered with lime and others charred to ash on pyres. It was a scene of unimaginable horror that shook even the toughest of soldiers to their core.

The liberation of Ohrdruf was a momentous occasion as it marked the first time that the U.S. Army had freed a Nazi concentration camp. Brigadier General Joseph F. H. Cutrona and the 89th Infantry Division led the charge, but it was the soldiers on the ground who bore witness to the atrocities that had been committed.

Upon hearing of the horrific discovery, General Dwight D. Eisenhower, Supreme Commander of the Allied Forces in Europe, made a visit to the camp on April 12, accompanied by Generals George S. Patton and Omar Bradley. After seeing the horrors of Ohrdruf with his own eyes, Eisenhower sent a cable to General George C. Marshall, the head of the Joint Chiefs of Staff in Washington, in which he described the atrocities he had witnessed.

Here is the actual cable message Eisenhower sent to Marshall:

WE CONTINUE TO DISCOVER GERMAN CONCENTRATION CAMPS FOR POLITICAL PRISONERS IN WHICH CONDITIONS OF INDESCRIBABLE HORROR PREVAIL. FROM EISENHOWER TO GENERAL MARSHALL FOR EYES ONLY. I HAVE VISITED ONE OF THESE MYSELF AND I ASSURE YOU THAT WHATEVER HAS BEEN PRINTED ON THEM TO DATE HAS BEEN UNDERSTATEMENT. IF YOU WOULD SEE ANY ADVANTAGE IN ASKING ABOUT A DOZEN LEADERS OF CONGRESS AND A DOZEN PROMINENT

EDITORS TO TAKE A SHORT VISIT TO THIS THEATER
IN A COUPLE OF C-54S, I WILL ARRANGE TO HAVE
THEM CONDUCTED TO ONE OF THESE PLACES WHERE
THE EVIDENCE OF BESTIALITY AND CRUELTY
IS SO OVERPOWERING AS TO LEAVE NO DOUBT IN
THEIR MINDS ABOUT THE NORMAL PRACTICES OF
THE GERMANS IN THESE CAMPS. I AM HOPEFUL
THAT SOME BRITISH INDIVIDUALS IN SIMILAR
CATEGORIES WILL VISIT THE NORTHERN AREA TO
WITNESS SIMILAR EVIDENCE OF ATROCITY.

FORTY-TWO
Speeding Ticket at 88

———— ～ ————

Papaw ambled into our farm's supply store and stuck his head in the office, "Why don't you ride up with me to the courthouse this Thursday about that speeding ticket I got last month."

I had almost forgotten about the ticket and inquired, "Why didn't you just mail in the payment instead of wasting a whole day at the courthouse? You already told me you were speeding; what's the point?"

He replied, "I just wanna talk to the judge about it, that's all."

"Suit yourself," I quipped. "I'll swing by the house and we'll head up to Wise after breakfast."

Upon our arrival at the courthouse, I couldn't help but take notice of the crowded courtroom. The bailiff instructed us to take our seats and then we all stood up as the honorable Judge Dotson made his entrance.

At Virginia traffic court, the proceedings kicked off with the Commonwealth Attorney reading out the names of traffic cases on the docket to see who showed up for the proceedings. Starting in alphabetical order, he recited a litany of names, and everyone present replied with "Here" or "Present" when their name was called.

When the name "Mr. Jimmie Galloway" was announced, Papaw sprang up and declared, "I'm so glad you called my name, young man!" All the while, he was sliding down the aisle, making his way toward the front of the courtroom.

The bailiff started to smile and raised his voice, saying, "Mr. Galloway, we're just taking roll right now to see which cases on the docket need to be heard by the judge, Sir!"

Unfazed, Papaw was already opening the little half door towards the judge's bench, "If you'd oblige me a little, young man, I won't take long." By now, he was looking up at Judge Dotson, "Judge, you remind me a lot of ole Judge Stump from back in the 1950s. Did you know that he shot a man dead for attacking a bailiff in the old courthouse? I hope you won't shoot me for wanting to come and ask you a question."

Judge Dotson and the whole courtroom burst into laughter. "Of course, I won't shoot you, Mr. Galloway. Come on up," he chuckled, even though Papaw was already leaning on his bench by now. Everyone was in on the joke, knowing they were in for a wild ride.

I was still sitting in my seat in the back of the courtroom, chuckling to myself, Here we go again. *They let him have an audience, and we're going to be here all day!*

Papaw held court in the courtroom, weaving a tapestry of tales that went back decades. He regaled the audience with stories of old courthouses, long since lost to the ravages of time and flame, and how this new building had been constructed during his tenure on the County Board of Supervisors in the 1970s.

He took pleasure in pointing out that he remembered the days before driver's licenses or permits were even a thing. Back then, if you had access to a car and a few dollars for gas, you were free to hit the open road. And if you knew how to drive, well, that was all the qualification you needed. In fact, he boasted, he had earned his pilot's certificate to fly planes years before he even bothered to get his driver's license… back before World War II.

Finally, Papaw had to take a breath of air and Judge Dotson seized the moment to speak, "Mr. Galloway, what did you want to ask me?" with a big smile.

Papaw puffed his chest out like a banty rooster and straightened his belt, "I almost forgot, but I wanted to talk to you about this speeding ticket I got."

Judge Dotson asked, "Sir, were you speeding?"

Papaw replied with bravado, "Well, yes, I was speeding because I don't go slow-poking around like some old man! But I wasn't driving recklessly. I can still drive like I was a pilot back in my younger days! I wanted to see if you could get rid of this ticket for me?"

Judge Dotson raised his eyebrows, scanning the courtroom of offenders with an amused expression. "Get rid of it? I don't know about that, Mr. Galloway. You just told me you were speeding, Sir."

Papaw paced in front of the judge's bench like a seasoned preacher. "Well, Son, I'm 88 years old and may not be long for this world. I've never had a ticket of any sort in my life and I'd hate to meet my Maker on Judgment Day with this speeding ticket tarnishing my spotless driving record."

Judge Dotson realized that his day was not going to proceed until this matter was resolved. "I tell you what, Mr. Galloway, I don't want to stand between you and a spotless driving record when you meet your Maker. How about you attend a driving school and we'll drop this whole thing? It'll be like it never happened."

A smile crept across Papaw's face, "You're a fine young man, Judge. Just tell my grandson back there where I need to go for this driving school thing and I'll be there ten minutes early. I don't skirt any chores!"

Papaw left the courtroom to a chorus of applause, probably making him the only man in Wise County history to do so.

From L to R: Jimmie Galloway, Governor Mark Warner, and John William Peace II (author of this book)

273

Galloway family early 1990s: from L to R, Jimmie Galloway, Graham Galloway, John Galloway, Julie (Ma) Galloway, Virginia (Jenny) Galloway

FORTY-THREE
Papaw's Favorite

———~———

Jimmie's life became a Papaw life. He was in his mid-80s, living on a quiet dairy farm within a mile of where he was born and raised after buying Clinch Haven Farms from Old Man Terpstra in 1972.

Papaw had just taken his work boots off on the front porch and was still sitting when his great-granddaughter, Shelby, (who lived on the farm down the driveway a little way) bounded through the screen door in front of him. She was in 5th grade and her class had been studying about World War II in history. She stood in front of Papaw and cocked her head to the side while throwing her pigtails behind her shoulders. She had a solemn look on her face, the look children have when they want answers to serious questions. "We've been studying about World War II and last night dad said that you were a war hero!? He said you were a pilot of a bomber plane and had earned a whole shoebox full of medals, all kinds of hero stuff. Is that true?"

Papaw just leaned back, grinned, and thought about how smart these kids are now. *They know so much more than when I was their age,* he thought. When Shelby was in kindergarten, they had studied about the Eiffel Tower and she had told her Papaw that when she grew up, she wanted to go visit that Eiffel Tower in Paris, France. He recalled thinking that he was probably in middle school or maybe even in high school before he even knew anything about the Eiffel Tower or Paris, France.

Papaw took a breath, "Well now, I was a bomber plane pilot and the Army did give me a whole bunch of medals. I'll have to show them to you sometime. As far as being a hero, Sweetie, I'm just a boy from Crackers Neck. I was just doing my job... I got an idea, let's go inside and get us some peach ice cream to eat, you and me?"

Shelby's face lit up, "I LOVE peach ice cream!" she exclaimed, grabbing Papaw's finger as they walked across the porch to the front door.

L to R: Brenda Helen Galloway Peace (namesake of the plane),
Shelby Ann Peace and Papaw

FOURTY-FOUR
Dinner's Ready

———————～———————

My son, Trey (Jimmie's grandson), walked down the hallway of Heritage Hall nursing home to visit Papaw. Jimmie had reached 95 years old and all the wear and tear on his body finally caught up to him. He had lived a healthy and independent life up until a few weeks before when he fell and broke some ribs which lead to a bad case of pneumonia.

While we waited right outside Jimmie's room, the doctor walked out and addressed both of us, simply answering the question I had asked, "How's he doing today?"

The doctor replied, "We're doing all we can, but I'm afraid everything is just worn out and starting to fail. We treat the lungs and his kidney function drops, next it's the liver and so on. Ninety-five years of age has finally caught up to him. Go on in though; he's in a great mood as usual!"

I responded, "Be careful if you're heading home, doc, it's getting real cold and the weatherman is calling for extremely frigid weather all week."

We entered the small room which had become his home for the past few days. The room was cozy but sterile with white walls and a few pieces of generic furniture. The TV was on, playing a football game in the background. Despite the uninviting surroundings, Papaw's smile lit up the room, "Come on in; I got the football game on," he said with a slight cough.

After exchanging pleasantries, Jimmie's expression turned serious as he began to share a dream he had the night before. He said, "It's been decades.... since right before the war... that I've recalled a dream!" His voice then grew soft as he described the vivid dream, recounting how he had awoken in his childhood bedroom to the smell of bacon and the sound of his mother's voice.

"In the dream, I got up and peeked my head out of the bedroom door, looked down our long hallway towards the kitchen, and there was Ma as plain as day," he said with a smile. "She was yelling down at me, 'Come on to the kitchen, Son. Dinner is ready!'"

Trey's eyes widened as he listened to the story, "Is that your Ma, the one everyone calls Little Granny?" he asked.

"Yep, it sure is!" Jimmie replied, his face glowing with the memory. "That dream was so real and wonderful! I could literally smell the bacon and feel the cold floor under my feet as I walked!"

As the conversation turned back to the football game, we all enjoyed each other's company. It was a simple moment, but one that would be cherished.

The next day, my cell phone rang and I learned the devastating news that Papaw had passed away during the night. I was heartbroken, but the memory of the dream brought a small measure of comfort.

"Dinner's ready, Papaw. Dinner's ready," I whispered to myself, knowing that my beloved grandfather was now with his mother and enjoying a home-cooked feast. She had called her son to dinner. Despite the sadness of the moment, I was deeply grateful for the years I spent with Papaw and the memory of his dream that would stay with me forever.

ABOUT THE COVER

———— ∼ ————

Seeing this old photograph again, Papaw let out a chuckle, "Just look at us, as innocent as a batch of puppies." His weathered hand reached out, brushing the edge of the picture with a tenderness belying his gruff exterior.

I understood the young bit, but the naive comment caught me off guard. So, I asked him about it. He just leaned back in his chair, a far-off look clouding his eyes, "Son, this was snapped at a shindig in Tampa Bay just after we got the word we were shipping out to Britain… shipping out to war. The shutterbug was just a hired gun, a tourist snapper, much like the ones you see hovering around theme parks or those floating cruise ships. I remember handing over my address and a bit of pocket change, half expecting the whole thing to be some kind of swindle."

"But wouldn't you know it," he continued, his voice gaining a note of surprise even after all these years, "the picture showed up in the mail." He pointed at the photograph, his finger hovering over the beaming faces of those young men. "See those grins? We were still wet behind the ears with not the foggiest idea about the hellfire we were walking into. We were all caught up in the rah-rah speeches and the shiny toys Uncle Sam handed us, convinced we were invincible. It's a wonder we didn't strut our way across the Atlantic."

His voice hitched a little, eyes clouding over as he finished, "But we paid the price in friends and brothers. So many barely made it back and so many more never made it." His words hung in the air, a sobering reminder of the cost of their naivety.

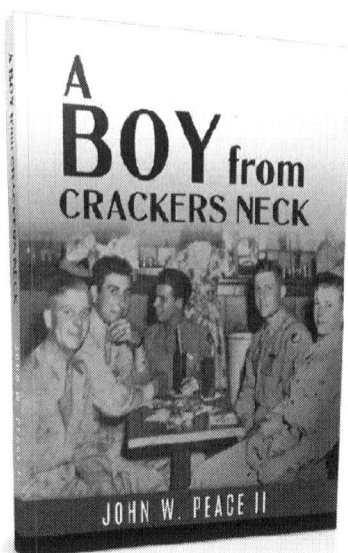

OTHER BOOKS BY JOHN W. PEACE II

Best Seller amazon.com

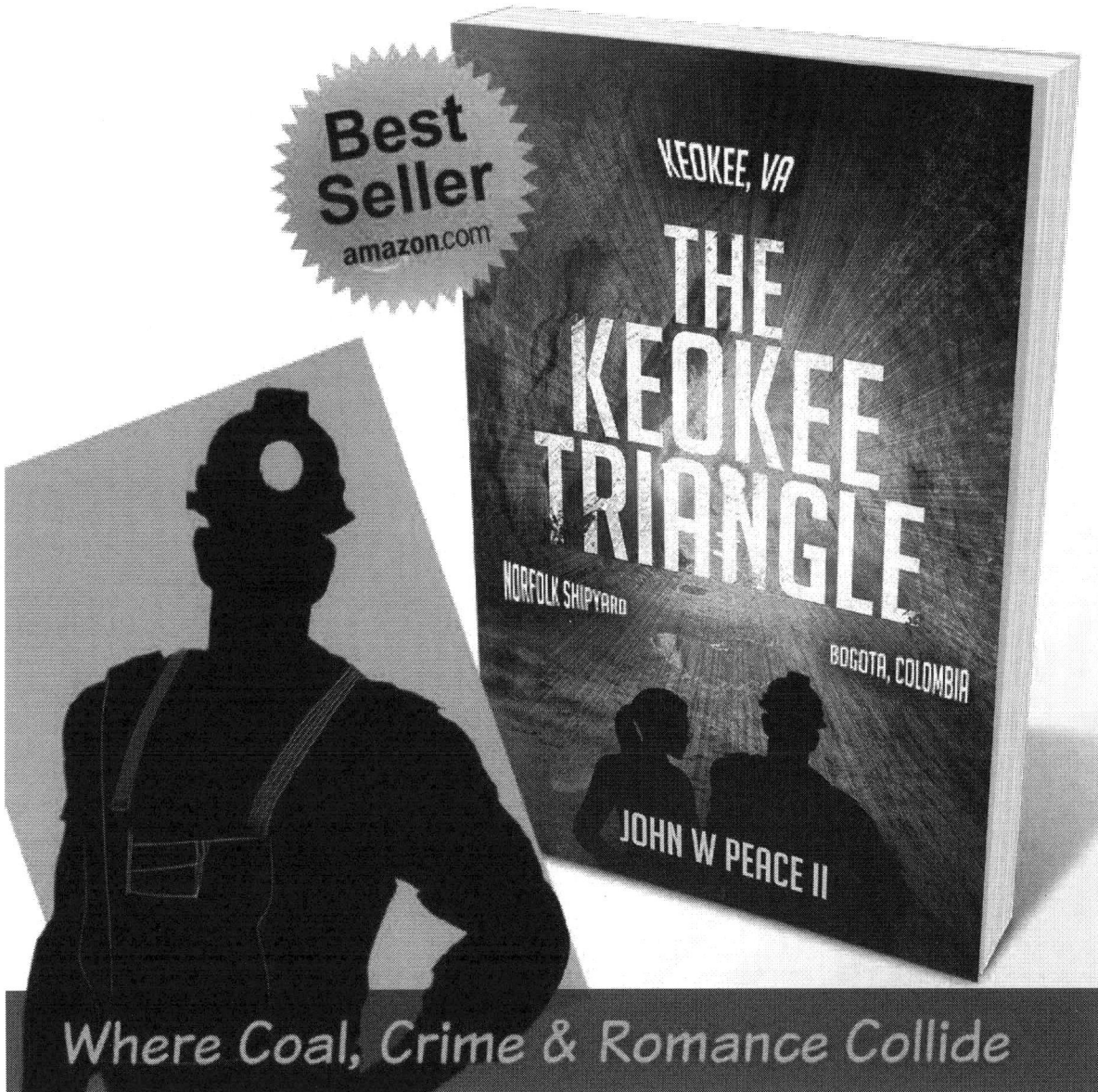

KEOKEE, VA

THE KEOKEE TRIANGLE

NORFOLK SHIPYARD

BOGOTA, COLOMBIA

JOHN W PEACE II

Where Coal, Crime & Romance Collide

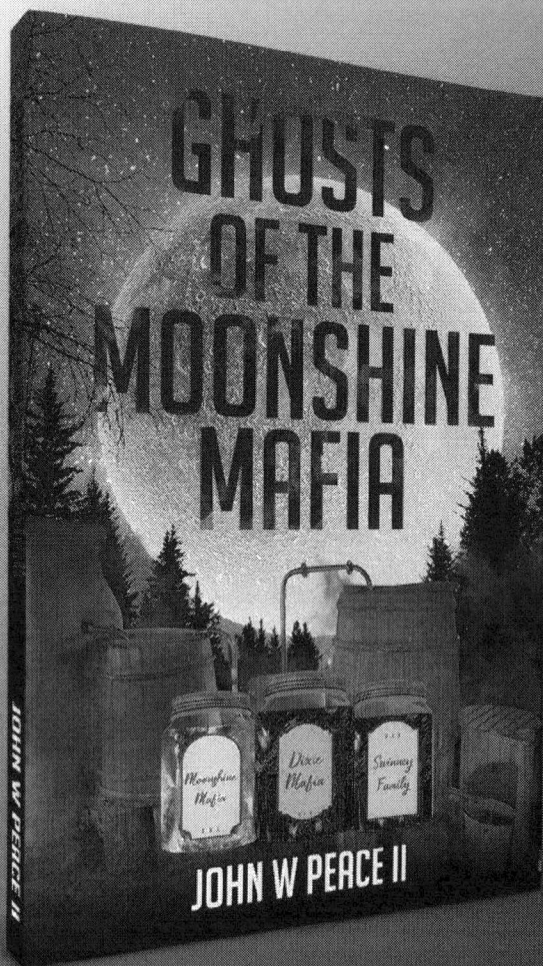

Manufactured by Amazon.ca
Bolton, ON